'This is exactly what we need! A beginner's introduction to analytical psychology which guides us through Jung's own words. For too long some have complained that Jung's *Collected Works* is obscure and confusing. Now Yeoman and Lu have given us this brilliant, compact book.'

Christopher Hauke, *Jungian analyst, London (S.A.P.) and New York (J.P.A.)*

'This book explains the whole of Jung's psychological theory clearly, concisely, and with optimal reference to the authority of Jung's own words. Remaining sensitive to the complexity and nuances of the many texts they survey, Yeoman and Lu's engagingly narrated journey through Jung's *Collected Works* provides the securest of foundations for deeper engagement with one of the culturally most important bodies of thought of the twentieth century.'

Professor Roderick Main, *University of Essex, UK*

'*The Collected Works of C.G. Jung: The Basics* succeeds in making the rich terrain of Jung's writing navigable while never reducing its true-to-psyche complexities. Essential reading for Jungians old and new, it presents the seminal ideas as evolving by exploring that which modernity has shorn, rejected, lost, or devalued.'

Professor Susan Rowland, PhD, *author with Joel Weishaus of* Jungian Arts-Based Research and the Nuclear Enchantment of New Mexico *(2021)*

'There's no way round it. You have to get into the *Collected Works* if you are serious about understanding Jung. But that isn't easy at all. No accessible guides exist to the massive collection of erudite, challenging, and illuminating volumes. Now we have an exceptional, basic guide to the actual writings. You will find it reliable, readable, and, at times, critical. The book is suitable for a variety of teaching contexts, both clinical and academic. And, for those into Jung who are on their own journey, it will be incredibly useful.'

Professor Andrew Samuels, *author of* Jung and the Post-Jungians

'These days we need more than ever to understand the ideas of C.G. Jung, yet the sheer size of his *Collected Works* can deter some readers from engaging with his complex (and often subtle) thought. Beyond the soundbites, the misrepresentations and the misprisions, *The Collected Works of C.G. Jung: The Basics* offers a sound and reliable account of a body of work that speaks to us more urgently than ever before. Essential reading for new as well as seasoned readers of Jung.'

Professor Paul Bishop, **PhD**, *William Jacks Chair of Modern Languages, University of Glasgow*

'*The Collected Works of C. G. Jung: The Basics* by Dr. Yeoman and Professor Lu offers a clear, concise, and well-synthesised presentation of the whole of Jung's *Collected Works*. Responsive to the expanding body of scholarship of the past 25 years in Jungian studies, the authors provide a remarkable, interwoven tapestry revealing the trajectory of the threads of Jung's key concepts. Tables provided throughout the book generate a wonderful map of this tapestry and will be of great use to students and researchers.'

Joe Cambray, **PhD**, *Past-President, Pacifica, Graduate Institute*

C.G. JUNG'S COLLECTED WORKS

This new introduction to Jung's *Collected Works*—written in lively and accessible style—provides a comprehensive guide to key concepts in analytical (Jungian) psychology while charting the creative evolution of Jung's thought through his own words.

Invaluable to both beginners and those more experienced with Jungian theory, this book provides tables listing key readings for further study of the *Collected Works*, clear explication of fundamental principles, chapter summaries, prompts for deepening a critical engagement with Jung's texts, a glossary of key terms, and suggestions for further reading.

This text will be an invaluable introduction for those coming to the *Collected Works* for the first time as well as a useful reference for readers familiar with the collection.

Ann Yeoman, **PhD**, Jungian Analyst, served as Dean of Students (New College, University of Toronto) where she developed and taught courses in Jungian Studies. She is the author of *Now or Neverland: Peter Pan and the Myth of Eternal Youth*. She now practises in Devon.

Kevin Lu, **PhD**, is Professor of Applied Psychoanalysis and Head of Department (Practice) at the Royal Central School of Speech and Drama, University of London.

The Basics Series

The Basics is a highly successful series of accessible guidebooks which provide an overview of the fundamental principles of a subject area in a jargon-free and undaunting format.

Intended for students approaching a subject for the first time, the books both introduce the essentials of a subject and provide an ideal springboard for further study. With over 50 titles spanning subjects from artificial intelligence (AI) to women's studies, *The Basics* are an ideal starting point for students seeking to understand a subject area.

Each text comes with recommendations for further study and gradually introduces the complexities and nuances within a subject.

BUSINESS ANTHROPOLOGY
Timothy de Waal Malefyt

EATING DISORDERS
Elizabeth McNaught, Janet Treasure, and Jess Griffiths

TRUTH
Jc Beall and Ben Middleton

PERCEPTION
Bence Nanay

C.G. JUNG'S COLLECTED WORKS
Ann Yeoman and Kevin Lu

For a full list of titles in this series, please visit www.routledge.com/The-Basics/book-series/B

C.G. JUNG'S COLLECTED WORKS

WORKS

THE BASICS

Ann Yeoman and Kevin Lu

Routledge
Taylor & Francis Group

LONDON AND NEW YORK

Designed cover image: bestdesigns © Getty Images

First published 2024
by Routledge
4 Park Square, Milton Park, Abingdon, Oxon OX14 4RN

and by Routledge
605 Third Avenue, New York, NY 10158

Routledge is an imprint of the Taylor & Francis Group, an informa business

© 2024 Ann Yeoman and Kevin Lu

British Library Cataloguing-in-Publication Data
A catalogue record for this book is available from the British Library

Library of Congress Cataloging-in-Publication Data
Names: Yeoman, Ann, 1945- author. | Lu, Kevin (Professor of applied psychoanalysis), author.
Title: C.G. Jung's collected works : the basics / Ann Yeoman and Kevin Lu.
Description: Abingdon, Oxon ; New York, NY : Routledge, 2024. |
Series: The basics series | Includes bibliographical references and index. |
Identifiers: LCCN 2023035836 (print) | LCCN 2023035837 (ebook) |
ISBN 9781138667006 (hardback) | ISBN 9781138667013 (paperback) |
ISBN 9781315619156 (ebook)
Subjects: LCSH: Jung, C. G. (Carl Gustav), 1875-1961. | Jungian psychology.
Classification: LCC BF173.J85 Y46 2024 (print) | LCC BF173.J85 (ebook) |
DDC 150.19/54--dc23/eng/20230926
LC record available at https://lccn.loc.gov/2023035836
LC ebook record available at https://lccn.loc.gov/2023035837

ISBN: 978-1-138-66700-6 (hbk)
ISBN: 978-1-138-66701-3 (pbk)
ISBN: 978-1-315-61915-6 (ebk)

DOI: 10.4324/9781315619156

Typeset in Bembo
by KnowledgeWorks Global Ltd.

Ann Yeoman dedicates this book to:

Michael Dixon, Fred Case, and David Clandfield
for the opportunities and fellowship afforded me
at New College, University of Toronto.

Kevin Lu dedicates this book to:

My parents (Tuong Dieu Lu and Lien Ho) and aunts
(Nu Lu, Co Lu, and Chau Le Lu) for supporting the
realisation of a dream.

CONTENTS

LIST OF TABLES

ACKNOWLEDGEMENTS

This book has been a long time coming. What seemed, on the surface, to be a manageable task—to write an accessible yet in-depth introduction to *The Collected Works* of C. G. Jung—became a daunting challenge that tested our resolve, decision making, knowledge of analytical psychology, and skills as writers. We wish to thank our editor, Sarah Rae, for her incomparable patience and understanding, and for giving us the necessary space to figure out what this book is about and how we wanted to frame what needed to be said. We would also like to thank Jaelyn Danielle Endris for her meticulous work on compiling the Index and Cara Fraser for thoroughly editing the manuscript.

Ann Yeoman and Kevin Lu

Acknowledgements! I go immediately to New College, University of Toronto. Thank you, Professor David Clandfield, former Principal of New College, for allowing me free range in the development of a Jungian Studies 'suite' of courses, supported by New College and the generous establishment of a trust fund by the late Marion and Ross Woodman. I loved designing and teaching those courses! And my thanks goes out to the wonderful, curious, bright, creative, and challenging students who signed up to find out about Jung! Those were special times. I miss them! The classes, the discussions, especially those 'after-hours' discussions, in which I learnt so much. Thank you. In writing the narrative for this book, I felt like I was back in the classroom, talking with all of you. And to Kevin Lu, a big thank you (I think!) for dreaming up this project in the first place.

Thank you to my long-suffering family, John and Jan, who have been wondering if this project would ever come to fruition; and to neglected friends who despite everything remained supportive and understanding.

Last but not least, I am grateful to my analysands, who keep me on my toes and with whom I continue to grow.

Ann Yeoman

I am indebted to the Lu family, who have made innumerable sacrifices to allow me to pursue my goals. I am particularly grateful to my sister, Karen, and her family (Brett, Adelyn, Gavin, and Bennett), for their warmth and support.

My time at the University of Toronto was life changing. I met some amazing people, and while time has an uncanny way of creating distance, how lucky am I to count you amongst my closest friends.

There is an alchemy to music—in performance, in the pursuit of combining words and sounds—that must be experienced to be fully appreciated. I am grateful to all the musicians and artists with whom I have had the pleasure of sharing a stage: "you've got soul."

Over the last 17 years, I have met many generous colleagues and intellectual giants. You have opened doors, shared your expertise graciously, and have helped me to navigate the quagmire that is Higher Education in the UK. I'm sorry I can't name you all here, but in particular, I would like to thank: Andrew Samuels, Roderick Main, Mark Saban, Renos Papadopoulos, Matt ffytche, Raluca Soreanu, Carolyn Laubender, Karl Figlio, Debbie Stewart, Alison Evans, Anne Snowling, Fiona Gillies, Susan Rowland, Joe Cambray, Paul Bishop, Chris Hauke, Dennis Merritt, Robin McCoy Brooks, Stephen Farah, Stefano Carpani, Brendan Callaghan SJ, Nadiya Shah, Nikolay Mintchev, William Sharp, Aaron Daniels, Greta Kaluževičiutė-Moreton, and Aaron Balick. I am grateful to Josette Bushell-Mingo, Mark Hunter, and Maria Delgado for the opportunity to join and represent the Royal Central School of Speech and Drama.

I wish to recognise my students, who have astounded me with their creativity, challenged me to think differently, and who have given me hope for a better and brighter future, especially: Frazer Merritt, Ris Swank, Andrew Howe, my PhDs (both past and present), especially Orsolya Lukács, Briony Clarke, and Louise Austin, and all the MAJ cohorts I had the pleasure of teaching.

There are those who leave such an indelible imprint on your life that to conceive of it without them would not only be unimaginable, but pure folly. My heartfelt thanks go to my wife, Grace, my children, Eric and Keira, John and Petina Hann, Branko Ozegovic, Tom Karczewski, and Angelo Mazzuca. My final expressions of gratitude belong to Professors Timothy Brook and Ann Yeoman, for altering the course of my life all those years ago.

Kevin Lu

ABOUT THE AUTHORS

Ann Yeoman, PhD, is a senior Jungian Analyst (C. G. Jung Institute) with over 25 years of clinical experience. She has now retired from the University of Toronto, where she served as Dean of Students (New College), adjunct faculty member, course designer and primary lecturer in Jungian Studies modules, and co-developer and director of a minor programme (Paradigms and Archetypes). She is the author of *Now or Neverland: Peter Pan and the Myth of Eternal Youth* (1998) and has published articles and chapters on Mervyn Peake's literature of the fantastic from an analytical psychological perspective. Ann has lectured and given workshops internationally. She is in private practice in South Devon.

Kevin Lu, PhD, is Professor of Applied Psychoanalysis and Head of Department (Practice) at the Royal Central School of Speech and Drama, University of London. He is the former Head of the Department of Psychosocial and Psychoanalytic Studies (University of Essex), was Director of the MA Jungian and Post-Jungian Studies between 2009 and 2022, and is now an Honorary Professor in PPS. He has served on the Executive Committee of the International Association for Jungian Studies and is a member of the Adjunct Faculty at Pacifica Graduate Institute. His publications include articles and chapters on Jung's relationship to the discipline of history, Arnold J. Toynbee's use of analytical psychology, critical assessments of the theory of *cultural complexes*, sibling relationships in the Chinese/Vietnamese Diaspora, Jungian perspectives on graphic novels and popular culture, and therapeutic, arts-based approaches to archival research. His papers on racial hybridity and archetypal thematic analysis (the latter co-authored with Ann Yeoman) were awarded the scholarship prize for best article published in the *IJJS* (2019 and 2023 respectively).

INTRODUCTION

The aim of this little book is to guide its readers on a journey of discovery which traces the creative evolution of C.G. Jung's thinking through *The Collected Works*. Our book is written for sixth form, undergraduate, and graduate students interested in learning or researching the fundamentals of Jungian psychology and the development of Jung's ideas. To this end, we will focus on the primary source—Jung's own writings, Jung's own words—using commentary and turning to interpretations of Jung's ideas by others solely in order to elucidate ideas and supply the historical and cultural context in which Jung was living and working. We will use the 'narrative' of each chapter to explain concepts, provide accessible examples, and supply the background information necessary to an understanding of the development of Jung's thinking. We may also draw from related or complementary disciplines, for example, neuroscience, literature, philosophy, and mythology, whenever their findings enable a deeper or broader understanding of Jung's ideas. Readers interested in delving into others' perspectives on Jung's writings, theories, and thought will find a short list of key interpretative studies at the end of this volume.

For the sake of accuracy and consistency, we have based the chronology of the publication of Jung's work (and, by extension, the chronology of the development of Jung's ideas) on the publication dates of the texts used for the English translations that comprise *The Collected Works*. At the end of each chapter, we provide tables indicating where in *The Collected Works* readers may pursue further research into topics we raise in our narrative. Because this book focuses on the fundamental concepts of Analytical Psychology, which is a huge

DOI: 10.4324/9781315619156-1

subject in itself, we regret that we will simply not have the room to trace Jung's application of his thinking to other disciplines and interests, such as religion, civilisation, history, and alchemy. However, we will provide an Epilogue! This will contain a listing of Jung's writings in *The Collected Works* that we have not been able to include in our book.

We hope the tables throughout our book will help readers develop their individual and particular investigations of Jung's ideas as we are well aware that these will vary greatly. Some readers may want to study analytical (Jungian) psychology because of their interest in psychology itself; others because of the applicability of Jung's thinking to diverse areas of study (from the humanities to the pure and applied sciences and the social and political sciences); still others because they are fascinated by the human psyche—how we 'tick,' the ever-challenging dynamics of personal and family relationships, and the ways in which human psychology generates systems of belief as well as social, cultural, and historical trends and events.

Jung was very prolific, which makes any study of his work rather intimidating. The scope of this book is consequently introductory and strictly limited to 18 of the 20 volumes of *The Collected Works* (volumes 19 and 20 cover the Bibliography and General Index). We understand how the sheer volume of *The Collected Works* alone may be daunting, even to students already well-versed in Jung's basic ideas. Therefore, in each chapter we highlight essential concepts (*persona, complex, archetype*, etc.) and key themes (*individuation, dreams, mythology, etc.*), and attempt to trace the development of Jung's thinking through his long lifetime.

We do not attempt to trace the complexity of Jung's thinking discoverable in his extensive correspondence or the many substantial volumes not included in *The Collected Works* (for example, his seminars on Nietzsche's *Thus Spoke Zarathustra* [1988], the *Vision Seminars* [1997], the seminars on *Dream Analysis* [1984], and his work on *Children's Dreams* [2008]), although we will draw on Jung's (1961/63) 'autobiography,' *Memories, Dream, Reflections,* on occasion (noting of course the robust debates that have occurred regarding the book's status as a reliable primary source [Shamdasani 1995; Elms 1994; Saban 2019]).

This book therefore presents a necessarily partial and rudimentary 'road map' highlighting the key developments in Jung's thinking and the key concepts of Analytical Psychology. When referencing material in *The Collected Works*, we use the method made popular by J. J. Clarke, which first indicates the volume in which the reference is found, followed by paragraph numbers (CW1:66 = *Collected Works vol 1*, paragraph 66). At the end of each chapter, you will find a list of reference material used in that chapter. At the end of the book, you will find suggestions for further reading and a Glossary of Terms.

We also realise that, apart from the vast amount of material in *The Collected Works*, many find Jung's idiosyncratic style and manner of writing difficult to follow! Jung's interests and the reach of his learning were unusually extensive; he was fluent in German, French, and English and knew ancient Greek and Latin, which means that his voracious reading and insatiable search for knowledge covered an extraordinarily wide range of disciplines, subjects, and cultural phenomena from the sciences, arts, humanities, and social sciences to the religions, rituals, and symbolism of cultures worldwide.

As Jung wrote in December 1956, less than five years before his death in 1961, "Any attempt at deeper penetration (of the human psyche) leads inevitably to the problem of the human mind *in toto*. The individual mind cannot be understood by and out of itself. For this purpose, a far more comprehensive frame of reference is needed: in other words, investigation of the deeper-lying psychic strata can be carried out only with the aid of other disciplines" (CW3:551). You will therefore find in Jung's writings consistent references not only to psychology, the medical arts, science, and psychotherapy but also to literature, art, architecture, philosophy, history, religion, mysticism, ritual, and symbolism drawn from cultures and traditions worldwide. This is because, as Jung reminds us, when we study human psychology, we study ourselves and, of course, we cannot get 'outside ourselves' in order to study ourselves from a relatively objective perspective. Consequently, Jung argues that because the "psyche expresses itself in all the activities and achievements of the human mind [...] (and) we can nowhere grasp the nature of the psyche *per se*, we must meet it, to study it, in its diverse and various manifestations: in life, art, history – the subject matter of humanistic enquiry" (CW15, p. 85). As a result, Jung explores every possible way in which the human psyche has expressed itself, and so revealed something of itself, through the millennia. Jung's allusions, analogies, and references are consequently often unfamiliar and obscure to the modern reader. Added to this is the fact that Jung frequently used the *process* of writing to clarify his own thoughts and help him work through complex problems.

Many of the essays in *The Collected Works* are well-argued lectures but some engage the reader in the process of arduous questioning and discovery in which Jung himself engaged *through the creative act of writing*. Don't expect *The Collected Works* to provide you with an ordered, accessible textbook! Better, perhaps, to immerse yourself in *The Collected Works* as a diver immerses him- or herself in untried waters to explore the mystery of an underlying coral reef. To this end, we will quote Jung's words as often as possible to help you appreciate the exploratory process that characterises much of Jung's writing—a process often obtuse and difficult to follow but, for those who persevere, one that promises rich rewards because it involves the reader in an active, critical evaluation of key questions about the psyche and the human condition that concern us all.

We hope that this little book will encourage you to engage *actively* with Jung's writings; we invite you to meet Jung the thinker, critically, analytically, and, above all, symbolically, and to discover analogies and metaphors that point to what might lie beneath the surface of things, motivating individual as well as collective (typical, group) behaviour and events. We hope you will develop your own way of questioning the human needs, psychological dynamics, and larger, collective demands of life that shape both individual biographies and the history of nations.

A final word: if, after dipping into our book, you want to explore Jung's writings, thought, and theory further, by all means use the many clear, concise explanations and interpretations of Jung's work that are readily available. BUT, please, always come back to Jung! Back to the primary source! We emphasise this for two reasons. Firstly, in the 1930s, Jung called his psychology Complex Psychology. This was because his research and therapeutic practice had resulted in a profound realisation of the extraordinarily *nuanced complexities* of the human psyche, which explains the often daunting (and sometimes tortuous) style of Jung's writing—elaborations, tangents, focus on detail, and untranslated Greek and Latin terms!—which, nevertheless, also promises rich rewards to the persistent reader. Secondly, in the making of this little book, we have been reading and rereading *Jung's* words and have been reminded, repeatedly, of the complexity and profundity of his thinking—its depth, breadth, precision, and occasional circuitous extravagances. So, although we focus on the evolution of Jung's thinking, traceable throughout *The Collected Works*, we also recommend a few volumes that you might find particularly useful. These are volumes of essays, many of which Jung revised and reworked, that represent Jung's mature reflections on key subjects, often spanning several decades. We refer you to volume 7 (*Two Essays on Analytical Psychology*), volume 8 (*The Archetypes and the Collective Unconscious*), and volume 18 (*The Symbolic Life*), which contain some often over-looked gems! Clinicians, or those aspiring to be clinicians, are referred to "The Psychology of the Transference" in volume 16.

REFERENCES

Elms, A. (1994) "The Auntification of C. G. Jung" in *Uncovering Lives: The Uneasy Alliance of Biography and Psychology*. New York: Oxford University Press, pp. 51–70.

Jung, C. G. (1953–83) *The Collected Works of C. G. Jung*, 20 vols. W. McGuire, H. Read, M. Fordham, G. Adler (Eds.). R. F. C. Hull (Trans.). London: Routledge & Kegan Paul; Princeton, NJ: Princeton University Press.

Jung, C. G. (1961/63) *Memories, Dreams, Reflections*. Recorded and edited by A. Jaffé. R. and C. Winston (Trans.). New York: Pantheon Books.

Jung, C. G. (1984) *Dream Analysis: Notes on the Seminar given in 1928 –1930*. W. McGuire (Ed.). Princeton, NJ: Princeton University Press.

Jung, C. G. (1988) *Nietzsche's Zarathustra: Notes of the Seminar given in 1934–1939*. J. L. Jarrett (Ed.). Princeton, NJ: Princeton University Press.

Jung, C. G. (1997) *Visions: Notes of the Seminar given in 1930–1934*, 2 vols. C. Douglas (Ed.). Princeton, NJ: Princeton University Press.

Jung, C. G. (2008) *Children's Dreams: Notes from the Seminar given in 1936–1940*. L. Jung and M. Meyer-Grass (Eds.). E. Falzeder and T. Woolfson (Trans.). Princeton, NJ: Princeton University Press.

Saban, M. (2019) *'Two Souls Alas': Jung's Two Personalities and the Making of Analytical Psychology*. Asheville, NC: Chiron Publications.

Shamdasani, S. (1995) "Memories, Dreams, Omissions." *Spring: Journal of Archetype and Culture*, 57, pp. 115–37.

THE GERMINATION OF C.G. JUNG'S INTERESTS AND IDEAS

Before a seed is able to germinate, grow into a mature plant, bloom and fruit, it must first be sown, preferably in fertile soil. The essential 'seeds' of Jung's mature thought are evident in the first three volumes of *The Collected Works* in which Jung's early psychiatric, experimental, and psychoanalytic work are to be found. Our first chapter will explore the significance of these 'seeds' to both Jung's early thinking and his later work and thought. The following chapters will trace the evolution of Jung's early insights and ideas as they develop into Analytical Psychology, the name Jung initially used to differentiate his own psychological and therapeutic method from that of Freud's psychoanalysis, although, as mentioned in our Introduction, in the 1930s Jung called his psychology Complex Psychology, in reference to the *complexity* of all psychical systems. However, Analytical Psychology became the accepted 'umbrella' term used to denote Jung's mature understanding of the structure and dynamics of the psyche, psychopathology, and the practice of psychotherapy, as well as his extensive application of psychological theory to the vast field of human endeavour and expression—from the arts and sciences, mythology and religion to history, culture, alchemy, the paranormal and more.

'Seeds':

If you are interested in tracking early 'seeds,' you might want to consult the five lectures that Jung delivered to colleagues at the Zofingia Society, the Swiss student fraternity he joined in 1895

DOI: 10.4324/9781315619156-2

shortly after enrolling as a medical student at Basel University. *The Zofingia Lectures* (1983) are published as *Supplementary Volume A* of *The Collected Works*. Jung's memories of significant childhood experiences and dreams that he believed shaped his life's path are to be found in *Memories, Dreams, Reflections* (1961/63).

STUDENT LIFE

Intimations of Jung's mature theory and the focus of his life's work may also be traced to his childhood, adolescent, and student experiences. However, we will begin with Jung's decision, towards the end of his medical studies, to pursue an apprenticeship and career in psychiatry rather than become a doctor of internal medicine as had been his initial focus. While studying for his final examination in psychiatry, Jung found himself deeply affected when he read in the preface to his textbook (von Krafft-Ebing 1888) that "psychiatric textbooks are stamped with a more or less subjective character" and major mental illnesses (i.e., schizophrenia, the psychoses) are "diseases of the personality" (Jung 1961/63, p. 108). Jung realised this meant that the previously assumed *objectivity* of the doctor is, in practice, an impossibility. Instead, the *whole* personality (the *subjectivity*) of the psychiatrist plays an integral role in the doctor-patient relationship, influences the treatment, and affects the outcome of the healing process. Likewise, the *whole* personality of the author of any psychiatric textbook inevitably shapes the way in which that author views and discusses both patients and mental illnesses. Von Krafft-Ebing, the author of the student Jung's textbook, considered mental illnesses "diseases of the personality," which suggested to Jung that psychiatrists need to treat the *whole* person—the patient's neurophysiology, psychology, and spirituality—body (physis), psyche, and soul—rather than focus solely on the illness as in some way *separate* from the full life and being of the individual, and therefore treatable as such. Jung's realisation was inspirational. It convinced him that a career in psychiatry would enable him to combine the two strands of his many interests—the empirical and scientific (biology, physiology, the natural sciences) and the more spiritual focus of humanistic studies (philosophy, religion, mythology, the arts). It shaped his worldview in general, and his approach to psychological theory and therapeutic practice in particular.

After medical school, in 1900, Jung had the good fortune to secure a post at the Burghölzli Psychiatric Hospital in Zürich, working under the guidance of its director, Dr. Eugene Bleuler. By 1902, Jung had completed his doctoral thesis in medicine and been appointed senior assistant staff physician at the Burghölzli. At this point, Bleuler asked him to work with a colleague, Dr Franz Riklin, on the application of the Word Association Test to psychiatric research and the treatment of psychoses.

Jung's doctoral thesis, "On the Psychology and Pathology of So-Called Occult Phenomena" (CW1), is a study of spiritualistic phenomena. It constitutes an early indication of how extensive the range of Jung's interests and psychological investigations were to become, and points to his later development of a model of the psyche and theory of the unconscious that Jung hoped would account not only for rational phenomena but also for irrational phenomena: the parapsychological, paranormal, and synchronistic. "On Synchronicity" (1951) and "Synchronicity: An Acausal Connecting Principle" (1952) may both be found in CW8.

THE WORD ASSOCIATION EXPERIMENT (WAE)

The Word Association Test had originally been devised by a British explorer, scientist, and psychologist, Sir Francis Galton (1822–1911), as a research tool to explore possible connections between an individual's intelligence (IQ) and the associations he or she made in response to a list of *stimulus words*. The Test was further developed as a tool for psychological research by Wilhelm Wundt (1832–1920), the founder of Experimental Psychology. Two psychiatrists, Emil Kraepelin and his pupil, Gustav Aschaffenburg, experimented with the Test as a diagnostic tool in an attempt to establish a link between a psychiatric patient's characteristic way of responding to the stimulus words and specific mental illnesses. Jung and Eugene Bleuler were both interested in the potential of the Test as a diagnostic tool for psychiatric pathologies; however, Jung was especially drawn to the Test because of the findings of an earlier researcher, Theodor Ziehen, who had discovered that when patients undergoing the Test *failed* to react to stimulus words in a timely fashion a "'relatively strong emotional charge' often occurred"—in other words, a disturbing idea or cluster of disturbing ideas had been activated (CW2:602, 29*n*). Jung was soon to rename the Word Association Test the Word Association Experiment (WAE) (*ibid.*:730) and to call the "cluster of disturbing ideas" 'constellated' (i.e., activated) in the patient a *complex* (adopting the term from Ziehen) or *feeling-toned complex of ideas*, because he found that the *feeling-tone* (emotional valence and intensity) was "common to all the individual ideas" that made up the cluster and served as the "cement that holds the complex together" (*ibid.*:733).

In *Experimental Researches* (CW2), Jung records the detailed and meticulous analysis of the results of his many years of work with patients using the WAE. Although the WAE is now somewhat out of fashion, it is nevertheless extremely effective and anyone interested in its use is advised to study CW2, and *The Psychology of Dementia Praecox* (1907) (CW3:1–316). A comprehensive summary of Jung's work with the Experiment is found in the 1935 Tavistock Lectures, in which Jung describes the Experiment as follows:

> The experiment is made [...] with a list of say a hundred words. You instruct the test person to react with the first word that comes into his mind as quickly as possible after having heard and understood the stimulus word. When you have made sure that the test person has understood what you mean you start the experiment. You mark the time of each reaction with a stop-watch. When you have finished the hundred words you do another experiment. You repeat the stimulus words and the test person has to reproduce his former answers. In certain places his memory fails and reproduction becomes uncertain or faulty. These mistakes are important.
> (CW18:98*ff*)

While the experiment was initially intended "for the study of mental associations," Jung soon discovered that more was to be learnt about the patient when involuntary *disturbances* occurred, such as prolonged response time, failure to respond, agitation, stammering, hesitation, repetitions, laughter, grimaces, changes in mood or demeanour, etc.). When the method and original aim of the association test were *disturbed* by the *autonomous behaviour of the psyche*,

Jung writes "[i]t was then that I discovered the feeling-toned complexes [...]" (CW8:195). Such disturbances "had always been registered before as *failures to react*" (i.e., as failures to react as anticipated by the doctor conducting the experiment).

Jung realised that disturbances occur "principally where a stimulus-word refers to a personal matter, which, as a rule, is of a distressing nature" (CW2:1350). References to *personal matter* were soon dropped "because such 'personal matter' is always a collection of various ideas, held together by an emotional tone common to all" (*ibid.*), i.e., a *complex*. Jung saw that all disturbed reactions to stimulus words "are beyond the control of the will" (CW18:101) as the word to which the patient is unable to respond *smoothly* "has hit [...] a complex, a conglomeration of psychic contents characterized by a peculiar or perhaps painful feeling-tone, something that is usually hidden from sight" (CW18:99). Jung called involuntary disturbances of his patients' responses to stimulus words *complex indicators*. They clearly showed the existence of an *unconscious* ("hidden from sight") dimension to the personality containing repressed or forgotten feelings, memories, and ideas which, when *constellated* (triggered, activated) by the stimulus word, disrupt and often override the conscious intentions of the patient.

Note Jung's comments on how methods and procedures 'work' in experimental psychology:

Modern psychology has one thing in common with modern physics, [which is] that its method enjoys greater intellectual recognition than its subject. Its subject, the psyche, is *so infinitely diverse in its manifestations, so indefinite and so unbounded, that the definitions given of it are difficult if not impossible to interpret*, whereas the definitions based on the mode of observation and on the method derived from it are—or at least should be—known quantities. Psychological research proceeds from these empirically or arbitrarily defined factors and observes the psyche *in terms of their alteration*. The psyche therefore appears *as the disturbance of the probable mode of behaviour* postulated by one or other of these methods. This procedure is [...] that of natural science in general. [...] *It has therefore long been recognized in experimental psychology, and above all in psychopathology, that a particular experimental procedure does not apprehend the psychic process directly, but that a certain psychic condition interpolates itself between it and the experiment, which one could call the 'experimental situation'.*

(CW8:194-96, emphasis added)

⊕

SUMMARY OF JUNG'S KEY DISCOVERIES FROM HIS WORK WITH THE WAE:

- Disturbed reactions to stimulus words "are not random" but *constellated* or activated by an *unconscious complex* (CW2:733-34)— sometimes a group of unconscious complexes
- Memory fails or is "seriously deranged" (i.e., in the second, *reproduction test*) where a complex (and accompanying strong affect) is operative (*ibid*.:747)
- "[T]he repressed complex can betray itself [...] even though it is unconscious [...] [and] split off from consciousness [...]. So far as I can see, where repressed complexes are concerned the same phenomenon occurs with normal, hysterical, and catatonic subjects; in normal cases there is a brief embarrassment or momentary blockage, in hysterical cases there is the well-known arbitrary amnesia, and in catatonic cases there is a complete barrier. The psychological mechanism, however, is the same" (*ibid*.:659)
- Examination of the patient's *associations* (memories, desires, anxieties) to stimulus word(s) eliciting disturbed responses leads to an understanding of the *content* and *meaning* of the underlying complex(es) and of "the intimate (i.e., unconscious) affairs of the subject," a procedure "of special importance in the psychological examination of patients" (*ibid*.:1350)
- In cases of a marked failure of memory, "the complex is stronger than the conscious will [such that] the subject [...] cannot will himself to remember. The complex plays the part of a second and stronger personality, to which ego-consciousness is subjected [demonstrating] the power of feeling-toned memories from which so many sensitive people suffer" (*ibid*.:901). By extension,

"The inability to remember in its various forms is the principal obstacle to analysis" (*ibid.*:902)

- Jung observed the universality of the feeling-toned complex (we all have them!) as well as the utility of the WAE to identify the repressed or unconscious complex that is the cause of an individual's neurotic, 'hysterical' or physical symptom: "In the depths of the mind of each [...] patient we always find an old wound that still burns or, in psychological terms, a feeling-toned complex" (*ibid.*:915)

- Jung realised that "Our association experiments have now also been able to demonstrate the same mechanism in cases of [...] *dementia praecox* (an early term for the disease now known as schizophrenia). In this, too, we are concerned with a complex buried in the depths of the mind which [...] causes many of the characteristic symptoms of this disease [...]" (*ibid.*:916)

- The WAE confirmed for Jung the psyche's capacity to "split," which means that, "within the scope of the normal individual [...] parts of the psyche detach themselves from consciousness to such an extent that they not only appear foreign but lead an autonomous life of their own" (CW8:253). The WAE also confirmed what Jung had noted in his doctoral research, namely, "the disaggregation (separation, falling apart) of psychic complexes" (CW1:93) and points to his later discussion of the inherent "dissociability of consciousness" in "On the Nature of the Psyche" (1954; orig. 1947, "The Spirit of Psychology").

Here is Jung on the **Dissociability of Consciousness:**

[...] a dissociation has two distinct aspects: in one case, there is an originally conscious content that became subliminal because it was repressed on account of its incompatible nature; in the other case, the secondary subject consists essentially in a process that never entered into consciousness at all because no possibilities exist there of apperceiving it ... ego-consciousness cannot accept it for lack of understanding, and in consequence it remains for the most part subliminal, although, from the energy point of view, it is quite capable of becoming conscious.

(CW8:366)

⊕

PRACTICAL APPLICATIONS OF THE WAE

Jung found the WAE of value in a number of applications, including (1) psychological investigation of so-called 'occult phenomena' and the paranormal; (2) psychological investigation of the function of *feeling-toned complexes* in 'normal subjects,' and cases of neurosis and psychosis; (3) psychophysical investigations, including the use of the WAE in the "'diagnosis' of a criminal case by study of the psychological make-up of the witness" (CW2:728), and in the development of lie-detection devices. Jung firmly establishes his work with the WAE as the foundation of his mature Complex Theory when he says, in a 1934 lecture delivered at the Federal Polytechnic Institute, Zürich: "the psyche is not an indivisible unity but a divisible and more or less divided whole. Although the separate parts are connected with one another, they are relatively independent, so much so that certain parts of the psyche never become associated with the ego at all, or only very rarely. I have called these psychic fragments 'autonomous complexes,' and I based my theory of complexes on their existence" (CW8:582). Our charts at the end of this chapter will help you locate Jung's commentary on points of specific interest, as well as provide details of various applications of the WAE.

SUMMARY

- We have seen how the key interests Jung held as a student influenced his career choice:
- The biological (natural) sciences AND humanistic studies (nature and spirit) come together in the discipline of a psychiatry that treats the whole person (psyche and soma)
- We have seen how Jung's work with the WAE led to his discovery of the COMPLEX and his recognition of the Dissociability of the Psyche
- We have touched on various pragmatic applications of the WAE, e.g., in criminal investigations (lie detection)

⊕

THE FEELING-TONED COMPLEX

The seeds that grew into Jung's elaboration of the *feeling-toned complex* as he worked on the WAE are also to be found in his doctoral dissertation. Inspired by Theodore Flournoy's earlier study of the experiences and revelations of a medium, Jung's dissertation presented a two-year study of the séances of his young (15-year-old) cousin, Hélène Preiswerk. Jung concluded that the 'spirits' his mediumistic cousin claimed to see and converse with, together with a mature, adult 'control spirit,' identified as 'Ivenes,' were *part-personalities* existing in the unconscious psyche which could manifest as 'persons' in trances, dreams, and visions. He also argued that these part-personalities (soon to be called *complexes*) were as yet undeveloped aspects of the personality in continual dynamic relationship with each other, and their 'existence' demonstrated how the future, more mature personality is in constant process of development *in the unconscious.*

Double Consciousness

Jung determined that the "phenomena of double consciousness" (or the emergence of part personalities) are "simply new character formations, or attempts of the future personality to break through, and that in consequence of special difficulties (unfavourable circumstances, psychopathic disposition of the nervous system, etc.) they get bound up with peculiar disturbances of consciousness" (CW1:166), these disturbances of consciousness "being closely connected with puberty" (*ibid.*), the developmental period during which profound changes occur in both psyche and *soma* (body).

Jung was impressed by "the strong tendency of the psychic elements towards autonomy" (CW1:159)—that is, the tendency of these unconscious psychic elements to operate outside the control of the will (in other words, they manifest as thoughts and behaviour which the individual experiences as something that cannot be controlled and consequently *cannot be helped*). This observation was repeatedly confirmed by the nature of patients' responses to stimulus words during the WAEs. Jung also found parallels between his own findings, the *subconscious fixed ideas* identified by French psychologist Pierre Janet (1859–1947) with whom Jung studied at the Salpêtrière for the winter semester in 1902–03, and Freud's *repressed wishes* and *traumatic memories* (see Freud's *The Interpretation of Dreams* [1900/13]). You will find Jung's doctoral dissertation ("On the Psychology and Pathology of So-called Occult Phenomena") in CW1, together with a number of short studies that focus on the role played by unconscious complexes (e.g., part-personalities, automatisms) in cases of mood disorder, cryptomnesia, misreading, simulated insanity, etc. (see box below). Those interested in the relationship of Jung's work with his cousin's 'unconscious personalities' to the development of his mature Complex Theory might want to focus on Part 3 of the doctoral dissertation, "Discussion of the Case" (CW1:72-150).

> **Cryptomnesia:** Jung defines cryptomnesia as "the coming into consciousness of a memory-image which is not recognized as such in the first instance, but only secondarily, if at all, by means of subsequent recollection of abstract reasoning" (CW1:138). Another, perhaps more accessible definition might be to call it 'unconscious plagiarism.' Something we might have heard told, seen, read, etc., is not consciously 'registered.' It 'by-passes' the conscious ego but can nevertheless re-emerge, much to the dismay of the 'unconscious plagiarist' who, even when confronted with undeniable evidence of the original source, cannot recall hearing, seeing, or reading it before.
>
> **Misreading:** saying a different word from that on the printed page.

In March 1911, the Australasian Medical Congress invited Jung (together with Freud and Havelock Ellis) to submit his findings from his work with the WAE and their implications for the understanding and treatment of the neuroses and psychoses (especially *dementia praecox* or schizophrenia). Jung's short paper was read at the Sydney meeting of the Congress that year and was later published as "On the Doctrine of Complexes," Appendix 4 of CW2. In this brief paper, Jung provides a helpful synopsis of his early work on complexes (collected in *Experimental Researches*—CW2—and "The Psychology of Dementia Praecox"—[CW3:1-316]). It affords a 'resting point' before we trace the development of his mature theory, summarised in "A Review of the Complex Theory" (1934) (CW8:194-219).

SUMMARY of the main points in Jung's own words:

1. "The association experiment provides the means of studying experimentally the behaviour of the complex [...]" (CW2:1352)

2. "[...] certainly in both the neuroses and *dementia praecox* (schizophrenia) the symptoms—whether of a somatic or of a psychic nature—originate from the complex [...]. While in hysteria there occurs usually a continuous accommodation to the surroundings, in consequence of which the complexes are subjected to continual alterations, in *dementia praecox* [...] the complexes are fixed, so that they usually arrest the progress of the general personality; [...] (However, *dementia praecox*) patients still possess a very vivid life of fantasy [...]. In fact, this is the workshop where delusions, hallucinations, etc., are produced from really sensible (i.e., rational) connections. The direction of thought is, however, entirely turned away from reality, and prefers thought-forms and material no longer of interest to modern man; hence many of these fantasies appear in a purely mythological garb" (*ibid.*:1354).

ILLUSTRATION: Jung provides a well-known example of the strange repetitive actions (evidence of a 'fixed' complex) of a woman suffering from schizophrenia that were, in fact, entirely rational, "produced from really sensible connections": "For decades she lay in bed, she never spoke or reacted to anything, her head was always bowed, her back bent and the knees slightly drawn up. She was always making peculiar rubbing movements with her hands so that in the course of the years thick horny patches developed on the palms. She kept the thumb and index finger of her right hand together as if sewing." When the patient died, Jung was able to ask her brother "if he remembered what had been the cause of his sister's illness. He told me that she had had a love-affair, but for various reasons it had come to nothing, and the girl had taken this so much to heart that she became melancholic. I asked who her lover was: he was a shoemaker. Unless we choose to see here some very strange play of chance, we must assume that the patient had kept the memory-image of her lover unaltered in her heart for thirty-five years" (CW3:358).

⊕

MORE ON THE FEELING-TONED COMPLEX

First: back to basics and beginnings. It is so easy, when reading Jung, or even commentary on Jung's ideas, to feel you have been plunged into the middle of a discussion that is fascinating, complex (sorry!), and meaningful but ... somehow, the meaning is elusive. You feel somewhat adrift, as though an essential introduction or step in the argument has been omitted. Jung was highly intuitive and 'intuitives' often jump from A to D in an argument or even start at D, leaving us, their readers, wondering how they 'got there' or, worse, doubting our ability to follow their thinking and understand their ideas. Before we explore the behaviour of complexes, complexes as 'part personalities,' etc., we need to have a sense of how these all-important psychic factors might form and develop in the human psyche; this takes us to beginnings and therefore to early childhood and the dawning of consciousness in the individual.

Jung is often charged with failing to work on the psychology of early childhood development, i.e., with 'beginnings.' He acknowledges that he "never made the child psyche an object of special research" (CW18:1823), but that the experiences of the child psyche collected from his psychotherapeutic practice did "give rise to a number of interesting observations, firstly in regard to adults who have not yet rid themselves of their disturbing infantilism, secondly in regard to the complex relations between parents and children, and thirdly in regard to the children themselves" (*ibid.*). Outside of *The Collected Works*, a volume was published by the Philemon Foundation entitled *Children's Dreams: Notes from the Seminar given in 1936–1940* (2008), a seminar presented at the Swiss Federal Institute of Technology (Zürich). The volume contains Jung's interpretation of children's dreams and the most extensive account of his psychology of childhood. There are also some important essays in CW17 (*The Development of Personality*) which include "Psychic Conflicts in a Child," "Child Development and Education," "Analytical Psychology and Education," "The Gifted Child," and sprinkled throughout *The Collected Works* are numerous gems of Jung's thoughts on developmental and childhood psychology. For our present purposes, Jung's reflections on the very earliest condition of infancy enable us to appreciate his understanding of how the complexes (conscious, semi-conscious, and unconscious) that characterise the personal psyche (see Chapter 3) come into being.

In Lecture 1 of CW18, Jung writes: "I would say that the thing that comes first is obviously the unconscious and that consciousness really arises from an unconscious condition. In early childhood we are unconscious and consciousness is rather the product of the unconscious" (CW18:15). The known and knowable (conscious experience) arises out of the unknown and unknowable (the unconscious—and it is important to remind ourselves, continually, that 'the unconscious' is not a *fact* or measurable factor but an *hypothesis*: Here is Jung: "When we say 'the unconscious' we often mean to convey something by the term, but as a matter of fact we simply convey that we do not know what the unconscious is. We have only *indirect proofs* that there is a mental sphere which is subliminal [...]. From the *products* which that unconscious mind produces we can draw certain conclusions as to its possible nature. But we must be careful not to be too anthropomorphic in our conclusions, because things might in reality be very different from what our consciousness makes them" ([CW18:11]—emphasis added).

Jung had a strong grounding in the biological sciences, and the relationship between soma (body) and psyche (spirit) engaged him for the whole of his life. His interest, however, focused increasingly on the psychic, spiritual side of the psyche/soma, spirit/matter equation. In the WAE, Jung was concerned with both *verbal* responses and *physical* reactions to stimulus words, that is, with body *and* psyche. He also worked almost exclusively with adults and his discussion focuses largely on the *behaviour* of the complex. Jung's account of the WAE was first published in psychiatric journals intended for a professional medical readership. Consequently, we appreciate that you might have felt a little overwhelmed when you found yourself immersed in the WAE earlier in this chapter! We hope the information in the following two paragraphs will help make Jung's theory of complexes, which we are about to explore, more accessible and answer any questions you might have, such as "how does it all begin?"; "how does a complex 'happen'?"; "what about the so-called archetypal nucleus of the complex?" etc., etc. We begin, thanks to the help of a smattering of basic neuroscience, with a very brief excursion into the way the *infant* brain 'works'!

HOW DO COMPLEXES 'HAPPEN?' A LITTLE NEUROSCIENCE ON THE INFANT BRAIN

It is important to remember that the human brain is far from fully formed at birth. The left hemisphere of the brain, which supports consciousness and cognition (our capacity for logical thinking), has not yet developed: the infant is a pre-verbal bundle of instinct and sensation. The right brain, or the right hemisphere of the brain, *is* up and running at birth. It processes emotional perception and bodily sensations and, at this stage of development, does all the work. The left hemisphere of the brain, which enables our capacity for language, cognition, analysis, and factual knowledge, does not start to come 'on-line' until the second year of life and, even then, is not fully developed. The right hemisphere records impressions, bodily sensations, physical reactions, smells, tastes, fears, trauma, joy, pleasure, a *felt-sense* of well-being, etc. It stores these experiences in what is called *implicit memory, emotional-* or *body-memory.* The contents of *implicit memory* are not retrievable, held, as they are, 'in the body,' that is, they are *unconscious.* At approximately age 2, *explicit memory* becomes possible with the development of the left hemisphere of the brain and its verbal and logical capabilities that gradually enable the infant to name, describe, and *situate* memories in the story line of his or her life; the development of the *cognitive* function of the left brain means that the contents of *explicit memory* are *retrievable,* able to be made *conscious.*

Even later, with the left hemisphere of the brain more fully developed, *implicit memory* continues to operate throughout life, as so much of our experience *in the world,* of necessity, bypasses conscious awareness, is suppressed or repressed. However, we are sure you will recognise that the unconscious contents of *implicit memory* recorded in infancy must have an especially significant formative impact on the infant as that impact was never mediated by language, logic, explanation, understanding (i.e., the influence of the left brain): something 'happens' and the infant is overwhelmed by affect, emotion, bodily sensation—from discomfort and hunger to fear, rage, panic. It is because *implicit memory* is irretrievable—there can be no conscious memory of its contents as specific, *understandable events*—the emotionally charged 'body-memories' and *affective* 'residue' of its impact remains. And *because* implicit memories remain unconscious, unknowable, and therefore untransformative, they continue to exert a powerful and disruptive influence on consciousness if and when activated or triggered by something in the *present* environment, when the infant is no longer an infant but an adult: "[t]hey [tend to] arise as a collage of sensations, emotions, movements and behaviours [and] appear and disappear surreptitiously. They are primarily organized around emotions and/or skills, or 'procedures'—things that the body does automatically [...]" (Levine 2015, p. 21).

THE PRIMARY PARENTAL COMPLEX

This brings us to a particularly useful discussion of complexes included in a lecture presented by Jung to the Congress of Swiss Psychiatrists (Zürich, 1928) and later published in German (1931) and English (1933):

> Experience shows us that complexes are infinitely varied, yet careful comparison reveals a relatively small number of typical primary forms, which are all built upon the first experiences of childhood. This must necessarily be so, because the individual disposition is already a factor in infancy; it is innate, and not acquired in the course of life. The parental complex is therefore nothing but the first manifestation of a clash between reality and the individual's constitutional inability to meet the demands it makes upon him. The primary form of the complex cannot be other than a parental complex because the parents are the first reality with which the child comes into conflict.

(CW6:927)

Jung goes on to say that what is important is "the special way" in which the parental complex (we all have one so this applies to us all!) "works its way out in the individual's life. And here we observe the most striking variations [...]" (*ibid.*:928). The complex has "a relatively small number of typical primary forms" yet can wreak havoc in the conscious lives of individuals in a variety of ways. Why might this be so?

At the core, or nucleus, of a complex Jung identifies an archetypal (typical or instinctual) dominant. We might think of this as a theme (e.g., mother/mothering); it functions as an *innate* predisposition or 'anticipation' (e.g., the infant's 'anticipation' of being mothered) that, once activated by an *external* stimulus (i.e., proximity of the actual mother), accrues to it an accumulation of sensations, feelings, experiences, beliefs, and memories bound to the archetypal, nuclear theme of 'mother.' Just as the genetic endowment of the human infant ensures that *physical* development, from conception to death, unfolds in a 'typical' but nevertheless individualistic way, so, too, we are each born with an *archetypal* endowment which promotes a 'typical' yet individualistic and endlessly varied development of personality and psychic (emotional and spiritual) life. It is not difficult to see that our archetypal endowment is closely aligned with the instincts: the baby's inborn archetypal need for positive mothering and nurture generates behaviour (crying when hungry, for instance) that ensures the basic survival instinct is met. In this way, the *unconscious* archetypal nucleus of a complex is a given, an instinct or human need that is *collective,* that is, common to us all. How a particular archetypal imperative (such as the need to be mothered, to be part of a community, to have a family) manifests, or 'looks in real life,' will differ from individual to individual. The 'complex' of experiences, memories, feelings, and ideas which accrues to the archetypal need to be 'mothered' will be different with each individual. My 'mother' complex will be different from yours because my experience of my mother was different from your experience of your mother. This is why Jung described complexes as the 'personifications' (or individualistic expressions or images) of their archetypal cores. It is also not surprising that the memories, fears, sensations, etc., adhering to the archetypal nucleus of such a key factor as 'mother' often result in a highly emotionally charged reaction—or behaviour—when that particular 'complex' is activated. The reaction or behaviour will, of course, depend on whether the infant's *personal* experience of 'being mothered' or 'parented' has resulted in a negative, positive, or ambivalent complex.

Example:

The archetypal survival instinct that is innate to the newborn baby has two 'poles': the baby needs physical nourishment to survive and also spiritual containment (e.g. the baby needs to be protected, held, feel secure, and welcomed into the world, loved). Without physical nourishment, the baby will not survive. Without sufficient spiritual nourishment, the baby may well develop a *negative* parental complex which becomes an inner voice telling her that she is not loved because not lovable, not good enough, etc.; she will be 'narcissistically wounded,' that is, wounded in her sense of selfhood and will lack self-confidence and self-esteem. The infant that experiences a secure, loving environment will develop a *positive* parental complex that ensures he will grow up to feel worthy, confident and grounded in a realistic sense of selfhood. From this example, I hope you can see how the archetypal/instinctual need for nurture becomes 'personalised' and 'particular' through the tenor and quality of each child-parent relationship. The *actual* parent 'humanises' (actualises, makes real) the *archetypal* parent, that is, the child's instinctual, archetypal need to be parented.

Jung writes that "complexes always contain something like a conflict [...]. At any rate, the characteristics of conflict—shock, upheaval, mental agony, inner strife—are peculiar to the complexes. (Thinking of our infant from the example above, we might see these 'characteristics of conflict' as arising from experiences of 'hunger,' 'discomfort,' 'pain,' 'fear,' etc.). These are the 'sore spots,' the *bêtes noires,* the 'skeletons in the cupboard' which we do not like to remember and still less to be reminded of by others, but which frequently come back to mind unbidden and in the most unwelcome fashion. They always contain memories, wishes, fears, duties, needs, or insights which somehow we can never really grapple with, and for this reason they constantly interfere with our conscious life in a disturbing and usually a harmful way" (*ibid.*:924).

The activation of disruptive (negative) complexes "means that something discordant, unassimilated, and antagonistic exists, perhaps as an obstacle, but also as an incentive to greater effort, and so, perhaps, to new possibilities of achievement. In this sense, therefore, complexes are focal or nodal points of psychic life which we would not wish to do without; indeed, they should not be missing, for otherwise psychic activity would come to a fatal standstill. They point to the unresolved problems in the individual, the places where he has suffered a defeat, at least for the time being, and where there is something he cannot evade or overcome—his weak spots in every sense of the word" (*ibid.*:925). In this statement, Jung argues that all "psychic material is grouped" or organised around complexes.

Complexes (whether conscious or unconscious) are the building blocks of the individual psyche. We might even say "Complexes 'R' Us"! They develop, as we have seen from our example of the 'mother' complex above, when inner meets outer, when an innate archetypal 'imperative' or instinctual need encounters outer reality and the encounter leaves an impression (conscious or unconscious) on psyche and soma. This is as true of the ego complex (yes, the 'ego' is also a complex), as it is of the mother, father, victim, saviour complex, or any of the well-known psychic components we will meet in Chapters 3 and 4, namely, *persona, shadow, anima, animus* … All are complexes, as all psychic content is 'grouped' into more or less autonomous clusters or 'complex' units—some conscious (that is, related to and under the purview of consciousness—we may well 'know' we have a 'father' *issue* or complex), others unconscious and, for that reason, all the more potentially disruptive to consciousness (leaving us wondering why we behaved in such an extreme, irrational manner, why we suddenly feel disoriented, speechless, "beside ourselves" with embarrassment or rage).

Jung writes, in Lecture 1 of the Tavistock Lectures (1935), "the nearest and dearest complex which we cherish is our ego. It is always in the centre of our attention and of our desires, and it is the absolutely indispensable centre of consciousness" (CW18:19). Jung describes the ego-complex in a healthy person as "the highest psychic authority. By this we mean the whole mass of ideas pertaining to the ego, which we think of as being accompanied by the powerful and ever-present feeling-tone of our own body" (CW3:82)— that is, the sense of 'I.' However, although the ego-complex may be "the psychological expression of the firmly associated combination of all body sensations [that] (good health permitting) weathers all psychological storms" (ibid.), it is nevertheless susceptible to being overpowered or displaced by a strong complex. How does a complex other than the ego-complex gain power? What happens when we find ourselves 'in the grip' of a complex? Here is Jung:

> […] [T]he ego-complex, by reason of its direct connection with bodily sensations, is the most stable and the richest in associations (*ibid.*:86). [However,] [r]eality sees to it that the peaceful cycle of egocentric ideas is constantly interrupted by ideas with a strong feeling-tone, that is, by affects (emotions). A situation threatening danger [or conflict, discomfort, anxiety, failure, ridicule, etc.—*authors*] pushes aside the tranquil play of ideas and puts in their place a complex of other ideas with a very strong feeling-tone. The new complex then crowds everything else into the background. For the time being it is the most distinct because it totally inhibits all other ideas; it permits only those egocentric ideas to exist which fit *its* situation, and under certain conditions it can suppress to the point of complete (momentary) unconsciousness all ideas that run counter to it, however strong they may be. It now possesses the strongest attention-tone (*ibid.*:84).

A helpful and most important point to keep in mind is Jung's realisation that the "essential basis of our personality is affectivity" (i.e., feeling, sentiment, emotion, and affect are primary and first registered in the body: we feel tears well up before we know why we are sad or moved). "Thought and action are," Jung writes, "only symptoms of (i.e., responses to) affectivity" (*ibid.*:78). In other words, what happens *inside* is a response to what happens to us on the *outside*, as well as serving as the motivating force for our own thoughts and actions.

Here is an example, from Jung, of how the basic "elements of psychic life, sensations, ideas, and feelings," (*ibid.*), shape thought and action through the concentration of affect; in other words, Jung's anecdote illustrates the activation of an unconscious complex which overpowers the ego:

> I was taking a walk with a very sensitive and hysterical gentleman. The village bells were pealing a new and very harmonious chime. My companion, who usually displayed great feeling for such chimes, suddenly began to rail at it, saying he could not bear that disgusting ringing in the major key, it sounded frightful; moreover it was a hideous church and a squalid-looking village. (The village is famous for its charming situation.) This remarkable inappropriate affect interested me and I pursued my investigations further. My companion then began to abuse the local parson. The reason he gave was that the parson had a repulsive beard and—wrote very bad poetry. My companion, too, was poetically inclined. Thus, the affect lay in poetic rivalry.
>
> (CW3:82)

Jung refers to the ego-complex as *primary* and other strong complexes that threaten to override the ego-complex as *secondary*. His realisation that the strong affectivity of a secondary complex often causes it to operate *as though it has a mind of its own* led him to describe such complexes as *autonomous,* possessing "all the characteristics of a separate personality" (CW2:1352), or splinter psyche (CW8:203). It follows, as Jung writes in "The Psychological Foundations of Belief in Spirits," that, with complexes often operating as 'separate personalities,' "the psyche is not an indivisible unity but a divisible and more or less divided whole. Although the separate parts are connected with one another, they are relatively independent, so much so that certain parts of the psyche never become associated with the ego at all, or only very rarely" (CW8:580). We don't want you to be alarmed by this observation, however, and can assure you that complexes operate continuously in the healthy psyche, mostly in association with, and under the purview of, the ego-complex. The ego-complex is the most important complex to emerge into consciousness in childhood. It is important because it is rooted in the body, in our sense that this is ME—body, mind, soul. It constitutes the *empirical personality* of an individual and serves as the centre of conscious awareness and the *carrier* of our sense of identity throughout life, who 'I' am now, was as a child, and have the potential to become in the future.

Jung once famously quipped "Everyone knows nowadays that people 'have complexes'; what is not so well known is that complexes can *have us*" (CW6:200). Unconscious complexes are more troublesome than those that are conscious (aligned with the ego-complex, one's conscious orientation and values) or semi-conscious. As we are not aware of unconscious complexes, they can more easily surprise us and derail the ego-complex (render us speechless, 'frozen,' fearful, devoid of confidence, etc.). This is particularly true of complexes that have been formed as the result of an acute or chronic (on-going) traumatic event or situation, especially in early childhood. In order to mitigate the disruptive and debilitating power of a strong, unconscious complex, we need to confront the complex and bring it to consciousness (and often we need help and support to do this). The powerful affect of the disruptive complex can be mitigated so that it loses its "automatic (i.e., instinctive) character and can be substantially transformed" (CW8:384) through rationalising (understanding) and personalis-ing it (exploring its relationship to one's conscious reality—"Do I really believe this?" "Is this how I want to behave?" "Are these truly my values?" "Am I reacting to what is happening now or to what happened to me as a child?" etc.). This healing process is ini-tiated through the differentiating, discerning courage and focus of the ego-complex. If it works, a 'new' complex or cluster of images, memories, sensations, and feelings develop to replace—or at least transform—the former disruptive complex. This tells us that com-plexes *can* be transformed! And not all complexes are negative! The term has, however, acquired negative connotations in the popu-lar imagination. While negative complexes that convince us we're unworthy, etc., can, of course, be pathological and cause neurotic suffering and serious mental illness, Jung regarded complexes as the natural and essential components of the healthy psyche. A positive mother or father or parental complex, for example, enables individuals to feel secure in the world, secure in themselves, realistically affirmative when faced with challenges, able to evaluate their own potential, etc.

In the table at the end of this chapter, you will find references to aspects of the complex not mentioned in this short narrative, such as the numinosity of complexes; more on the relationship of complexes to archetypes; why some complexes remain unconscious; 'spirits' as manifestations of complexes of the *collective unconscious* (see chapter 4); the relationship of complexes to dreams; complexes as the *via regia* (royal road) to the unconscious (in contrast to Freud's contention that the dream is the *via regia* to the unconscious); the autonomy of the complex; the complex as the 'architect' of the personality and of dreams, and more.

Enjoy your pursuit of Jung's ideas, following the guidance provided in Tables 1.1 and 1.2 below.

SUMMARY

We have looked at:

- Jung's early interests: nature/biological sciences and spiritual/humanistic studies
- His choice of psychiatry as a career as it treats the whole personality (psyche and soma; spiritual and physical experience)
- Jung's work with the Word Association Experiment which enabled him to discover the presence and dynamics of the complex as a structural component of the psyche
- The pragmatic applications of the WAE, including lie detection
- Jung's developing theory of the Feeling-Toned Complex
- "How does a complex 'happen'?" and the importance of experiences of early infancy
- A little neuroscience: the development of the infant brain
- The parental complex; the 'mother' complex
- The ego-complex (more on this in Chapter 3)
- Affectivity (emotion) as the basis of personality

⊕

REFERENCES

Freud, S. (1900/13) *The Interpretation of Dreams*. New York: Macmillan.

Jung, C. G. (1961/63) *Memories, Dreams, Reflections*. Recorded and edited by A. Jaffé. R. and C. Winston (Trans.). New York: Pantheon Books.

Jung, C. G. (1983) *The Collected Works of C. G. Jung: Supplementary Vol. A: The Zofingia Lectures*. J. Van Heurk (Trans.). Princeton, NJ: Princeton University Press.

Jung, C. G. (2008) *Children's Dreams: Notes from the Seminar Given in 1936-1940*. L. Jung and M. Meyer-Grass (Eds.). E. Falzeder and T. Woolfson (Trans.). Princeton, NJ: Princeton University Press.

Von Krafft-Ebing, R. (1888) *Lehrbuch der Psychiatrie: auf klinischer Grundlage für praktische Ärzte und Studirende*. Stuttgart: Ferdinand Enke.

Levine, P. (2015) *Trauma and Memory: Brain and Body in a Search for the Living Past: A Practical Guide for Understanding and Living with Personal Trauma*. Berkeley, CA: North Atlantic Books.

Table 1.1 Word Association Experiments

CW2, in which analyses of WAE case studies are recorded, is extremely detailed and may strike the reader as inaccessible. This table directs readers to key aspects of the test procedure and case analyses, and to *applications* of the experiment to subjects of more general interest: How psychic associations 'work,' WAE and memory, psycho-pathology, psychology of family units, and crime; the table lists two later works (1911, 1935) in which Jung summarises his work with the WAE. See the next table for (feeling-toned) complexes.

TOPIC/ KEYWORDS	LOCATION	DESCRIPTOR
Test Procedures	CW2:7-19 (1904)	Procedural details of how the Association Tests are set up for the experiment—number and type of stimulus words—nouns, verbs, etc.—Stages of the procedure/test, etc.
Classification of types of associations	CW2:20-113 (1904)	How association works in the psyche. Types of association, e.g., internal (cherry, apple = both fruit), objective (snake, poisonous), external (ink, pen), egocentric (praise, me), etc.
Test Results for Normal Subjects	CW2:114-498 (1904)	Detailed analyses of test results of a number of educated women and men, uneducated women, uneducated men.
WAE and Memory	CW2:639-659 (1905)	"Experimental Observations on the Faculty of Memory": two case studies of memory failure in the *reproduction* part of the test due to activation of feeling-toned complexes.

(Continued)

Table 1.1   (Continued)

TOPIC/ KEYWORDS	LOCATION	DESCRIPTOR
Significance of WAE to psychopathology	CW2:863-917 (1906)	Association mechanism discovered to follow certain laws potentially important to understanding psychopathological states (hysteria/neurosis, dementia praecox/schizophrenia).
WAE and the family	CW2:999-1014 (1909)	WAE applied to 24 families to investigate the psychology or 'constellation' of the family unit: role of education, attachment patterns, unconscious affective states of parents on children, etc.
WAE and crime	CW2:1316-1347 & 1357-1388 (1908)	Contribution of the WAE to criminology and the detection of evidence in 2 short articles: "New Aspects of Criminal Psychology," "On the Psychological Diagnosis of Evidence: The Evidence-Experiment in the Näf Trial" (Zurich, 1934).
Jung's retrospective (1911) reflections on significance of WAE & complex theory to the diagnosis and treatment of mental illness	CW2:1349-1356 (1913)	Succinct review of WAE and development of Complex Theory: "My theoretical views on the neuroses and certain psychoses—especially dementia praecox—are founded upon the psychological outcome of the *association experiment*" (by extension, on the Complex Theory that developed out of Jung's work with the WAE). Key points of Complex Theory: primary and secondary complexes, affect-intensity and autonomy of the complex, power of a complex to temporarily replace the ego, characteristics of a powerful complex to act as a separate personality, 'possession,' behaviour of complexes in hysteria/neurosis and dementia praecox (schizophrenia), "more or less autonomous complexes occur everywhere, even in so-called normal (mentally healthy)" individuals.
Tavistock Lectures: Comprehensive, summary of Jung's work with the WAE	CW18:97 *ff* (1935)	Summary of test procedures; recognition that "originally the experiment was […] meant for […] the study of mental association" (diagnosis of psychiatric pathologies); types of disturbance; analysis of case test results with diagrams; discussion with attendees of lecture.

Table 1.2 Complexes

TOPIC/ KEYWORDS	LOCATION	DESCRIPTOR
What is a complex? **Formation of the complex around nuclear element; behaviour; affect; numinosity, etc.**	CW8:18 *ff* (1948)	Based on his work with the WAE, Jung's Theory of Complexes is central to his model of the psyche and understanding of analytical psychology. Jung's exploratory work on complexes is recorded in CW2 (*Experimental Researches*); a later paper, "On Psychic Energy," (CW8:342–443) provides a comprehensive, meticulous (and difficult!) account of all aspects of the phenomenon of the complex and the 'dynamics' of the human psyche: useful 'map' on which to 'pin' the components of Jung's theory located elsewhere in CW.
Physical symptoms	CW2:727 (1906) CW2:816 (1906/1909)	Physical and psychic symptoms as manifestations of pathogenic complexes; hysteria and obsessive phenomena as symptoms of a complex. Complex often associated with a particular body part (found in common expressions, e.g., "I can't stomach this," "he is a pain in the neck," etc.)
Primary complex	CW2:610 *ff* (1905/1906)	Difference between ego (primary) complex and a secondary complex. Feeling-toned complexes influence and compete with the intentions of the ego complex.
Secondary complex	CW2:861 (1906/1909)	"The complex has an abnormal autonomy in hysteria and a tendency to an active separate existence, which reduces and replaces the constellating power of the ego-complex. In this way a new morbid personality is gradually created [...] This secondary personality devours what is left of the normal ego and forces it into the role of a secondary (oppressed) complex."

(Continued)

Table 1.2 (Continued)

TOPIC/ KEYWORDS	LOCATION	DESCRIPTOR
Ego-complex **Centre of consciousness: sense of who 'I' am; sense of continuity: 'me' as a child, an adult, etc.**	CW3:82 *ff* (1907)	"The ego-complex in a normal (healthy) person is the highest psychic authority. By this we mean the whole mass of ideas pertaining to the ego, which we think of as being accompanied by the powerful and ever-present feeling-tone of our own body." "The ego is the psychological expression of the firmly associated combination of all body sensations. One's own personality is therefore the firmest and strongest complex, and (good health permitting) it weathers all psychological storms."
	CW8:387, 430 (1954)	Ego-complex as an individual's empirical personality. Complexity of ego-complex: "the light of consciousness has many degrees of brightness, the ego-complex many gradations of emphasis." Ego as "hard-and-fast complex which, tied to consciousness and its continuity, cannot easily be altered, and should not be altered unless one wants to bring on pathological disturbances."
Splitting/ Complex as psychic fragment	CW2:712 (1906)	Splitting of the personality (multiple personalities) understood as splitting of complexes—aspects of the personality that do not want to know each other.
	CW8:253 (1937)	The psyche's tendency to split, leading to the autonomous life of psychic components manifests not only in severe cases but as complexes in 'normals.' "Complexes are psychic fragments which have split off owing to traumatic influences or incompatible tendencies." Complexes interfere with intentions of the will (ego), disturb conscious performance, **behave like independent beings.**
Being in the 'grip' of a complex	CW3:84-88 (1907)	What happens when we are in the 'grip' of a complex; how a complex gains power; the perseverance and return of complexes; the chronic effects of a complex.
	CW8:200 (1948)	"Everyone knows [...] that people 'have complexes.' What is not so well known, [...] is that complexes can *have us*."

(Continued)

Table 1.2   (Continued)

TOPIC/ KEYWORDS	LOCATION	DESCRIPTOR
Aim of education	CW3:90-91 (1907)	Aim of education: to instil positive (life-affirming) complexes in the child—so the effect of a complex extends from emotion, through thought to action.
Autonomy of Complex	CW3:102-04 (1907)	Autonomous complexes that hinder, eclipse or displace the ego-complex. The effect of an autonomous complex on ego-consciousness/ the ego-complex.
Numinosity; 'Possession' by complex;	CW7:387 (1916/1928)	Autonomous complexes as disturbing factors that disrupt conscious control and act like 'disturbers of the peace.' Complexes and 'possession,' – the process of freeing oneself from 'possession' by a complex.
Psyche as Divided Whole;	CW8:580 *ff* (1948)	Psyche as "more or less divided whole"—*not* an indivisible unity—Role of ego-complex; relation or 'association' of complexes to ego-complex.
Manifestations of autonomous complex/ projection;		"Autonomous complexes appear most clearly in dreams, visions, pathological hallucinations, and delusional ideas. Because the ego is unconscious of them, they always appear first in projected form." Ways in which autonomous complexes manifest. Spirits as manifestations of autonomous complexes. Distinction between **spirit** and **soul** and differentiation of **soul and spirit complexes.**
Soul & spirit — Complexes of personal uncs./ collective uncs.		
Effects/causes	CW8:590 *ff*	"The personal unconscious [...] contains complexes that belong to the individual and form an intrinsic part of his psychic life." What happens when a complex which ought to be associated with the ego becomes "lost," i.e., unconscious; and when "a complex of the collective unconscious becomes associated with the ego."
	CW8:593 *ff*	*Soul* correlative with autonomous complexes of personal unconscious, *spirits* with collective unconscious.
	CW8:600	Effects of an autonomous complex (both psychical and physical). And causes (including 'loss of soul').
	CW9i:220 (1950)	*Telepathic effects* of autonomous complex. "Possession [...] as identity of ego personality with a complex."

(Continued)

Table 1.2   (Continued)

TOPIC/ KEYWORDS	LOCATION	DESCRIPTOR
Complexes and Dreams	CW3:122; 133 (1907)	Dreams = Symbolic expressions of the complexes. Jung saw the Complex as *via regia* (royal road) to the unconscious over the Dream (Freud); complex *the architect of the Dream*.
	CW3:141 (1907)	For the 'normal' individual to free himself of obsessive complexes, *displacement* is often used; an hysteric can be cured if the therapist is able to induce a new complex that will obsess the patient (fighting a complex with another, new complex).
Displacement Overcoming a complex	CW9i:184 (1954)	A complex can be overcome if lived out to the full (made conscious).
'Correction' of complexes	CW8:383 *ff* (1954)	Feeling-toned complexes that remain unconscious do not change in the same way as when conscious. To be 'corrected,' complexes need to be made conscious; they "lose their automatic character and can be substantially transformed." Dialectic discussion with complexes becomes possible.
"On the Doctrine of Complexes" **Concise 'story' of Jung's work with WAE and development of his thinking on the complex (to 1911)**	CW2:1349-56 (1913)	*Comprehensive early summary of the WAE and its findings.* Behaviour of the complex and close relation of the complex to neurosis. Includes all-encompassing definition of primary (ego) complex vs. secondary complex. Jung argues that 'normals,' neurotics, and schizophrenics all suffer from the autonomy of complexes: the autonomous complex as source of all psychological difficulties: "[...] certainly in both the neuroses and dementia praecox (schizophrenia) the symptoms— whether of a somatic or of a psychic nature— originate from the complex as [...] described in detail by the school of Freud." Behaviour of complexes in neurosis and dementia praecox.

(Continued)

Table 1.2   (Continued)

TOPIC/ KEYWORDS	LOCATION	DESCRIPTOR
Nuclear complexes: Oedipus/Electra	CW4:562-63 (1916)	Jung still incredibly supportive of Freud's ideas but beginning to diverge from Freud. For Jung, a *fixation* on infantile fantasies causes neurosis; everyone possesses these fantasies, yet some are not fixated on them. The 'nuclear' complex: Oedipus /Electra. For Jung, the past can only provide so much information; the present as a moment demanding a new psychological perspective.
Jung's 1934 "A Review of the Complex Theory"	CW8:194-219 (1948)	***Thorough retrospective on Jung's Complex Theory.*** Review of the WAE; clear definition of 'feeling-toned complex'; complex theory and French school of dissociationism (Janet): the fragmentary personality and the complex; autonomy of complexes; splinter psyches; the personification of complexes in dream figures; aetiology of complexes originating in trauma; complexes as living units of the psyche and *via regia* to the unconscious; the complex as architect of dreams and symptoms (psychic and somatic).
Elucidation and Review/Tavistock Lectures	CW18 (1935) 5 Lectures, pp. 5–182	***Fundamental Psychological Conceptions—A dynamic, comprehensive review of key theories, including the Complex Theory. Discussion with lecture attendees.***
The Mother Complex	CW9i:161 *ff* (1954)	Chapter 3 in "Psychological Aspects of the Mother Archetype." Mother's role in the development of the mother complex; effects of mother complex on son; and daughter; adult men and mother complex; finely differentiated *eros* (relatedness); same-gender relationships; Don Juanism; negative mother complex.

JUNG, FREUD, AND THE DEVELOPMENT OF JUNG'S WORK ON PERSONALITY TYPES

In this chapter we will look at Jung's relationship with Freud, his devastating break with Freud, the 'creative illness,' and 'confrontation with the unconscious' that followed, together with the ideas that Jung formed during this period of his life, as they were to form the bedrock of his model of the psyche. We will also discuss Jung's Theory of Psychological Types (his theory of the different 'types of consciousness') as they reflect his struggle to understand the cause of the differences between his, Freud's, and Adler's ideas and psychotherapeutic methods.

JUNG'S RELATIONSHIP WITH FREUD

By 1906, Jung had been working on the Word Association Experiment at the Burghölzli Mental Hospital (the Psychiatric Clinic associated with the University of Zürich) for six years. He had published his findings, established a reputation as a researcher, and was focused on an academic career. However, a combination of events, most notably Jung's study of Freud's *The Interpretation of Dreams* (1900/13) and writings on the causes and treatment of the neuroses, led to a shift in Jung's focus and the start of his work as a psychoanalyst. In his reading of Freud's work, Jung found that many of Freud's theories corroborated his own ideas deduced from close observations of psychiatric patients in the Burghölzli and subjects undertaking the Word Association Test.

In 1906, however, neither Freud nor his psychoanalytical theories were accepted by the academic world. Both were discredited and often ridiculed. Jung nevertheless refused to ignore the impact of

DOI: 10.4324/9781315619156-3

Freud's contribution on his own research; he felt that to deny Freud's influence would be disingenuous, a lie. Consequently, Jung found himself defending Freud publicly at lectures, conferences, and in academic papers despite, as he writes in his autobiography, warnings "that if I remained on Freud's side and continued to defend him, I would be endangering my academic career" (1961/63, p. 148).

Jung sent Freud a copy of his research on the Word Association Experiment in 1906 and a correspondence ensued. Then, in early 1907, after Jung sent Freud his book, "The Psychology of Dementia Praecox" (*dementia praecox* = schizophrenia, see CW3), Freud invited Jung to Vienna. At their first, now-famous meeting in March, 1907, the two men talked for 13 hours! A professional friendship followed, mostly through correspondence. An important result of the collaboration between Jung and Freud was the foundation in 1910 of the International Psychoanalytic Association. Jung served as president of the Association from its founding until 1913, when he was forced to recognise that Freud's and his own ideas diverged on key issues to such an extent that the breakdown of their relationship had become inevitable.

Freud (born May, 1856) was almost 20 years older than Jung (born July, 1875). At their first meeting, each man was impressed by the other. As the younger of the two, Jung felt he had a great deal to learn from the more experienced Freud. Jung recalls, in his 1959 BBC interview with John Freeman (1959/78), that in Freud's presence he mostly listened. Nevertheless, during that first significant and intense encounter, Jung found himself neither unquestioning nor uncritical of certain of Freud's ideas and theories. Even before the two men corresponded or met, Jung had openly published his concerns, along with his appreciation of Freud, in the July, 1906 Preface to "The Psychology of Dementia Praecox":

> Even a superficial glance at my work will show how much I am indebted to the brilliant discoveries of Freud. [...] Fairness to Freud, however, does not imply, as many fear, unqualified submission to a dogma; one can very well maintain an independent judgment. If I, for instance, acknowledge the complex mechanisms of dreams and hysteria (the neuroses), this does not mean that I attribute to the infantile sexual trauma the exclusive importance that Freud apparently does. Still less does it mean that I place sexuality so predominantly in the foreground, or that I grant it the psychological universality which Freud, it seems, postulates in view of the admittedly enormous role which sexuality plays in the psyche. As for Freud's therapy, it is at best but one of several possible methods,

and perhaps does not always offer in practice what one expects from it in theory. Nevertheless, all these things are the merest trifles compared with the psychological principles whose discovery is Freud's greatest merit [...].

(CW4, pp. 3–4)

Despite his claim (above) that "one can very well maintain an independent judgment," in the face of Freud's often dogmatic insistence on the unquestionable validity of his theory and method and on his younger colleague's allegiance, Jung was troubled by a growing awareness of how significantly his ideas and observations differed from those of Freud. On their voyage together from Europe to Clark University, Massachusetts, in 1909, where both Freud and Jung had been invited to lecture, Jung suffered serious misgivings about Freud's interpretation of one of his dreams, yet he remained silent. In his autobiography, Jung writes: "I felt violent resistance to [...] [Freud's] [...] interpretation. I also had some intimation of what the dream might really mean. But I did not then trust my own judgment, and wanted to hear Freud's opinion. I wanted to learn from him" (1961/63, p. 139). Jung came to appreciate this dream as perhaps *the* most important, transformative dream of his life. In the following two boxes, you will find Jung's dream and his (much later) reflections on its meaning and significance to his understanding of the structure of the human psyche and to the development of the theory and practice of Analytical Psychology on which he worked for the rest of his life. You may well be familiar with this dream from your reading of Jung's 'autobiography' (*Memories, Dreams, Reflections*), from biographies of Jung or from books by commentators on Jung. Although long, the dream is cited below in its entirety because of its profound impact on Jung and his thinking.

"I was in a house I did not know, which had two stories (*sic.*). It was 'my house.' I found myself in the upper story (*sic.*), where there was a kind of salon furnished with fine old pieces in rococo style. On the walls hung a number of precious old paintings. I wondered that this should be my house, and thought, "Not bad." But then it occurred to me that I did not know what the lower floor looked like. Descending the stairs, I reached the ground floor. There everything was much older, and I realized that this part of the house must date from about the fifteenth or sixteenth century. The furnishings were medieval; the floors were of red brick. Everywhere it was rather dark. I went from one room to another, thinking, "Now I really must explore the whole house." I came upon a heavy door, and opened it. Beyond it, I discovered a stone stairway that led down into the cellar. Descending again, I found myself in a beautifully vaulted room which looked exceedingly ancient. Examining the walls, I discovered layers of brick among the ordinary stone blocks, and chips of brick in the mortar. As soon as I saw this I knew that the walls dated from Roman times. My interest by now was intense. I looked more closely at the floor. It was of stone slabs, and in one of these I discovered a ring. When I pulled it, the stone slab lifted, and again I saw a stairway of narrow stone steps leading down into the depths. These, too, I descended, and entered a low cave cut into the rock. Thick dust lay on the floor, and in the dust were scattered bones and broken pottery, like remains of a primitive culture. I discovered two human skulls, obviously very old and half disintegrated. Then I awoke" (Jung 1961/63, pp. 158–59).

As Jung writes in his 'autobiography,' Freud became fixated on the image of the two skulls, insisting they indicated "that secret death-wishes were concealed in the dream" (*ibid.*, p. 159) and wanting to know towards whom Jung harboured death wishes. Jung struggled to satisfy Freud with an answer ("My wife and my sister-in-law" [*ibid.*]) which was, in fact, a deceit to avoid conflict with his mentor. Before this dream, Jung had already been asking himself a number of questions: "On what premises is Freudian psychology founded? To what category of human thought does it belong? What is the relationship of its almost exclusive personalism to general historical assumptions?" (*ibid.*, p. 161). In this next box are Jung's reflections on the answers to his questions he found in the dream's imagery:

"It was plain to me that the house represented a kind of image of the psyche—that is to say, of my then state of consciousness, with hitherto unconscious additions. Consciousness was represented by the salon. It had an inhabited atmosphere, in spite of its antiquated style. The ground floor stood for the first level of the unconscious.

The deeper I went, the more alien and the darker the scene became. In the cave, I discovered remains of a primitive culture, that is, the world of the primitive man within myself—a world which can scarcely be reached or illuminated by consciousness. The primitive psyche of man borders on the life of the animal soul, just as the caves of prehistoric times were usually inhabited by animals before men laid claims to them" (1961/63, p. 160).

"My dream was giving me the answer (to the questions posed above). It obviously pointed to the foundations of cultural history— a history of successive layers of consciousness. My dream thus constituted a kind of structural diagram of the human psyche; it postulated something of an altogether *impersonal* nature underlying that psyche. It 'clicked,' as the English have it—and the dream became for me a guiding image which in the days to come was to be corroborated to an extent I could not at first suspect. It was my first inkling of a collective *a priori* beneath the personal psyche. This I first took to be the traces of earlier modes of functioning. Later, with increasing experience and on the basis of more reliable knowledge, I recognized them as forms of instinct, that is, as archetypes" (*ibid.*, p. 161).

SUMMARY

- We have discussed Jung's reading and appreciation of Freud's work; and his championing of Freud in the face of criticism of Psychoanalytical Theory, despite his own misgivings about some of Freud's ideas
- We have noted how Jung makes contact with Freud, and that the two men meet and are impressed by each other
- We have identified Jung's growing awareness of the divergence of his and Freud's ideas
- and noted a turning point in their relationship: the voyage to the USA; Jung's differences from Freud clarified by their discussion of Jung's Dream of the Multi-storey House

⊕

JUNG'S BREAK WITH FREUD

The dream (above) had a profound effect on Jung, reawakening an earlier interest in archaeology and mythology from his student days, and leading him to discover Friedrich Creuzer's *The Symbolism and Mythology of Ancient Peoples* (1822). Jung recalls the profound impact of Creuzer's book:

> [It ...] fired me! I read like mad, and worked with feverish interest through a mountain of mythological material, then through the Gnostic writers, and ended in total confusion. I found myself in a state of perplexity similar to the one I had experienced at the clinic when I tried to understand the meaning of psychotic states of mind. It was as if I were in an imaginary madhouse and were beginning to treat and analyze all the centaurs, nymphs, gods, and goddesses in Creuzer's book as though they were my patients. While thus occupied I could not help but discover the close relationship between ancient mythology and the psychology of primitives, and this led me to an intensive study of the latter.
>
> (1961/63, p. 162)

Fascinated also by the recently published fantasies of a young American woman, "Miss Miller," Jung was "struck by the mythological character of the fantasies. They operated like a catalyst upon the stored-up and still disorderly ideas within me" (*ibid.,* pp. 162–63). This inner creative turbulence resulted in the publication in 1912 of Jung's next book, *Wandlungen und Symbole der Libido* (published in English in 1917 as *Psychology of the Unconscious,* with an extensive revision by Jung in 1952 re-titled *Symbols of Transformation* and published in 1956 as volume 5 of *The Collected Works*).

Below is an excerpt from Jung's Foreword (written in 1950) to the *revised edition* of *Symbols of Transformation,* in which Jung reflects back on the book's genesis and why it "stood in urgent need of revision" 38 years after its original publication date. Jung's Foreword also makes clear why this book's publication in 1912 definitively broke his 'silence' and precipitated his eventual break with Freud:

> I have never felt happy about this book, much less satisfied with it: it was written at top speed [...]. The whole thing came upon me like a landslide that cannot be stopped. The urgency that lay behind it became clear to me only later: it was the explosion of all those psychic contents which could find no room, no breathing-space, in the constricting atmosphere of Freudian psychology and its narrow outlook. I have no wish to denigrate Freud, or to detract from the extraordinary merits of his investigation of the individual psyche. But the conceptual framework into which

he fitted the psychic phenomenon seemed to me unendurably narrow. I am not thinking here of his theory of neurosis, [...] or his theory of dreams, [...] I am thinking more of the reductive causalism of his whole outlook [...] [particularly] [...] his earlier views, which move within the confines of the outmoded rationalism and scientific materialism of the late nineteenth century.

(CW5, p. xxiii)

Jung stalled the publication of *Symbols of Transformation* because he knew it would cost him his friendship with Freud. He was unable to write for two months and the question kept going round in his head: "Should I keep my thoughts to myself, or should I risk the loss of so important a friendship?" (1961/63, p. 167). Jung *did* publish *Symbols of Transformation*. And it *did* cost him his friendship with Freud. It also cost him his relationships with most of his friends and colleagues, and tarnished his reputation, as many in the psychoanalytic community declared his book to be rubbish (*ibid.*). As Anthony Stevens (1990) summarises, in *Symbols of Transformation* Jung "announced his hypothesis of a collective unconscious, [...] rejected Freud's view of libido as exclusively sexual, [...] that the Oedipus or Elektra complex was a developmental stage through which all boys and girls passed [...] [and] that [...] attachment [to] or [...] conflict (with parental figures) was inevitably sexual" (p. 22).

JUNG'S "CONFRONTATION WITH THE UNCONSCIOUS"

Following the dissolution of his relationship with Freud, Jung was isolated professionally and alone with himself. He resigned from his presidency of the International Psychoanalytic Association in 1913 and relinquished his lectureship at the University of Zürich at the end of the 1913–14 academic session; he had already left his post at the Burghölzli in 1909.

Over the next five years, Jung experienced what Henri Ellenberger, Stevens, and others, including the authors of this book, understand as a *creative illness* but which Jung's critics have variously described as "a breakdown, a psychosis" (Stevens 1990, p. 7). Jung was 38 in 1913, and Ellenberger (1970) reminds us that Freud suffered a comparable experience at around the same age: "The creative illnesses of both these men succeeded a period of intense preoccupation with the mysteries of the human soul. Both [...] cut or restricted to the minimum their ties with the university and professional or scientific organizations. Both suffered symptoms of emotional illness [...] [and] [...] underwent self-imposed psychic exercises, each according to his own method: Freud by free association, endeavouring to recover the lost memories of his early childhood; Jung by forced imagination (i.e., active imagination) and the drawing of his dreams" (p. 672). Jung kept himself grounded in the reality of everyday life through his private practice, focus on his family, and his military responsibilities during WW1 "amounting to a few months every year" (*ibid.*, p. 670).

In his 'autobiography,' Jung refers to this period of intense inner work as his "Confrontation with the Unconscious" (1961/63). It was his *nekyia* or *katabasis,* his descent to the underworld, the depths of the unconscious, which Jung considered to be "the real, subterranean life of the psyche" (CW5, p. xxvi). The dreams, visions, fantasies, and images that assailed Jung during this 'experiment,' which lasted until his recovery on the eve of WWI Armistice Day in 1918, provided him with the raw material on which he would work for the rest of his life. Jung writes:

> When I parted from Freud, I knew that I was plunging into the unknown. Beyond Freud, after all, I knew nothing; but I had taken the step into darkness. [...] It has taken me virtually forty-five years to distil within the vessel of my scientific work the things I experienced and wrote down at that time (i.e., 1914-1918). [...] The years when I was pursuing my inner images were the most important in my life—in them everything essential was decided. It all began then; the later details (i.e., the defining and description of terms, concepts and psychic dynamics that constitute Analytical Psychology) are only supplements and clarifications of the material that burst forth from the unconscious, and at first swamped me. It was the *prima materia* for a lifetime's work.
>
> (1961/63, p. 199)

SUMMARY

- We have noted Jung's introverted period of work on what was to become CW5, *Symbols of Transformation,* in which he introduced his hypothesis of the collective unconscious and openly rejected Freud's central tenets on the nature of *libido,* sexuality, the Oedipal/Electra complex,

- and the awakening of Jung's interests in mythology, Gnosticism
- We discussed Jung's hesitation to publish *Symbols of Transformation* for fear of losing Freud's friendship
- his break with Freud
- and Jung's *creative illness* and 'confrontation with the unconscious'

A BRIEF DIVERSION

THE RED BOOK (AND THE BLACK BOOKS)

The Black Books (2020) refer to Jung's private, personal journals which he kept for many years as a young man and a student. He abandoned his journal when, in 1902, he became engaged to his future wife, Emma Rauschenbach. One late entry, cited in Sonu Shamdasani's (2009) commentary on *The Red Book,* indicates Jung's shift of focus at that time from the inner to the outer world: "I am no longer alone with myself, and I can only artificially recall the scary and beautiful feeling of solitude. This is the shadow side of the fortune of love" (p. 196). There followed an extraverted period during which Jung achieved international recognition, worldly success, wealth, and happiness. Yet, as Murray Stein (2012) points out, "[...] a period of doubt had settled into his mind [...] as he was struggling with Freud, with other personal relationships, with his ground-breaking work, *Transformations and Symbols of Libido* (*Symbols of Transformation*), and above all with himself" (p. 284). And in November 1913, at the time of his break with Freud, Jung started writing in his private journal once again. This marked the beginning of work on *The Red Book* or *Liber Novus* (*New Book*), which contains Jung's record of his *confrontation with the unconscious* and its aftermath. "Between November 12, 1913 and April 19, 1914, he (Jung) wrote the entries into his diary that would become the basis for *Liber Primus* (Book One) and *Liber Secundus* (Book Two) of *The Red Book* [...]. Th[is] period [...] constitutes his most intensive engagement in active imagination. The remaining important imaginal material [...] was produced intermittently until the middle of 1916. After that, he continued working on the commentaries and interpretations of the material generated in active imagination, as well as on the calligraphy and paintings [...]" (*ibid.,* p. 282).

What *is* *The Red Book*? It was published in 2009. It is a feast for the mind and soul, and its exquisite calligraphy and beautiful, evocative paintings an aesthetic treat for the eye. "What Jung has done is to bring the mysteries forward from ancient mythological and theological enactments into the psychological domain of an individual, describing essentially the same mystery within the consciousness of a modern personality. It is a re-enactment of ancient mysteries but in a modern context [...]. We can read *The Red Book* as an account of a symbolic process of divinization of the human within the privacy of an individual psyche, [...] as (a realisation) of the dimension of transcendence within the psyche" (Stein 2012, p. 294).

JUNG ON HIS DIFFERENCES FROM FREUD AND THE SUBJECTIVITY OF EXPERIENCE

We noted above that his *creative illness* provided Jung with material from the unconscious on which he worked for the following decades and out of which he distilled his model of the structure and dynamics of the human psyche (see Chapters 3 and 4). Jung also worked to understand the devastating impact of his break with Freud. This led him to address personal as well as purely ideological and intellectual differences between himself and Freud. Jung also reflected on his differences with Alfred Adler, Adler's Individual Psychology, and the possible cause of Adler's own break with Freud.

Jung's conclusions? In an open, reflective—and self-reflective—article published in 1929, 16 years after his break with Freud, Jung writes: "Philosophical criticism (i.e., critical examination of one's vision, ideas and assumptions) has helped me to see that every psychology—my own included—has the character of a subjective confession" (CW4:774). In other words, the way in which we understand ourselves, and experience and understand the world, is shaped by our subjectivity, who we are as individuals. An individual's vision of world, self, and others is a (naturally limited) expression of him- or herself; and that vision expresses *a truth*, the observing individual's 'truth,' not The Truth (should such a thing ever be possible to attain!). Jung argues that the closest one can get to 'the truth' is 'true expression,' which "consists in giving form to what is observed" (CW4:771). Here is Jung on Freud:

> What Freud has to say about sexuality, infantile pleasure, and their con-flict with the 'reality principle,' as well as what he says about incest and the like, can be taken as the truest expression of his personal psy-chology. It is the successful formulation of what he himself subjectively observed. [...] By his own subjective confession, Freud has assisted at the birth of a great truth about man. He has devoted his life and strength to the construction of a psychology which is a formulation of his own being . . .
>
> (CW4:772)

... as has Jung! ... as has Adler ... as do founders of systems, philosophies, schools of thought, etc., ... and as do we all in shar-ing our perspectives and stories with others. And, again, here is Jung on Freud's and Adler's different standpoints and schools of psychology:

> Working with the same empirical material as Freud, he (Adler) approached it from a totally different standpoint. His way of looking at things is at least as convincing as Freud's, because he too represents a psychology of a well-known type. I know that the followers of both schools flatly assert that I am in the wrong [...]. Both schools, to my way of thinking, deserve reproach for over-emphasizing the pathological aspect of life and for interpreting man too exclusively in the light of his defects. [...] For my part, I prefer to look at man in the light of what in him is healthy and sound, and to free the sick man from just that kind of psychology which colours every page Freud has written.
>
> (CW4:774)

In the same essay, "Freud and Jung: Contrasts," written in 1929, Jung clarifies his own 'attitude' and picture of the world, the founda-tion on which Analytical Psychology was built:

> In my picture of the world there is a vast outer realm and an equally vast inner realm; between these two stands man, facing now one and now the other, and, according to temperament and disposition, taking the one for the absolute truth by denying or sacrificing the other. [...] This picture is hypothetical, of course, but it offers a hypothesis which is so valuable that I will not give it up. [...] This hypothesis certainly came to me from an inner source, though I might imagine that empirical findings had led to its discovery. Out of it has grown my theory of types, and also my reconciliation with views as different from my own as those of Freud.
>
> (CW4:777–78)

Elsewhere, Jung pinpoints the essential attitudinal differences between his, Freud's, and Adler's 'schools' and methods when he identifies the premises informing Freud's Psychoanalysis and Adler's Individual (or Ego) Psychology as *causal* (based on cause and effect) and *reductive* (or *mechanistic*), and those of Analytical Psychology as *synthetic* (or *constructive*) and *progressive* (or *finalistic,* i.e., purposive, oriented to a future goal). Jung discusses these different descriptive approaches to theory, psychotherapeutic method, and the dynamics of psychic energy (how psychic energy 'works' and 'behaves') in some detail in Chapter XI, "Definitions," of *Psychological Types* (1921). (This chapter, as its title suggests, contains 'definitions' of the terms and concepts fundamental to Jung's own Analytical Psychology which he would further differentiate and develop for the remainder of his life.)

Here are a few key observations on the reductive and constructive methods:

> The reductive method is oriented backwards, in contrast to the constructive (*synthetic*) method [...]. The interpretive methods of both Freud and Adler are reductive, since in both cases there is a reduction to the elementary processes of wishing (Freud) or striving (Adler), which in the last resort are of an infantile or physiological nature.
>
> (CW6:788)

The reductive method primarily seeks the causes of psychological disturbance in the literal events, persons, and situations and memories of childhood. Jung understands the *constructive* (or *synthetic*) method as the antithesis of the reductive method:

> The constructive method is concerned with the elaboration of the products of the unconscious (dreams, fantasies). It takes the unconscious product as a symbolic expression which anticipates a coming phase of psychological development.
>
> (*ibid.*:701)

When Jung says he understands an unconscious 'product' (i.e., dream/fantasy image, feeling, idea) "as a symbolic expression which *anticipates* (authors' emphasis) a coming phase of psychological development" (*ibid.*), he is describing the *progressive* focus of his own method, based on his observation of a natural movement in the psyche towards consciousness. "The aim of the constructive (synthetic) method, therefore, is to elicit from the unconscious product a meaning that relates to the subject's future attitude" (*ibid.*:702).

A PAUSE AND A RECOMMENDATION

Before moving to Jung's theory of types, or Typology, we highly recommend Jung's 1929 essay, "Freud and Jung: Contrasts" (CW4, *Freud and Psychoanalysis*). It offers a concise appreciation of the chief differences in attitude, understanding of the human psyche, and the psychological systems of both Freud and Jung. Certainly, Jung had felt that Freud, for the most part, discounted experience of the spirit in his approach to the human psyche. In his reflections, Jung looks forward as well as backward, outlining what he feels to be the focus and goal of the rest of his life's work: "We moderns are faced with the necessity of rediscovering the life of the spirit; we must experience it anew for ourselves. It is the only way in which to break the spell that binds us to the cycle of biological events" (CW4:780). The essay is clear, succinct, robust—and short! In it, Jung clarifies his understanding of the term 'spirit' and readily acknowledges criticisms levelled against his own thinking and the tenets and hypotheses of his developing Analytical Psychology.

As the title suggests, all essays in CW4 (*most* of which were published between 1906 and 1916) focus on Freud, Psychoanalysis, Jung's response to Psychoanalysis, and his analyses of the key differences between Analytical Psychology (the Zürich School) and Psychoanalysis, between Freud's, Adler's, and his own thinking. If Jung's relationship to Freud and Psychoanalysis, and this stage of his personal and professional development are of interest, CW4 is for you!

SUMMARY

- We have explored Jung's argument that all psychological systems have the character of a subjective confession
- and his realisation: the closest we come to the 'truth' is the 'true expression' of necessarily subjective observation and experience
- We reviewed the differences between Freud's, Adler's, and Jung's standpoints or ways of seeing the world
- and noted Jung's 'picture of the world': a vast outer realm and equally vast inner realm
- We also noted the goal of Jung's life's work: to rediscover the life of the spirit
- and that Jung understood Freud's 'method' as causal and reductive, and his own as synthetic (constructive) and progressive

> • Important point: Jung observed a natural movement towards consciousness in the psyche, an idea fundamental to Analytical Psychology and his therapeutic method (see Chapter 5, especially *Individuation*)

AN INTRODUCTION TO JUNG'S THEORY OF PSYCHOLOGICAL TYPES

As Jung acknowledges, his 'struggles' with Freud, precipitating his *creative illness,* fuelled his need to *understand* what had happened, and why. This served as the catalyst for the development of his theory of typology, published in 1921 as *Psychological Types* (CW6). When Jung was working on the Word Association Experiment at the Burghölzli Hospital, he and his colleague, Franz Riklin, had recognised that, as well as responses to the stimulus words being affected by the activation of unconscious complexes, they were also influenced by the 'individual character' of the subject. John Beebe (2006), in his chapter on Psychological Types in *The Handbook of Jungian Psychology,* cites Jung's and Riklin's identification, at that time, of two 'types' of character or personality: "(1) A type in whose reactions, subjective, often feeling-toned experiences are used; (2) A type whose reactions show an objective, impersonal tone" (p. 131). Introversion. Extraversion. Jung associated the hysteric's "intensity of feeling" with extraversion, and the schizophrenic's lack of intensity with introversion (*ibid.*). Jung was soon to refer to an individual's 'type' as his or her *personal equation.*

ALERT!

John Beebe observes that most people assume that 'types' refer to 'types of people,' while in fact "for Jung, they were types of *consciousness,* [...] characteristic orientations assumed by the ego in establishing and discriminating an individual's inner and outer reality" (*ibid.,* p. 130). As you read on, access this topic in the CW through Table 2.1 at the end of the chapter, and no doubt try to 'type' yourself and your friends, **remember John Beebe's words!**

Jung's early work on typology, first presented in 1913, focused on introversion and extraversion, and the opposition of two 'functions,' thinking and feeling (evaluating). At this point, Jung was identifying 'thinking' with introversion, and 'feeling' with extraversion. Working with Toni Wolff, an analyst and collaborator who helped Jung formulate and clarify many of his key concepts such as *anima, animus* (see Chapter 4 below), and psychiatrist and colleague Dr Hans Schmid-Guisan, with whom he corresponded on the 'question of types' in 1915–16 (Jung 2013), Jung soon identified thinking and feeling as *rational* 'functions' of consciousness, and intuition and sensation as irrational or *non*-rational 'functions' (i.e., beyond the control of rational consciousness). The *creative illness*, which in 1913 pulled Jung from a busy, extraverted life into a period of extreme introversion, followed by a return in 1918 to extraverted engagement with the world, convinced him that extraversion and introversion are *complementary attitudes* rather than opposing ways in which consciousness *functions.*

The terminology used by Jung to describe the typology of the personality (which one might arguably dub his "psychology of consciousness") has become part of our everyday language: introversion, extraversion, 'thinker,' 'intuitive,' etc., are common parlance. This poses a potential problem! We can slip easily (that is, unconsciously) into taking this language, which is at best *descriptive of various and variable processes,* literally, as fact; we may all too readily identify ourselves as a particular 'type': "I *am* an extravert," "I *am* an introverted thinking type," etc. No! Every healthy personality is more than *just* a particular 'type.' In the healthy, evolving personality, 'types' are not 'fixed.' To identify (with a 'type' or with something or someone, actual, fictional, imaginary, etc.) perhaps makes us feel 'safe' (for a while) but is by definition limiting and liable to inhibit the natural unfolding and development of the conscious personality, cutting us off from our as yet unlived (still unconscious) potential. (See "Distortion, Falsification, and Transcendence of Type" below.) Remember Beebe's cautionary wisdom, cited above: Jung's familiar 'types' do not describe types of *people* but types, or characteristic orientations, of *consciousness*!; and one's conscious orientation can become increasingly more differentiated as the personality develops through the natural process of ***individuation*** (see Glossary and Chapter 4).

AN ASIDE: THE MYERS–BRIGGS TYPE INDICATOR (MBTI)

You have probably heard of, or taken, the MBTI 'test.' Your friends might have referred to themselves as an INTP or an ESTJ type. The MBTI is a reasonably accurate tool designed to help us understand our *current* 'characteristic orientation' to both inner and outer reality. It can be helpful to individuals wanting to understand how they 'tick'; it is widely used by businesses, institutions, PR, and advertising firms, etc., in their development of leadership and management training programmes, promotional and advertising strategies. The test was developed in the 1940s by mother and daughter team Katherine Briggs and Isabel Myers; both were fascinated by Jung's system of psychological types, on which it is based. The MBTI introduces some different terms—e.g., judgment and perception in place of rational and irrational. It was originally designed to help people discover their strengths, weaknesses, likes, and dislikes in order to facilitate a choice of career, so it links results to specific professions, as well as to propensities, e.g., INTJ = The Architect; ENFI = The Giver. It is easy to assume, given the MBTI's 16 very specific types, that 'types' are 'fixed.' However, as we noted above, introversion and extraversion are *complementary* attitudes and the degree to which one dominates consciousness in any given circumstance or period of life may vary considerably. While the MBTI suggests we are each a 'type' throughout life, Jungian thought argues that the 'functions' can be differentiated with the growth of consciousness and development of the personality, enabling one to *consciously* develop and engage particular functions as needed. 'Type' can be *transcended* (see below).

Have fun with the MBTI! but study CW6 for the 'real thing': a rich exploration of types—"psychic processes that can be shown to be typical" (CW6, p. xv)—which, yes, may certainly help you recognise your own *characteristic orientation* and *type of consciousness*. Note: The Singer–Loomis Inventory of Personality (SLIP) developed in 1980 assesses the *degree of differentiation* of each of the eight function-attitudes (extraverted thinking, introverted thinking, etc.) (Macdonald and Holland 1993).

The 'functions' (thinking, feeling, intuition, sensation) may also *be developed consciously* when we engage actively (i.e., consciously) in our own psychological, spiritual growth (i.e., in the process of individuation—the development of personality and potential). One's personal journey is enhanced through disciplines and practices such as psychoanalysis, psychotherapy, spiritual practice, meditation, yoga, as well as physical training, education, travel, music, art. To learn most effectively about Typology and how personality and potential are developed, first heed Jung's reminder that Typology is not a rigid system of classification:

> [...] far too many readers have succumbed to the error of thinking that Chapter X ("General Description of the Types") represents the essential content and purpose of the book (*Psychological Types*), in the sense that it provides a system of classification and a practical guide to a good judgment of human character. Indeed, even in medical circles the opinion has got about that my method of treatment consists in fitting patients into this system and giving them corresponding "advice." [...] [T]this kind of classification is nothing but a childish parlour game [...]. My typology is [...] a critical psychology dealing with the organization and delimitation of psychic processes that can be shown to be typical.
>
> (CW6, pp. xiv–xv)

In Jung's opinion, the most important chapters of *Psychological Types* are the earlier chapters, as they describe "the *processes* (authors' emphasis) in question with the help of various examples" (*ibid.*); and Jung recommends that readers immerse themselves in Chapters II and V ("Schiller's Ideas on the Type Problem," and "The Type Problem in Poetry: Carl Spitteler: *Prometheus and Epimetheus*") if they really want to understand his work on typology, before reading his "general descriptions" of the eight 'types' in Chapter X.

Ellenberger (1970) argues that as "[m]ost accounts of Jung's psychological types are oversimplified" (p. 700), Chapter X of CW6, nevertheless remains the definitive text for an accurate yet, as its title suggests, *general* description of the types. (Note: Ellenberger's book, *The Discovery of the Unconscious*, was published in 1970; since then a number of excellent works have been published which both explicate and build on Jung's Typology—See Recommended Reading at the end of this book.) In Chapters I through IX of CW6, Jung explores the question of types or attitudes of consciousness in works by philosophers, poets, physicians, and thinkers from the classical age, through the medieval period, to Schiller, Nietzsche, William James, and others; the list includes Eastern philosophy, Gnosticism, and writings of the Church Fathers (Tertullian, St, Augustine …). Jung's Psychology of Types clearly rests on a centuries-old conversation on the subject, in itself evidence that there are, and no doubt have always been since the dawn of consciousness, two visions or (at least) two ways of perceiving the world. The breadth of his research and extent of his reading also shows how, during this period—1913–20—Jung deepened his knowledge to an extraordinary degree by immersing himself in a study of the world's cultural and spiritual heritage.

THE FOUR TEMPERAMENTS—Greek physician and thinker, Hippocrates (c. 460–377 BC)

Hippocrates came up with the idea, through careful observation of the natural world and the human body in sickness and in health, that a *balance* between what he considered the four essential bodily fluids was necessary to maintain good health. The four fluids were: phlegm, blood, yellow bile, and black bile. He even linked these fluids to the seasons and to diet, and also developed his theory of four temperaments: people tend to be **melancholic, sanguine, choleric,** or **phlegmatic** (i.e., pensive/sad, optimistic/confident, angry/irascible, or calm/unemotional). You can see how two of Hippocrates' temperaments tend towards introversion, two towards extraversion. Hippocrates' ideas influenced medicine and descriptions of a person's temperament for approximately two thousand years (even today we may talk of someone being melancholic).

SUMMARY

- We noted Jung's early observation that 'individual character' as well as an activated complex influenced the results of the Word Association Experiment
- We introduced a box about the Myers–Briggs Type Indicator test

- We outlined the extent of Jung's early research that forms the basis of his developed theory of psychological types
- We noted Jung's insistence that typology is not a rigid system of classification but a finely differentiated description of psychic processes that are typical
- And we also noted John Beebe's reminder that Jung's theory of types describes types of conscious orientation rather than types of people

ANOTHER (NECESSARILY SIMPLIFIED) SUMMARY OF THE 'ATTITUDES' AND 'TYPES'

First, a summary of Jung's developed Psychology of Types provided by Henri Ellenberger (*ibid.,* pp. 701–02). Ellenberger's summary is quoted in full in the box below, followed by an anecdotal sketch of the occasion of a dinner party to which various 'types' are invited. You can perhaps apply what you are learning about typology by imagining the conversation that might have occurred around the dinner table, given the 'types' present!

HERE IS HENRI ELLENBERGER ... with a proviso: remember this was written in the late 1960s:

The notion of introversion and extroversion (*sic*) and of the four functions enabled Jung to establish a system of eight psychological types, of which four are extroverted and four are introverted.

The *thinking-extroverted** type directs his life and that of his dependents according to fixed rules; his thinking is positive, synthetic, dogmatic. The *feeling-extroverted* type keeps to the values he has been taught, respects social conventions, does what is proper, and is very emotional. The *sensation-extroverted* type is pleasure-loving, sociable, and adjusts himself easily to people and circumstances. The *intuition-extroverted* type shows insight in life situations, detects and is attracted by new possibilities, is talented for business, speculation, and politics. Then we have the *thinking-introverted* type who is described at length by Jung who appears to have taken Nietzsche as his model for it: a man who lacks practical sense, he isolates himself after unpleasant experiences with his fellow men, desires to go to the bottom of things, and shows great boldness in his ideas, but is often hindered by hesitations and scruples. The *feeling-introverted* type is an unassuming, quiet, oversensitive individual, difficult to understand by his fellow men; in the case of a woman, she exerts a mysterious power over extroverted men. The *sensation-introverted* type is also a quiet person who looks upon the world with a mixture of benevolence and amusement, and is particularly sensitive to the aesthetic quality of things. The *intuitive-introverted* type is a daydreamer who ascribes the utmost value to his inner trend of thought and who is easily considered odd or eccentric by the others.

As a mnemotechnic (memorising–*authors*) device Ania Teillard imagined the story of a dinner party of the psychological types: The perfect hostess (*feeling-extroverted*) receives the guests with her husband, a quiet gentleman who is an art collector and expert in ancient paintings (*sensation-introverted*). The first guest to arrive is a talented lawyer (*thinking-extroverted*). Then comes a noted business-man (*sensation-extroverted*) with his wife, a taciturn, somewhat enigmatic musician (*feeling-introverted*). They are followed by an eminent scholar (*thinking-introverted*) who came without his wife, a former cook (*feeling-extroverted*), and a distinguished engineer (*intuitive-extroverted*). One vainly waits for the last guest, a poet (*intuitive-introverted*) but the poor fellow has forgotten the invitation.

(*'Type' is usually described by the attitude followed by the function, e.g., *introverted thinking*. We have followed Ellenberger's method (*thinking-extroverted*) in this quotation from his book. Elsewhere in our narrative we adopt the more familiar practice, i.e., *introverted thinking*.)

INTROVERSION AND EXTRAVERSION

In Freud's and Adler's theory and practice, Jung saw how each man's dominant *attitude* (introversion or extraversion) shaped his thinking, method, and world-view: "With Adler the emphasis is placed on a subject who, no matter what the object, seeks his own security and supremacy; with Freud the emphasis is placed wholly upon objects, which, according to their specific character, either promote or hinder the subject's desire for pleasure" (CW7:59). Jung understood Adler as predominantly introverted, and Freud as extraverted. This is how Jung describes the two attitudes in "The Problem of the Attitude-Type" (CW7:62).

> *Introversion* [...] is normally characterized by a hesitant, reflective, retiring nature that keeps itself to itself, shrinks from objects, is always slightly on the defensive and prefers to hide behind mistrustful scrutiny. *Extraversion* [...] is normally characterized by an outgoing, candid, and accommodating nature that adapts easily to a given situation, quickly forms attachments, and, setting aside any possible misgivings, will often venture forth with careless confidence into unknown situations. In the first case obviously the subject, and in the second the object, is all-important.

We do not understand why some individuals adapt to life predominantly in one way or the other. Jung seemed to think that the reason for the two attitude-types embodying the antithesis of each other very likely has a biological foundation:

> There are in nature two fundamentally different modes of adaptation which ensure the continued existence of the living organism. The one consists in a high rate of fertility, with low powers of defence and short duration of life for the single individual; the other consists in equipping the individual with numerous means of self-preservation plus a low fertility rate. [...] [Similarly] the peculiar nature of the extravert constantly urges him to expend and propagate himself in every way, while the tendency of the introvert is to defend himself against all demands from outside, to conserve his energy by withdrawing it from objects, thereby consolidating his own position.

> (CW6:559)

In a nutshell, the more introverted person is concerned with and stimulated by the inner, subjective world, whereas the more extraverted person's attention is drawn to events, objects, and persons in the outer world. Both 'attitudes' describe the way in which psychic energy (interest, attention, valuing) habitually flows: with the introvert to the inner world; with the extravert to the outer world. With the introvert, the *subjective,* inner experience is of greatest interest and value, i.e., the *effect* or impact of an outer object or experience on the inner world. The extravert, however, values and is stimulated by the *object* or (so-called) objective reality. Introverts are happy with their own company; extraverts thrive in the company of others (as long as there are not too many introverts around!). A person's dominant 'attitude' is evident from very early in life; it is seemingly innate, a 'given,' and can be seen in the behaviour of infants (how content they may be on their own in the pram; how much they are drawn to or retreat from strangers, or new objects in the home, etc.).

Remember that the 'attitudes' are seen as *complementary* rather than *opposed*. This means that nobody is a 'pure' introvert or extravert— that would be untenable. Earlier in this chapter we saw how Jung's life shifted from one dominated by extraversion to one characterised by introversion at the onset of his *creative illness,* followed by a more extraverted engagement with the world upon his recovery in 1918. The more 'differentiated' one becomes, that is, the better we understand the dynamics and vagaries of our *natural* orientation to the world (i.e., the degree to which we favour introversion or extraversion), the better we are able to call upon our complementary attitude, as appropriate and useful, in different situations. Demands of the outer world also help us to differentiate our less dominant attitude, although it will always remain 'in the shadows' to some degree. This also applies to the 'functions' (thinking, feeling, sensation, intuition). As Marie-Louise von Franz writes (1996) on the art of interpreting fairy-tales: "The more you have differentiated your functions, the better you can interpret because you must circumambulate a story as much as possible with all your functions" (p. 11). Differentiation of the functions and attitudes allows one to 'interpret' more profoundly one's experiences of both of the outer and inner world and, consequently, to live more consciously and closer to one's full potential. Jung's tale, below, helps us understand the characteristics of, and dynamics between introverts and extraverts:

JUNG'S TALE OF THE EXTRAVERTED AND THE INTROVERTED YOUTHS

Let us suppose two youths rambling in the country. They come to a fine castle; both want to see inside it. The introvert says, "I'd like to know what it's like inside." The extravert answers, "Right, let's go in," and makes for the gateway. The introvert draws back— "Perhaps we aren't allowed in," says he, with visions of policemen, fines, and fierce dogs in the background. Whereupon the extravert answers, "Well, we can ask. They'll let us in all right"—with visions of kindly old watchmen, hospitable seigneurs, and the possibility of romantic adventures. On the strength of extraverted optimism they at length find themselves in the castle. But now comes the dénouement. The castle has been rebuilt inside, and contains nothing but a couple of rooms with a collection of old manuscripts. As it happens, old manuscripts are the chief joy of the introverted youth. Hardly has he caught sight of them than he becomes as one transformed. He loses himself in contemplation of the treasures, uttering cries of enthusiasm. He engages the caretaker in conversation so as to extract from him as much information as possible, and when the result is disappointing he asks to see the curator in order to propound his questions to him. His shyness has vanished, objects have taken on a seductive glamour, and the world wears a new face. But meanwhile the spirits of the extraverted youth are ebbing lower and lower. His face grows longer and he begins to yawn. No kindly watchmen are forthcoming here, no knightly hospitality, not a trace of romantic adventure—only a castle made over into a museum. There are manuscripts enough to be seen at home. While the enthusiasm of the one rises, the spirits of the other fall, the castle bores him; the manuscripts remind him of a library; library is associated with university, university with studies and menacing examinations. Gradually a veil of gloom descends over the once so interesting and enticing castle. The object becomes negative. "Isn't it marvellous," cries the introvert, "to have stumbled on this wonderful collection?" "The place bores me to extinction," replies the other with undisguised ill humour. This annoys the introvert, who secretly vows never again to go rambling with an extravert. The latter is annoyed with the other's annoyance, and he thinks to himself that he always knew the fellow was an inconsiderate egotist who would, in his own selfish interest, waste all the lovely spring day that could be enjoyed so much better out of doors (CW7:81).

So what happened? Jung argues that the two were in happy symbiotic, or complementary mode before entering the castle. Then they each 'flip' to their shadow attitude: the introvert who had been reluctant to enter the castle now doesn't want to leave; the extravert who couldn't wait to get inside the castle wants to be outside in the spring sunshine. The introvert is now fascinated by the *object* (the manuscripts); the extravert has lost all interest in the object of his initial interest (the castle). The introvert became extraverted (focusing on the 'object,' speaking with enthusiasm to the curator), the extravert introverted (brooding on the 'subject,' his own subjectivity, his boredom). Most interesting of all is that both youths become unsociable! This suggests that they do not have a differentiated, conscious understanding of their 'attitude-types' that would enable either of them to recognise what had happened … and to mend the rift that had occurred between them. Remember, however, that before they entered the castle and flipped into their shadow attitudes, they were perfectly happy and compatible, as is usually the case with people with complementary attitudes. This is why Jung writes that marriages between opposing, complementary attitude-types are usually extraordinarily successful (CW17:324–45).

THE FUNCTIONS

About the functions: basically, Sensation tells us that something exists, that something *is*; Thinking tells us *what* it is; Feeling (Evaluating) tells us if it is good, bad, indifferent, i.e., what is its *worth*; and Intuition tells us what we might do with it, what its *possibilities* may be. Sensation connects us to the world through the senses; Thinking through the logical processes of the mind; Feeling through the capacity to evaluate the worth of a thing; and Intuition to the inherent possibilities of a thing or situation. Jung placed the four functions on two intersecting axes—see diagram below—Thinking and Feeling on what he called the Rational Axis, because both Thinking and Feeling are rational thought processes—i.e., what does this mean? what is this worth?; and Intuition and Sensation on the Irrational Axis (or the Axis that eludes conscious control)—because both Intuition and Sensation experience and respond to what IS: what *exists* (Sensation); what *might be* (Intuition). Thinking and Feeling have to do with judgment, evaluation; Intuition and Sensation with perception (Figure 2.1).

As you can see from the diagram, each of the four functions can be either extraverted or introverted—just never both at the same time! Below is a brief description of how the functions and attitudes are seen to 'work' together:

On the two axes, one 'rational,' the other 'irrational' (non-rational), you will see that Thinking is *opposed* to Feeling, as Intuition is *opposed* to Sensation. This means that when Thinking

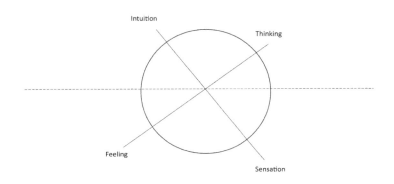

Figure 2.1   The attitudes and functions of an introverted intuitive thinking type.

is operative, there is no room for Feeling, and *vice versa*. The same applies to Intuition and Sensation: when Intuition is operative, with light bulbs going off and dreams of possibilities not yet realised, there is no room for Sensation to ground an experience in the body and the here-and-now of the outer world. While the 'attitudes' (introversion and extraversion) are seemingly innate and can be recognised when one is still an infant, the 'functions' *develop*. There is invariably one function that becomes the primary or Superior Function and dominates how an individual typically behaves and responds to lived experience. The function that is on the same axis and therefore *opposes* the superior function is referred to as the *inferior,* undeveloped, or *shadow* function. This function often asserts itself in a rather undifferentiated, instinctual way when the superior function becomes excessively one-sided. Everyone develops a Superior or preferred function which, like all functions, can be either introverted or extraverted. If Thinking is the *superior*, primary function, Feeling will be the *inferior*, fourth function. *Inferior* feeling will be introverted if *superior* thinking is extraverted; it will be extraverted if thinking is introverted. When thinking and feeling are the superior and inferior functions, respectively, intuition and sensation, on the opposite axis, become the auxiliary (secondary) and tertiary (third) functions: one will be the secondary, auxiliary function, the strongest and most conscious after the primary, superior function; the other third, tertiary function will be less conscious.

Ideally, as Marie-Louise von Franz (1996) suggests, one needs to develop the less conscious functions. To do this, it is often helpful to see the four functions not as positioned on a cross, which suggests they are static, fixed, but as the four compass points, with the 'needle,' or conscious focus of ego-consciousness, intentionally pointing to one, then another, as necessary. If one knows one's superior function, i.e., how one typically meets the challenges of the inner or outer world, one can learn to engage, consciously, other less conscious functions. For example, after the initial excitement of a 'light bulb' moment, someone with superior, extraverted intuition may want to check out their 'big idea' by activating a feeling response and asking if it is *worthwhile*; then move to thinking to check the *logic* of the vision; and finally turn to sensation to ask how it can be *realised*. (Another metaphor you might find useful: the 'circle of functions' may be seen, in the example provided above, to work like a medicine wheel.) As less- or unconscious functions are made conscious and become increasingly accessible to the will of the ego, the personality becomes more cohesive, flexible, and whole. If we understand psychic health as the attainment of wholeness, then we can see how healing results from a growth in consciousness through the differentiation of both the attitudes and functions.

BRIEF OVERVIEW OF THE FUNCTIONS

Sensation

Sensation is on the irrational axis. It is a *perceiving* function. Sensation is about experiencing the world by means of the senses, perceiving and recognising what *is* through the body. That might make one think that Sensation 'types' are invariably introverted (experiencing life in and through the physical senses) but that is not so. **Extraverted Sensation** is focused on external reality and there is little or no concern for subjective (inner) experience. The *outer* object takes precedence over any *inner*, subjective response. In other words, Extraverted

Sensation creates a strong and sensuous tie between the subject and the external world. As Jung writes:

> Objects are values in so far as they excite sensations, and, so far as lies within the power of sensation, they are fully accepted into consciousness whether they are compatible with rational judgments or not. The sole criterion of their value is the intensity of the sensation produced by their objective qualities. [...] Hence the orientation of such an individual accords with purely sensuous reality.
>
> (CW6:605)

Extraverted sensation supports a well-developed sense of objective facts but generates little or no support for abstract, or inner, reality. Those with extraverted sensation as their superior function have no problem with external reality, remembering details, appointments, whether they locked the car, etc. They enjoy social gatherings, sport (often extreme sport), and tend to do things just because they are there to be done. They notice details: a change of hairstyle or cologne; the sensual and sexual needs of a partner. However, their pursuit of sensation can become all-consuming (Sharp 1987, p. 57).

The opposing function to extraverted sensation is Introverted Intuition, which concerns everything that cannot be seen, heard, smelled, touched, tasted, in other words, everything that is the extreme opposite of sensate experience. So, the 'inferior' or 'shadow' function, introverted intuition, often manifests in a negative way; experiences that for the introverted intuitive are positive, devolve into dark fantasies and premonitions, suspicions, catastrophic thinking, etc., in the extraverted sensation type. This may happen when any function becomes extremely one-sided, opening consciousness to the danger of being overpowered by the unconscious inferior, shadow function that opposes it. However, this does not need to happen. If the inferior function (in this case, introverted intuition) *balances* the excesses of extraverted sensation, the effect can be an advantageous 'softening' of the main function: "More usually, the compensating inferior function (to extraverted sensation) simply imparts a rather charming air of inconsistency to the personality [...] [such as] a childish interest in the occult or sudden spiritual insights" (*ibid.,* p. 58).

Introverted Sensation "is guided by the intensity of the subjective sensation excited by the objective stimulus" (CW6:650). Jung explains how "Introverted sensation apprehends the background of the physical world rather than its surface. The decisive thing is not the reality of the object, but the reality of the subjective factor,"

(CW6:649); in other words, "[…] perception is oriented to the meaning that adheres to objects rather than to their inherent physical properties" (Sharp 1987, p. 81).

Extraverted Intuition is the opposing, inferior function to Introverted Sensation. This means that whereas the extraverted sensation type picks up intuitions that concern the inner self and immediate environment of the *subject*, the introverted sensation type tends to intuit dynamics in the *object,* in outside world. The resultant tendency is then to foment dark fantasies of what might happen not only to themselves and their immediate community but on a national or global level, to humankind as a whole (*ibid.,* p. 83). When the opposing inferior function of extraverted intuition balances introverted sensation in a positive way, it can help the introverted sensation type escape the tunnel of his or her own fantasy-making and start to intuit *possibilities* rather than predominantly negative outcomes.

Intuition

Like sensation, intuition is a *perceiving* function. Unlike sensation, intuition perceives what is unconscious, possibilities not realisable by any of the other functions. In the Extraverted Intuitive type, Jung writes that:

> The intuitive function is represented in consciousness by an attitude of expectancy, by vision and penetration; but only from the subsequent result can it be established how much of what was 'seen' was actually in the object, and how much was 'read into' it. Just as sensation, when it is the dominant function, is not a mere reactive process of no further significance for the object, but an activity that seizes and shapes its object, so intuition is not mere perception, or vision, but an active, creative process that puts into the object just as much as it takes out.

> (CW6:610)

Extraverted Intuition is focused on the outer world—things, events, people; it has the ability to sense what is going on below the surface—and see into the soul (Sharp 1987, p. 59). Intuition is powerful and, when it is 'in full swing,' the other functions, especially sensation, are more or less disabled and unavailable to conscious control sensation. The extraverted intuitive is quickly bored, always on the lookout for new possibilities and challenges. Extraverted intuition can 'see' the finished home in the forest where the sensation type registers only trees, however extraordinary those trees may be. Similarly, extraverted intuitives can see the possibilities in individuals, in creative work, in business ventures, especially possibilities for others, while often not realising very much for themselves. They are good at starting projects but not so good at finishing them!

With **Introverted Intuition**, the focus is on the inner world; "it does not concern itself with external possibilities but with what the external object has released within" (CW6:656), and:

> [...] perceives all the background processes of consciousness with almost the same distinctness as extraverted sensation registers external objects. [...] therefore, unconscious images acquire the dignity of things. But, because intuition excludes the co-operation of sensation [...] the images appear as though detached from the subject, as though existing in themselves without any relation to him (the subject)."
>
> (CW6:657)

Introverted Intuition, focused on possibilities and not-yet-realised futures, is often the superior function of the poets and visionaries of a society, the day-dreamers with whom pragmatic parents, teachers, and employers can lose patience! They often lack good judgment and have difficulty expressing their thoughts and feelings (other than through their art). And they often have little connection to their physical needs, to the body. Introverted intuitives can be grossly misunderstood and seen to be ineffectual dreamers, yet Jung has this to say about their value to the collective:

> The perception of the images of the unconscious, produced in such inexhaustible abundance by the creative energy of life, is of course fruitless from the standpoint of immediate utility. But since these images represent possible views of the world which may give life a new potential, this function, which to the outside world is the strangest of all, is as indispensable to the total psychic economy as is the corresponding human type to the psychic life of a people. Had this type not existed, there would have been no prophets in Israel.
>
> (CW6:658)

Jung considers that, while incomprehensible and frustrating to the rational types, introverted types on the irrational axis (intuitive or sensate) are of great value in a world of increasingly utilitarian, scientific, technical, and economic priorities. While introverted intuitives are often vague about and disconnected from the 'real world,' missing appointments, getting lost, losing important documents, etc.,

> [v]iewed from a higher standpoint, they are living evidence that this rich and varied world with its overflowing and intoxicating life is not purely

external, but also exists within. [...] In their own way, they are educators and promoters of culture. Their life teaches more than their words. From their lives, and not least from their greatest fault—their inability to communicate—we may understand one of the greatest errors of our civilization, that is, the superstitious belief in verbal statements, the boundless overestimation of instruction by means of words and methods.

(CW6:665)

Thinking

Thinking, together with Feeling, is on the rational axis. This means that if thinking is the superior function, feeling will be the opposing inferior function. If the superior function is extraverted, the inferior function will be introverted, and *vice versa*. Either intuition or sensation will serve as the auxiliary (secondary) function; the same applies for the tertiary function.

Thinking is concerned with facts, logic, the intellect. It has "no necessary connection with intelligence or the quality of thought, it is simply a process" (Sharp 1987, p. 44). The focus of **Extraverted Thinking** is on the outer world, objective data, outer circumstances. Extraverted thinkers can "bring clarity into emotional situations" (*ibid.*, p. 45), and bring order to chaos. They may often be formulaic, traditional, and conservative in their thinking, with a tendency to rigidity, espousing idealistic principles, rules, and truths, with little or no access to subjective feeling. As introverted feeling is the opposing semi- or unconscious 'shadow' function, the extraverted thinker will tend not to value and therefore prioritise the cultivation of friends, interest in the arts, aesthetic taste, or social and family time.

The motivation of the **Introverted Thinking** type, although focused on outer objects, is subjective, coming from within and concerning the effect of the outer on the inner world.

> (The introverted thinker) formulates questions and creates theories, [...] opens up new prospects and insights, but with regard to facts (his) attitude is one of reserve. [...] of paramount importance is the development and presentation of the subjective idea, of the initial symbolic image hovering darkly before the mind's eye.
>
> (CW6:628)

Introverted thinkers are concerned with clarification, bringing order, filling in gaps, precision, creating theories, and developing subjective ideas for their own sake (such as philosophers, mathematicians). Marie-Louise von Franz (1971/79) describes introverted thinkers as:

> [...] people who are perpetually trying to prevent their colleagues from getting lost in experiments and who, from time to time, try to get back to basic concepts and ask what we are really doing mentally.
>
> (p. 41)

Anthony Stevens (1994) makes an astute observation when he argues that Jung, in describing the introverted thinker, is in all probability describing himself! Stevens adds that "Jung's theory of psychological types is a good example of introverted thinking in action: it is a carefully thought-out system, devised in neat opposites and balances, then imposed, like all typologies, on the psychological data" (p. 93). Introverted thinking types are happy to be left alone in their studies with time to explore the thoughts that come to them as though unbidden, i.e., from the inner realm of the unconscious.

Because the opposing inferior function to thinking is feeling, both extraverted and introverted thinkers form somewhat 'sticky attachments' when it comes to relationships. Again, von Franz (1971/1979) argues that:

> The inferior feeling of both types (introverted and extraverted thinking) is sticky, and the extraverted thinking type has that kind of invisible faithfulness which can last endlessly. The same is true for the extraverted feeling of the introverted thinking type, except that it will not be invisible. [...] It has that kind of sticky, dog-like attachment which, especially to the beloved, is not amusing. You could compare the inferior feeling of an introverted thinking type to the flow of hot lava from a volcano—it only moves about five feet an hour, but it devastates everything in its way.
>
> (p. 43)

Those charming but annoyingly obtuse and unrelatable 'absent-minded professors' are no doubt introverted thinking types, as are those attentive souls in academic writing centres who help us clarify our arguments, and edit our essays with exquisite attention to detail.

Feeling

Feeling is on the rational axis. 'Feeling' is in many ways an unsatisfactory term for a 'function' that has nothing to do with emotion (so often a synonym for feeling). In Jung's typology, **Extraverted**

Feeling is about judgment and valuing: is this worthwhile or not? Jung writes:

> Extraverted feeling has detached itself as much as possible from the sub-jective (inner) factor and subordinated itself entirely to the influence of the object (outer reality). Even when it appears not to be qualified by a concrete object, it is none the less still under the spell of traditional or generally accepted values of some kind.
>
> (CW6:595)

The extraverted feeling type adjusts to the outer, social setting and tries to ensure there is harmony in the immediate environment. Remember that, in the description of the dinner party quoted by Ellenberger (above), the 'perfect hostess' is an extraverted feeling type!

> Without extraverted feeling, a 'civilized' social life would be virtually impossible. Collective expressions of culture depend on it. Out of extra-verted feeling people go to the theatre, to concerts, to church and the opera; they take part in business conventions, company picnics, birthday parties, etc.
>
> (Sharp 1987, p. 50)

The problem for extraverted feeling types is that they become so tied to the 'object,' in terms of convention, social protocol, and doing the 'right thing,' that they lose touch with their inner world and what is going on in themselves. This means their social skills start to ring hollow, in danger of becoming mere gestures with little or no trace of the warmth of genuine regard.

Introverted thinking is the opposing function to extraverted feeling and, although extraverted feeling types may think a lot, thinking does not displace feeling. "Everything that fits in with objective values is good, and is loved, and everything else seems to [...] exist in a world apart" (CW6:598). When thoughts persist that are perceived as negative because they do not 'fit' the feeling type's objective values, the experi-ence can be overwhelming. The negative thoughts then turn inward and the extraverted feeling type, hating to be alone with such thoughts, seeks the company of friends or some other form of diversion.

Introverted Feeling, like introverted thinking, is concerned pri-marily with subjective, inner reality, not with the object or outer world. Jung suggests that the expression "still waters run deep" applies to this type (CW6:640):

> (Introverted feeling) is continually seeking an image which has no existence in reality, but which it has seen in a kind of vision. It glides

> unheedingly over all objects that do not fit in with its aim. It strives after inner intensity, [...]. The depth of this feeling can only be guessed—it can never be clearly grasped. It makes people silent and difficult of access [...].
>
> *(ibid.:*638)

Introverted feeling types, focused intensely on inner images and values, are habitually quiet, so difficult to understand and get to know. Their inner feelings are seldom communicated to others. Yet they have a positive influence on others. Marie-Louise von Franz (1971/79) writes:

> Introverted feeling types [...] very often form the ethical backbone of a group; without irritating the others by preaching moral or ethical precepts, they themselves have such correct standards of ethical values that they secretly emanate a positive influence on those around them. One has to behave correctly because they have the right kind of value standard, which always suggestively forces one to be decent if they are present. Their differentiated introverted feeling sees what is inwardly the really important factor.
>
> (p. 49)

Extraverted thinking is the inferior function of the introverted feeling type. With its realistic adherence to concrete facts, extraverted thinking often works in a positive, compensatory way to mitigate what Jung describes as "the mysterious power of intensive feeling (of the introverted feeling type to turn) [...] into a banal and overweening desire to dominate, into vanity and despotic bossiness" (CW6:642).

DISTORTION, FALSIFICATION, AND TRANSCENDENCE OF TYPE

Earlier in this chapter we saw that *attitude* (whether an individual is naturally more introverted or extraverted) appears to be innate, or at least we seem to be born with a predisposition to favour one of the two attitudes. The *functions* develop later, as the brain develops and as the individual responds and adapts to the family ethos, social norms, education, etc. This means that *adaptation* plays a key role in the development of the superior and auxiliary functions. However, there will often be an indication, observable early in a child's development, of the function that might *naturally* develop as the child's *superior* function. This is because the function in question is *syntonic*, or in alignment, with the child's (as yet undeveloped) individual propensities, talents, and capacities—for example, one child in a family may love to curl up in a corner, reading and drawing, while a sibling (even a twin!) may be slow to read but quick with numbers and problem-solving, and happier outdoors than in. If two such siblings are supported to develop their natural interests and talents, they will no doubt follow different paths in life and experience themselves as having very different 'typology.'

The impact on us of our environment in our early years is enormous. Children absorb the ethos and values of care-givers, parents, relatives, siblings, and the cultural, socio-economic, and educational milieu in which they are raised. The development of *functions,* essentially the superior and auxiliary functions, is consequently very much a process of adaptation to the only environment or 'world' the child has ever known. If the functions validated at home and, later, at school are *syntonic* with a child's natural abilities, that child will typically thrive. If they are *dystonic* (i.e., not a good 'fit' with the child's natural disposition and talents), he or she may struggle, usually without knowing why. We speak of a ***distortion of type*** when a child, whose natural disposition might be, for example, that of introverted intuition, is born into a high-achieving academic family. As the expected and only known route to success and validation is an academic career, the child adapts by unconsciously fashioning him- or herself as a 'thinking' type. This may at first work well, as thinking can often support or complement intuition as an auxiliary or secondary function ... until the child is no longer a child ... perhaps even 'middle-aged' ... and suddenly finds that the zest for life, interest in things academic, and enthusiasm for the chosen profession evaporates, as if over-night. Life loses its savour; work becomes meaningless. Jung writes that when a distortion or falsification of 'type' occurs in childhood, "the individual becomes neurotic (i.e., one-sided) later, and can be cured only by developing the attitude consonant with his nature" (CW7:560). The difficult work, first to acknowledge, then develop one's natural attitude and the neglected, often despised, functions of consciousness, presents a huge challenge that amounts to a crisis of identity: "Who am I if I am no longer an X ...?" "How can I tell my family and friends I am not who I—and they—thought I was?" "Who am I?" "What am I going to *do*?" The hard work of realising one's natural but unvalued capacities and a way of being in the world that supports their development can, however, result in a transformative growth of the personality and a new life.

A distortion or *falsification* of type can also result from an individual's *identification* with a particular 'type.' Remember John Beebe's warning that typology describes orientations of consciousness, ways of perceiving and responding to life experiences; it does not describe *people. Type*, and '*typing*' oneself and others, tends to belong to one's development in the first half of life, when one is adapting to life, forging a career, honing skills, focusing on a professional training, etc. A falsification of 'type' at this stage of life happens when an individual is encouraged to develop functions that might not reflect a natural disposition, and when that individual, as a result, then rigidly identifies as a particular 'type': "I am a thinking type; I am an introvert" ... "that's why I see the world as I do; that's why I have the career I have; that's simply who I am." We are sure you can see that this attitude, although justified, is nevertheless limiting, and can also serve as a bit of a cop out! For example, "Oh! I am an introverted intuitive. Please don't expect me to run for any political position. It's not my responsibility to deal with community issues. That's simply not who I am."

This brings us to the *transcendence* of type. We have seen that the (necessary) development of a rather one-sided typology is largely unavoidable in the first half of life. However, there are some people who can never be 'typed,' even in the first half of life. Their environment and innate disposition equip them to develop not simply the superior function and auxiliary functions but a more comprehensive range of functions. Jung found in talking to farmers and local Swiss living in the countryside that many often seemed to be more 'rounded' or 'whole' in that they were able to utilise the appropriate attitude and a variety of functions as needed. There are, then, individuals who are never 'types.' But the majority of us who can be identified (or who identify!) as 'types' in our early years, also have the potential to *transcend* that potentially limiting typology to become far more of a well-rounded and conscious *individual*. Understandably, when one is young there is a need to be part of a group, to identify as a 'this' or a 'that,' which serves one well as one finds one's way in the world. However, when that 'identity' or 'type' no longer seems to 'fit,' that is when the opportunity to 'transcend' type starts to push one to develop neglected (or even despised) functions. This opportunity enables one truly to become an *individual* and grow beyond the former 'type' that confined one to a *collective* identity and *persona* (see Chapter 3). The transcendence of 'type' enables us to become the unique individuals we all have the potential to be, and is the goal of the process of *individuation* (see Chapter 5).

SUMMARY

In the last section of this chapter we have:

- Discussed the two 'attitudes'—Introversion and Extraversion
- Provided a short summary of the 'functions'
- And briefly discussed the concepts of
  - The Distortion of Type
  - The Falsification of Type, and
  - The Transcendence of Type

REFERENCES

Creuzer, F. (1822) *Symbolik und Mythologie der alten Volker, besonders der Griechen,* 2nd ed. Leipzig: Bei Carl Wilhelm Leske.

Ellenberger, H. (1970) *Discovery of the Unconscious: The History and Evolution of Dynamic Psychiatry.* New York: Basic Books.

Freud, S. (1900/13) *The Interpretation of Dreams.* New York: Macmillan.

Jung, C. G. (1953–83) *The Collected Works of C. G. Jung,* 20 vols. W. McGuire, H. Read, M. Fordham, G. Adler (Eds.). R. F. C. Hull (Trans.). London: Routledge & Kegan Paul; Princeton, NJ: Princeton University Press.

Jung, C. G. (1961/63) *Memories, Dreams, Reflections.* Recorded and edited by A. Jaffé. R. and C. Winston (Trans.). New York: Pantheon Books.

Jung, C. G. (2009) *The Red Book: Liber Novus.* S. Shamdasani (Ed.). M. Kyburz, J. Peck and S. Shamdasani (Trans.). New York: W. W. Norton & Company.

Jung, C. G. (2013) *The Question of Psychological Types: The Correspondence of C. G. Jung and Hans Schmid-Guisan, 1915–1916.* J. Beebe and E. Falzeder (Eds.). E. Falzeder and T. Woolfson (Trans.). Princeton, NJ: Princeton University Press.

Jung, C. G. (2020) *The Black Books,* 7 vols. S. Shamdasani (Ed.). M. Liebscher, J. Peck and S. Shamdasani (Trans.). New York: W. W. Norton & Company.

Jung, C. G. and Freeman, J. (1959/78) "The 'Face to Face' Interview" in W. McGuire and R. F. C. Hull (Eds.). *C. G. Jung Speaking: Interviews and Encounters.* London: Thames & Hudson, pp. 410–25.

Macdonald, D. A. and Holland, C. J. (1993) "Psychometric Evaluation of the Singer-Loomis Inventory of Personality" in *Journal of Analytical Psychology*, 38(3), pp. 303–20.

Shamdasani, S. (2009) "Liber Novus: The 'Red Book' of C. G. Jung" in C. G. Jung, *The Red Book: Liber Novus*. S. Shamdasani (Ed.). M. Kyburz, J. Peck and S. Shamdasani (Trans.). New York: W. W. Norton & Company, pp. 193–221.

Sharp, D. (1987) *Personality Types: Jung's Model of Typology*. Toronto: Inner City Books.

Stein, M. (2012) "How to Read *The Red Book* and Why" in *Journal of Analytical Psychology*, 57(3), pp. 280–98.

Stevens, A. (1990) *On Jung*. London: Routledge.

Stevens, A. (1994) *Archetype Revisited: An Updated History of the Self*. London: Brunner-Routledge.

Von Franz, M. L. (1971/79) "The Inferior Function" in *Lectures on Jung's Typology*. New York: Spring Publications, pp. 1–72.

Von Franz, M. L. (1996) *The Interpretation of Fairy Tales*. Boston, MA: Shambhala.

Table 2.1 Psychological Types

TOPIC/KEY WORDS	LOCATION	DESCRIPTOR
Development of Typology	CW7:56 *ff* (1917/1926)	Development of Psychological Types (his *psychology of consciousness*) attributed to Jung's need to understand differences between Freud's, Adler's, and his own thinking.
	CW6:88 *ff*	Freud's psychoanalysis identified as "a psychology of instinct" and Adler's "an ego-psychology."
(Differences between Freud, Adler, Jung; subjectivity of each model of psyche; opposing attitudes to experience)	CW4:745–65, 768–84	*These passages in CW4 detail Jung's realisation that the differences between his and Freud's psychologies stem from "essential differences in our basic assumptions," i.e., in type; that each model of the psyche is a personal, subjectively coloured confession; and the impact of one's own 'personal equation' (attitude and psychological 'type') on all aspects of one's life is inevitable.* In his original model, Jung describes eight types (i.e., four *functions,* two *attitudes*), but does not foreclose the possibilities of others (fn. 2).

(Continued)

Table 2.1 (Continued)

TOPIC/KEY WORDS	LOCATION	DESCRIPTOR
	CW6:970 *ff* (1921/1923)	Goal of psychological types is not "to classify human beings into categories" but "to provide a critical psychology which will make a methodological investigation and presentation of the empirical material possible" (986). Typology provides guidelines to "reduce the chaotic profusion of individual experiences to [some] kind of order," and "understand the wide variations that occur among individuals." Also helps therapists better understand their own "personal equation" and inferior functions, which can influence therapeutic alliance.
Two Attitudes: Introversion and Extraversion	CW7:62 (1917/1926) CW6:5 *ff* (1921/1923)	The two fundamental attitudes, *introversion* and *extraversion*. Jung's observation that differences exist between extraverted and introverted individuals leads to identification of four psychological functions (thinking, feeling, intuition, sensation). Each function is shaped by either introversion or extraversion (7).
	CW6:687 *ff*	'Attitude' is the psyche's *a priori* predisposition and readiness "to act or react in a certain way" to external stimuli. Denotes "presence of a certain subjective constellation, a definite combination of psychic factors or contents, which will either determine action in this or that definite direction, or react to an external stimulus in a definite way."
	CW6:902	One attitude operates consciously, the other unconsciously. Potential one-sidedness of predominant attitude compensated by unconscious counter-position.
As the movement of libido	CW6:835	Attitudes described as "the predominant trend of the movement of *libido* (psychic energy)": in the introvert, psychic energy flows to the external stimulus, then back to the subject; with the extravert, psychic energy flows to and remains with the external stimulus.

(Continued)

Table 2.1   (Continued)

TOPIC/KEY WORDS	LOCATION	DESCRIPTOR
Introversion and Extraversion	CW6:562–67;	Description of The General Attitude of Consciousness of the *extraverted type*, and
	568–76	The Attitude of the Unconscious
	CW6:620–25;	Description of The General Attitude of Consciousness of the *introverted type*, and
	626–27	The Attitude of the Unconscious
	CW6:860 *ff* (1913)	Succinct overview of intellectual precursors.
	CW7:62 (1917/1926)	**Introversion** "characterized by a hesitant, reflective, retiring nature that keeps itself to itself, shrinks from objects and is always slightly on the defensive and prefers to hide behind mistrustful scrutiny." **Extraversion** "characterized by an outgoing, candid, and accommodating nature that adapts easily to a given situation, quickly forms attachments, and [...] will often venture forth [...] into unknown situations."
	CW6:5 *ff* (1921/1923)	**Introversion** values the subject, **extraversion** values the object. "Every human being possesses both mechanisms as an expression of his natural life-rhythm [...]" (6).
	CW6:972 *ff* (1936) & CW6:562 *ff*	**Extraversion** concerned with the external object and happenings, a desire to influence and be influenced by events. A danger of superficiality in relationships. The ethics of extraverts exhibit a highly collective nature "with a strong streak of altruism" aligned with public opinion. Jung discusses shadow side of extraversion: reluctance "to submit [...] motives to critical examination" (973).
	CW6:976 *ff* & CW6:626 *ff*	**Introverts** focus on the subject, retreat from the object, distance themselves from social gatherings, often feel lost in such situations (976), prefer their own company and working alone (977). **Extreme introversion** leads to a compensatory reaction from the unconscious. Negative attributes of introversion are highlighted (976), before elaborating introversion's redeeming and essential contributions (979): The introvert's "retreat into himself is not a final renunciation of the world, but a search for quietude, where alone it is possible for him to make his contribution to the life of the community" (980).

(Continued)

Table 2.1   (Continued)

TOPIC/KEY WORDS	LOCATION	DESCRIPTOR
Functions	CW6:7 (1921/1923)	Psychological functions are shaped by the predominant attitude. As with the attitudes, one function will dominate (superior function).
	CW6:731	Function: "a particular form of psychic activity that remains the same in principle under varying conditions," a "manifestation of libido" which remains constant. Two functions are classified as 'rational' (thinking/feeling), two as 'irrational' (intuition/sensation). Each function is distinct; can neither be reduced nor related to another function.
Thinking	CW6:577 *ff* (1921/1923)	Characteristics of the thinking function; the thinking function when modified by extraversion, and how it is shaped by an introverted attitude.
	CW6:628 *ff*	Thinking facilitates cognition and judgment. Distinction between *active* vs. *passive* thinking corresponds to Jung's distinction between *directed* and *fantasy* thinking.
	CW6:830 *ff*	Thinking is a rational function "because it arranges the contents of ideation under concepts in accordance with a rational norm of which [one] is conscious (832)."
Feeling	CW6:595 *ff* (1921/1923)	Jung describes feeling and elaborates on the extraverted feeling type.
	CW6:638 *ff*	Introverted feeling is described.
	CW6:724 *ff*	Feeling considers value, whether something is important or unimportant. "Feeling is a process that takes place between the *ego* [...] and a given content, [...] that imparts to the content a definite *value* in the sense of acceptance or rejection [...]." Feeling can also manifest as mood. Feeling is a form of judgment (725). Feeling *function* distinguished from *affect* (emotion). Jung distinguishes between *abstract* and "ordinary concrete feeling" (727). Feeling is a rational function.

(Continued)

Table 2.1 (Continued)

TOPIC/KEY WORDS	LOCATION	DESCRIPTOR
Intuition	CW6:610*ff* (1921/1923)	Extraverted intuition is explored.
	CW6:601 *ff*	Introverted intuition is described.
	CW6:770 *ff*	Intuition sees hidden possibilities. It "mediates perceptions in an *unconscious way*," and is an instinctive apprehension of contents that present as "whole and complete." Intuitive knowledge possesses an "intrinsic certainty and conviction." A distinction between *subjective* and *objective* forms of intuition is made (771). Intuition" stands in a compensatory relationship to sensation and, like it, is the matrix out of which thinking and feeling develop as rational functions" (772). Differentiation between introverted and extraverted intuition (773).
Sensation	CW6:604 *ff* (1921/1923) CW6:647 *ff*	Jung defines extraverted sensation and the extraverted sensation type, and introverted sensation and the introverted sensation type.
	CW6:792 *ff*	Sensation conveys concrete reality through our senses, (hearing, tasting, etc.). It "mediates the perception of a physical stimulus." Jung differentiates sensation from feeling and distinguishes between *concrete* and *abstract* sensation (794). Sensation and intuition are opposites or "two mutually compensating functions" (795). Sensation as an *irrational* function (796).
Rational and Irrational Functions	CW6:835 (1921/1923)	The four functions may be organised on two axes: *rational* and *irrational*. Thinking and feeling are on the rational axis, intuition and sensation on the irrational axis.
	CW6:983 (1936)	Irrational functions are "concerned simply with what happens and with actual or potential realities." The rational functions and irrational functions are diametrically opposed to each other on their respective axes.

(*Continued*)

Table 2.1 (Continued)

TOPIC/KEY WORDS	LOCATION	DESCRIPTOR
Primary/Superior Function	CW6:502 *ff* (1921/1923)	One function (the superior, primary, or directed function) usually invested with more energy and *libido*. Identification with the directed/superior function invaluable for adaptation but can lead to an impoverishment of the individual: the more libido channelled to one function, "the more [one] withdraws libido from the other functions." This may lead to self-alienation or a dissociation of the personality, as "the self-regulation of the living organism requires [...] the harmonizing of the whole human being [...]" (504).
	CW6:575 & 667	The superior function "is the most conscious." It is "always an expression of the conscious personality, of its aims, will, and general performance [...]"
	CW6:763	The demands of society often cause individuals to develop the function that aligns with collective expectations and will lead to social success. Identifying with the most developed function "gives rise to the various psychological *types*."
Auxiliary Function	CW6:666 *ff* (1921/1923)	Alongside the superior function, a secondary, "less differentiated function [...] is invariably present in consciousness and exerts a co-determining influence." It is not, "an absolutely reliable and decisive factor but comes into play more as an auxiliary or complementary function." Auxiliary function cannot be opposed to the dominant function, (feeling cannot be the auxiliary function to thinking as "it is [...] too strongly opposed to thinking." If superior function is rational, auxiliary will be irrational.

(Continued)

Table 2.1 (Continued)

TOPIC/KEY WORDS	LOCATION	DESCRIPTOR
	CW6:904 *ff* (1923)	Jung on **unconscious functions.** "When a function is not at one's disposal, when it is felt as something that disturbs the differentiated function [...] it has all the qualities of a quasi-unconscious function" (906). A function repressed into the unconscious "remains undeveloped, fused together with elements not properly belonging to it [...]" (907). The attitude of undeveloped functions is opposed to the dominant attitude of the personality (908): "the unconscious feelings of the thinking type are of a singularly fantastic (i.e., irrational) nature [...]" (906), e.g., the undeveloped feeling of an **extraverted** thinker will be **introverted.**
Inferior Function	CW7:85 *ff* (1917/1926)	Sensitiveness is a strong sign of inferiority. The inferior function may also be felt to be autonomous; "[...] it attacks, it fascinates and so spins us about that we are no longer masters of ourselves [...]." It is important to facilitate the development of the inferior function (86).
	CW6:670 (1921/1923)	The inferior function may best be developed via the auxiliary function in order to adequately protect "the conscious standpoint"—"in the case of a rational type via one of the irrational functions."
	CW6:763 *ff*	The inferior function "lags behind in the process of *differentiation*." It "reverts to the archaic stage" of development but may be brought to consciousness through realisation of the archaic fantasies it generates.
	CW9i:430 *ff* (1948)	*The four functions as represented in fairytales*, with the inferior function as the Achilles heel "of even the most heroic consciousness" (430). "Like the devil who delights in disguising himself as an angel of light, the inferior function secretly and mischievously influences the superior function most of all, just as the latter represses the former most strongly" (431).
Falsification of type	CW6:560 (1921/1923)	A distortion (falsification) of type may occur in early development—due to parental and environmental influences—causing psychological difficulties in later life.

THE STRUCTURE OF THE PSYCHE I

This chapter introduces key concepts of Jung's model of the psyche: consciousness; ego; persona; the personal unconscious; the shadow. We will refer back to topics already discussed (the complex, typology), and point forward to topics (archetypes, the collective unconscious, individuation, etc.) to be covered in Chapters 4 and 5. We hope, from this 'cross-referencing,' you will start to appreciate the nuanced complexity of Jung's thinking about the nature of the psyche, that elusive energic system in which all 'parts' affect each other as well as the whole.

CONSCIOUSNESS

Before we can talk about the perhaps more enticing topic of the *unconscious*, we need first to consider the great mystery that is 'consciousness.' We tend to take 'consciousness' for granted. After all, as soon as we wake up in the morning, we are, as far as we are aware, 'in' consciousness until we go to sleep! Our consciousness is, fundamentally, our *awareness*—of ourselves, others, and the world around us. Because 'consciousness' is our usual and familiar state of being when we are awake, we tend not to wonder about it very much at all. And we tend not even to register many of the subtle states, thresholds, degrees, and qualities of consciousness that nevertheless are operative in both our waking and sleeping lives. Yet 'conscious,' 'conscious mind,' and 'consciousness' occupy almost 13 columns in the index of Jung's *Collected Works*! These references to consciousness are descriptive. They refer to very specific *qualities* of consciousness, such as 'rational consciousness,' 'the dissociability

DOI: 10.4324/9781315619156-4

of consciousness,' 'the one-sidedness of consciousness,' and 'sub-liminal consciousness,' and also to the way in which consciousness *behaves* or *functions,* as we have already seen in Chapter 2 when we explored Jung's Theory of Typology or *types of consciousness.* But what of 'consciousness' itself, as a phenomenon? What *is* it? Jung writes: "consciousness is the most remarkable of all nature's curiosities" (CW8:695); and "Where does consciousness come from? What is the psyche? At this point all science ends" (CW11:533). So it seems that consciousness is a 'wonder of the world,' a 'curiosity,' or 'miracle of nature' similar to matter, for while we may describe matter and study how it behaves, we cannot (yet) define what it *is*!

There is evidence in the *Zofingia Lectures* (1983), ideas presented to peers during Jung's student days, that Jung's fascination with the phenomenon of consciousness was awakened from an early age. We have seen, in Chapters 1 and 2 of this book, how Jung devoted the early years of his professional life to the Word Association Experiment, studying the *disturbances to consciousness* he witnessed in the responses of his test subjects to certain stimulus words. We learnt that Jung soon attributed such disturbances to the presence of unconscious *complexes* activated by those stimulus words. *Psychological Types,* as we have also seen, grew out of his work with the Word Association Experiment and elaborates what may be called Jung's theory or *psychology of consciousness.* In his chapter on Definitions in *Psychological Types,* Jung writes:

> By consciousness I understand the relation of psychic contents to the ego, in so far as this relation is perceived as such by the ego. Relations to the ego that are not perceived as such are *unconscious*. Consciousness is the function or activity which maintains the relation of psychic contents to the ego. Consciousness is not identical with the *psyche,* because the psyche represents the totality of all psychic contents, and these are not necessarily all directly connected with the ego, i.e., related to it in such a way that they take on the quality of consciousness. A great many psychic complexes exist which are not all necessarily connected with the ego.
>
> (CW6:700)

Elsewhere Jung puts the same point perhaps more clearly: "Consciousness can even be equated with the relation between the ego and the psychic contents" (9i:490). So ... does Consciousness = Ego (ego = 'I') + Psychic Contents (e.g., memories, perceptions, emotions, ideas, fantasies, bodily sensations, and intentions)? Can we understand Consciousness as an individual's awareness or *experience of being conscious of something,* i.e., Consciousness = I (ego) + the *specific* psychic content of consciousness (the idea, emotion, memory, etc.) on which I am *currently* focused? Common sense and experience tell us that not *all* the psychic contents of consciousness to which I may have access can be 'in focus' at any given time. However, the equation of consciousness "with the relation between the ego and the psychic contents," cited above, describes our *experience* of consciousness or of 'being conscious' of this or that; in other words, it describes *ego-consciousness* but not the degrees and subtleties of awareness that lie beyond the reach of the ego, of which there are many.

Murray Stein (1998), in his introductory text to Jung's understanding of the psyche, reminds us that humans are not the only conscious or aware beings:

> Other animals are conscious as well, since obviously they can observe and react to their environments in carefully modulated ways. Plants' sensitivity to their environment can also be taken as a form of consciousness.
>
> (p. 16)

What distinguishes the conscious awareness of humans from other beings, as far as we know, is our capacity for *self*-awareness, *self*-reflection, and *self*-consciousness. Yet this quality of consciousness, centred in the *ego* (in 'I'), does not include a fully conscious awareness of the *body* in which it is 'housed,' or of the totality of the *psychic system,* the immeasurable unconscious, *psychic unknown* which eludes the reach of ego-consciousness:

> Many physiological processes never pass over into the psyche, even into the *unconscious* psyche. In principle, they are incapable of ever becoming conscious. It is evident that the sympathetic nervous system, for instance, is for the most part not accessible to consciousness. As the heart beats, blood circulates, and neurons fire, some but not all somatic processes can become conscious.
>
> (*ibid.,* pp. 24–25)

It is consequently important to bear in mind what Jung has to say or, rather, the *very little* he feels it is possible to say about consciousness *per se.* Also important to note, in your further reading, are the myriad subtle, equivocal, and nuanced ways (often appearing contradictory!) in which Jung explores or, rather, *circumambulates* this elusive mystery that nevertheless constitutes the core of our humanity. Here are Jung's thoughts from *Memories, Dreams, Reflections,* recorded approximately 40 years after the 1921

German publication of *Psychological Types* in which he first 'defined' consciousness:

> When one reflects upon what consciousness really is, one is profoundly impressed by the extreme wonder of the fact that an event which takes place outside in the cosmos simultaneously produces an internal image, that it takes place, so to speak, inside as well, which is to say: becomes conscious.
>
> (1961/63, p. 394)

It is equally important to keep in mind that consciousness, in Jung's experience of psychic reality, is an *epiphenomenon*, albeit of essential and defining significance for the human race. As an *epiphenomenon,* consciousness:

> does not create itself—it wells up from unknown depths. In childhood it awakens gradually, and all through life it wakes each morning out of the depths of sleep from an unconscious condition. It is like a child that is born daily out of the primordial womb of the unconscious. In fact, closer investigation reveals that it is not only influenced by the unconscious but continually emerges out of it in the form of numberless spontaneous ideas and sudden flashes of thought.
>
> (CW11:935)

So those brilliant ideas and thoughts are not *ours*, that is, they are not intentional products of our *conscious* minds, after all. They are products of the ever-creative and generative unconscious that erupt into the conscious mind. Humbling, perhaps, for the ego! But these products of the unconscious are nevertheless gifts, with which comes the responsibility to use them well lest they sink back into the unconscious. In other words, we each need to relate to, focus on, value, and *realise* those ideas and thoughts as consciously and creatively as possible. This brings us to the critical psychic 'organ' or function at the heart of conscious awareness, the ego, and the relationship of the ego both to consciousness and to what remains, permanently or temporarily, unconscious. But first:

1. A WORD OF WARNING ABOUT THEORY:

Jung, in his 1938 Foreword to "Psychic Conflicts in a Child": "Theories in psychology are the very devil. It is true that we need certain points of view for their orienting and heuristic value; but they should always be regarded as mere auxiliary concepts that can be laid aside at any time. We still know so very little about the psyche that it is positively grotesque to think we are far enough advanced to frame general theories. We have not even established the empirical extent of the psyche's phenomenology: how then can we dream of general theories? No doubt theory is the best cloak for lack of experience and ignorance, but the consequences are depressing: bigotedness, superficiality, and scientific sectarianism" (CW17, p. 7). A theory, like a model, does not establish that this or that 'thing' is 'just so.' It tells us as much or more about the theoriser because theory illustrates the mode of observation of the theorist.

2. A WORD OF WARNING ABOUT TERMINOLOGY:

We might say that terms, however useful, are also "the very devil." Jung: "Psychology has still to invent its own specific language. When I first started giving names to the attitude-types I had discovered empirically, I found this question of language the greatest obstacle. I was driven [...] to fix definite boundaries to my concepts [...]. In so doing, I inevitably exposed myself to the [...] common prejudice that the name explains the thing" (CW8:224). Psychological terms (*persona, shadow, anima*) at best *describe* or point to a psychic dynamic, imperative, or experience. The terms should *not* be understood as referring to *things* or *entities* or anything *metaphysical,* but inner, psychic dynamics and experiences. This is inevitably difficult to grasp until one has had an equivalent experience, an Aha! moment when one can say "Oh, so *that* is what Jung means by *anima*," "*Now* I get what Jung means by a *complex*." All language, even so-called scientific language, as Nietzsche insisted, is metaphorical, and therefore imprecise, equivocal. Words can never equate to the thing or experience they designate and describe. So while language may be humanity's greatest achievement and tool, it is also a limitation.

EGO

In *Jung's Map of the Soul: An Introduction,* Murray Stein writes:

> Fundamentally, the ego is a virtual center of awareness that exists at least from birth, the eye that sees and has always seen the world from this vantage point, from this body, from this individual point of view. In itself it is nothing, that is, not a thing. It is therefore highly elusive and impossible to pin down. One can even deny that it exists at all. And yet it is always present. It is not the product of nurture, growth, or development. It is innate.
>
> (1998, p. 19)

'Ego' is the Latin word for 'I.' As we have seen from our discussion above, 'consciousness' or 'awareness' emerges out of the unconscious and, as Stein emphasises, exists from birth, if not before. It is, however, only when infants are usually in their second year (12–18 months) that a coherent sense of 'I,' 'Me,' and 'Mine' develops. This stage of development marks the emergence, at the centre of awareness, of what we can call *ego.* From this point onwards, rather than a cry indicating a need, we hear "*I* want …," "*I* am hungry."

Once the sense of 'I' emerges into consciousness, it starts to weave a cohesive thread of continuity and identity—a narrative—throughout an individual's life. Even though we are in many ways very different at 20 or 50 or 80 from how we were at 4, there nevertheless persists a strong sense of identity—or 'I-ness'—that assures us we are the same person, no matter what challenges and changes time and circumstance have wrought upon us. On the one hand, then, 'ego' may be understood as a *descriptive term* for the sense of a continuity of identity that becomes apparent in infancy and remains with us throughout our lifetime. On the other hand, through the repeated challenges and demands of both the outer and inner worlds, the 'ego-complex' takes shape as an increasingly effective 'executive' functional psychic 'organ' at the centre of consciousness, acquiring specific competencies such as the ability to focus, to discriminate, to choose, and to say "No!": "'no!' and 'I won't!' are exercises that strengthen the ego as a separate entity and as a strong inner center of will, intentionality, and control" (*ibid.,* p. 30).

One's sense of 'I' and the attributes of ego-consciousness are shaped by one's environment, family, educational and cultural milieu, by one's adaptation to social and later professional expectations, etc. They are also shaped by the inner pressure of instinctual, emotional needs, arising in the body, and by the growth and maturation of the body itself. The inextricably intertwined (neuropsychophysiological) development of body, mind, and psyche is the product of the natural, archetypical unfolding, in every individual, of the human life cycle, driven by the mystery we call the 'life force'. This life force, as 'architect,' ordering principle, and archetypal imperative shaping the maturation of mind, body, and soul from conception to death, Jung called the Self. (It is useful to use a capital 'S' in order to distinguish the Self from the small 's' self which refers to the subjective sense of 'I' and self grounded in ego-consciousness.) An analogy is perhaps useful at this point: we might think of the Self, the creative, energic principle that shapes the human being (and all living beings, each in its own characteristic way) as analogous to the invisible dynamic principle that renders each snowflake, every crystal 'true to type' and recognisable for what it is, yet at the same time unique. So the life of each human being, at once both typical and individual, is borne through all the stages of life by the creative imperative that is dubbed, for want of a better word, the Self. This concept will be explored in more depth in Chapter 4.

Back to the development of ego-consciousness. A secure and loving family environment enables a child to develop a strong and flexible ego or sense of selfhood. A strong ego is not an arrogant, self-centred ego but one that can 'stand' in its own values and experiences while also appreciating that another 'ego' or person may hold different values and have had experiences different from one's own. A strong, flexible sense of selfhood enables engagement with the 'other,' with difference, while a fragile, inflexible ego tends to be abrasive and loud in order to bolster itself, puff itself up, while masking its vulnerability, its lack of sustainable values and openness to difference. We speak of a 'narcissistic' individual when we encounter someone who seems to be all about 'me,' how wonderful 'I' am, yet in many cases this behaviour is an indication that underneath the seeming self-assurance there lies a profound lack of self-esteem, an emptiness and insecurity, and nagging questions such as 'who *am* I?' 'what am I?' 'Why am I?' "A strong ego," Stein reminds us, "is one that can obtain and move around in a deliberate way large amounts of conscious content. A weak ego cannot do very much of this kind of work and more easily succumbs to impulses and emotional reactions" (*ibid.,* p. 20).

Although Jung often *appears* to use 'ego' and 'consciousness' as interchangeable, as synonyms, he does not, in the end, equate 'ego' with 'consciousness.' Jung places 'ego' as a 'complex' at the *centre* of the 'field' of consciousness:

> By ego I understand a complex of ideas which constitutes the centre of my field of consciousness and appears to possess a high degree of continuity and identity. Hence I speak of an *ego-complex*.
>
> (CW6:706)

You might remember from our discussion of complexes in Chapter 1 that Jung describes the human psyche as a conglomerate of 'complexes,' each with an archetypal, instinctual 'core' of cohesive meaning. The ego-complex is therefore one of many but an extremely important complex as it carries an individual's sense of continuity and identity. Being one of many complexes, the ego does not *equate* to consciousness or to the psyche as a whole, although it might *feel* like it is the 'whole' because we are all, for the most part, 'in' or identified with the ego complex. The ego is, then, a *content* of consciousness; a *part* of one's psychic wholeness, that hypothetical wholeness which embraces not only all that is not yet conscious or has by-passed consciousness, but all that will never attain consciousness (which includes the archetypal, instinctual, and deeply somatic levels of being).

We have so far noted that the ego provides one with a sense of the continuity of one's identity. The ego is also the seat of our capacity to will, intend, focus, discriminate, discern, prioritise, make choices and decisions, and act. In its 'executive' role as the focal point and centre of the 'field' of consciousness, the ego has a degree of freedom. However, as a *content* of a 'field' of consciousness larger than itself, and a *part* of an indefinable *whole* which embraces psyche and soma, conscious and unconscious, it is affected by outer and inner stimuli and events, and is therefore also limited and vulnerable. As we saw in Chapter 1, the ego-complex can all too readily be disabled and overridden by the activation of a powerful unconscious complex, by impulses or powerful emotions, just as it can be debilitated by the impact of external events. When such experiences are neither too extreme nor potentially damaging to the psyche, however, "collisions" with the inner and outer worlds are essential to the growth and development of a resilient ego:

> Although its bases are themselves relatively unknown and unconscious, both psychic and somatic, the ego is a conscious factor par excellence. It is even acquired, empirically speaking, during the individual's lifetime. It seems to arise in the first place from the collision between the somatic

factor and the environment, and, once established as a subject, it goes on developing from further collisions with the outer world and the inner.

(CW9i:6)

The ego that "goes on developing" supports the unfolding of the personality and the growth of consciousness, largely through the differentiation of the functions, as discussed in Chapter 2. We will talk in more depth about the development of the personality and the growth of consciousness in Chapter 5 when we discuss Jung's concept of *Individuation*. In the meantime, we would like to introduce a metaphor that those new to Jung's ideas might find helpful to their understanding of the relationship of the ego both to consciousness and to psychic content that is either temporarily or permanently unconscious. Let us imagine, for a moment, the ego as a swimmer: The swimmer functions at the interface of two realms, dependent on both the air she breathes and the water on the surface of which she floats; the swimmer is part in and part out of both the world above and the world below; she can swim forwards into the future, backwards into the past; she can swim on her back, facing the sky, perhaps aspiring to the heights; she can peer into the water, trying to understand what lies in the depths; she can swim to shore or further out to sea.

The ego is, then, like the double-faced Roman god, Janus, after whom January is named. Like Janus, the ego may look both ways, change its focus from inner to outer, and *vice versa*. The healthy mature ego can, therefore, succeed in establishing a bridge between inner and outer experience and, as Edward Edinger (1972) describes in *Ego and Archetype,* an ego–Self *axis* which connects the individual 'I' (one's subjectivity) and centre of conscious awareness to the totality of the *objective* psyche or *psychic unknowable*, that is, to the Self as 'orchestrator' of every human life. While the psyche, like the body, seems to strive for homeostasis and balance, the fragile ego may be vulnerable to becoming overwhelmed or fascinated by the *numinous* god-like power of the unconscious, in which case it may become identified with it: "I am invincible," "I am Superman," etc. Such a state of affairs is referred to as an *inflation* of the ego, described as an "Expansion of the personality beyond its proper limits [...] (which) produces an exaggerated sense of one's self-importance and is usually compensated by feelings of inferiority" (i.e., the psyche's attempt to restore homeostasis) (Jung 1961/63, p. 396). Inflation may become pathological in cases of identification with a religious or historical figure; it can also be caused by an unrealistic identification with the persona (see below).

In his essay, "The Stages of Life," first published in German in 1930, Jung describes the work of the first half of life (early adulthood to mid-life) as usually impelled by the need to establish oneself in the world. In terms of our metaphor above, this would see our swimmer leave the sea for at least a significant period of living on dry land:

> Achievement, usefulness and so forth are the ideals that seem to point the way out of the confusions of the problematic state (i.e., adolescence). They [...] guide us in the adventure of broadening and consolidating our physical existence; they help us to strike our roots in the world [...]. [...] We limit ourselves to the attainable, and this means renouncing all our other psychic potentialities.
>
> (CW8:769-70)

Embracing "all our other psychic potentialities" is typically the work of the second half of life.

SUMMARY

- Jung's lifelong fascination with the 'miracle' of consciousness
- Conscious awareness as an *epiphenomenon* that "does not create itself" but gradually emerges from the unknown depths of both body and psyche
- Development of the sense of a continuity of identity, the sense of 'I'
- Ego as complex at the centre of the 'field' of consciousness. In 'collisions' with inner and outer worlds, the ego develops ways to meet and manage life: thinking, will, intention, agency, discernment, valuing, etc.
- Ego-consciousness enjoys a degree of freedom as the focal point of consciousness. It is, however, not identical with consciousness but a *part* of consciousness, vulnerable to intrusions of the *psychic unknown*, in the form of unconscious complexes
- Ego-inflation: the expansion of the personality beyond its proper limits
- Focus of the first half of life tends to be on establishing oneself in the world, i.e., in the collective, through the development of appropriate competencies

⊕

PERSONA

For the work of the first half of life, the ego adopts and develops a 'skin,' the psychic organ or complex that Jung refers to as the *persona*. The word *persona* originally described the theatrical mask worn by actors in ancient Greece to convey to members of the audience (who might be sitting too far away to see the actual features of the actors' faces) the *role* and *character* each was playing. Embedded in every mask was a rudimentary megaphone to amplify and project the voice of the actor. Jung adopted the term, *persona,* to describe the 'face' we each present to the world. The persona serves to protect vulnerable, and conceal (or mask) undesirable aspects of the personality, amplify traits that will serve us well in the world, and also project the essential qualities of a person's character. In this way, it is a *functional* complex "that comes into existence for reasons of adaptation or personal convenience, but is by no means identical with the individuality. The persona is exclusively concerned with the relation to objects" (CW6:801). The persona is also *necessary,* as it enables individuals to insert themselves into "a social network of communication," for communication "needs an intermediary, or medium, because there is no such thing as pure communication" (Humbert 1988, p. 51). Elie Humbert, a French analytical psychologist and one of the last analysts to be trained by Jung, is regretful that "Jung wrote so little about the persona because his way of seeing it has the value of acknowledging the importance of the human stage or theater [...]. The persona makes it possible for the subject to be 'present' while maintaining a certain 'distance' from others by means of social roles. That is to say, the persona allows for communication" (*ibid.,* pp. 51–52) between discrete, separate individuals.

The development of the persona begins early in life. Infants and young children learn very quickly the kinds of behaviour that win praise and approval from parents and teachers, and those that result in punishment or the withdrawal of love. Behaviours and traits that do not receive approval are usually denied or repressed and contribute to the formation of yet another complex, the personal *shadow*, which we will discuss below. As complexes, both persona and shadow may be understood as *part personalities* (as discussed in Chapter 1), or examples of *character-splitting*. As Jung writes on "traces of character-splitting in normal individuals,"

> One has only to observe a man rather closely, under varying conditions, to see that a change from one milieu to another brings about a striking alteration of personality, and on each occasion a clearly defined character

emerges that is noticeably different from the previous one. [...] A particular milieu necessitates a particular attitude.

(CW6:798)

While Jung considers the persona to embody an individual's *attitude* to the outer world, he raises the question of what happens when a person adopts two very different attitudes in vastly different milieus, "Which is the true character, the real personality?" (*ibid.*). Jung's answer?

> In my view the answer to the above question should be that such a man has no real character at all: he is not individual but collective, the plaything of circumstance and general expectations. Were he individual, he would have the same character despite the variation of attitude. He would not be identical with the attitude of the moment, and he neither would nor could prevent his individuality from expressing itself just as clearly in one state as in another. Naturally he is individual, like every living being, but unconsciously so. Because of his more or less complete identification with the attitude of the moment, he deceives others, and often himself, as to his real character.
>
> (*ibid.*:799)

And Stein (1998) points out that while the persona adopted in a particular environment enables us to act appropriately and is therefore "a feature of character [...], the longer an attitude persists and the more frequently it is called upon to meet the demands of a milieu, [...] the stronger and the more entrenched it becomes," (p. 112), that is, the more *unconscious* the adoption of a particular persona, the more 'collective' the individual becomes, with the 'true' personality becoming less evident as a result.

We mentioned above that the ego may become *inflated* if displaced by another complex of which it is unconscious or overridden by an intrusion of unconscious archetypal energy. The ego's vulnerability to inflation suggests that, despite its functioning as the centre and focal point of consciousness, the ego is nevertheless partially unconscious. Jung emphasises that "inflation is a regression of consciousness into unconsciousness. This always happens when consciousness takes too many conscious contents upon itself and loses the faculty of discrimination" (CW12:563), i.e., when the ego loses focus, forgets what it *is* and what it is *not*. The ego may also become inflated by unconsciously identifying with an idealised persona, or image of itself. The individual then becomes more than, better than, smarter than others, a brittle shell that is 'nothing but' the idealised persona or role with which he or she is identified. Rigidity sets in, the ego loses its freedom, and development is compromised: the lawyer is the lawyer at work, at home, in social situations; the only-mother is forever only mother; the eternal adolescent never does manage to grow up. When identified with the persona, the ego can only orient itself outwardly; it cannot respond to inner promptings or experience itself as being other than or more than the persona; it cannot take off the actor's mask. Identification with the persona consequently means identification with a prescribed, collective role, a 'false self,' which results in the eclipse of individuality, of personality. However, *deflation* may also eclipse individuality by flooding the ego with a sense of worthlessness, hopelessness, insignificance, and depression. The ego identifies with the persona of the victim, outsider or failure. In either case—inflation or deflation (negative inflation)—the discerning, differentiating, mediating role of the ego is usurped and rendered dysfunctional because unconscious.

But let us not forget that the persona does play an essential role, to the extent that Jung refers to that role as archetypal and the persona as an archetype, that is, an intrinsic component of the core psychic totality. The fundamental function of the persona is adaptation: In the healthy personality, the persona changes and adapts; it *transforms* as one moves from one stage of life to another (i.e., from childhood to adolescence; adolescence to adulthood; middle- to old-age); it may be *consciously* 'worn' and utilised as the individual matures, develops new interests, changes careers, and embraces various social and familial roles, such as those of mayor, politician, educator, spouse, parent, grandparent … as the life cycle unfolds. Stein (1998) writes that "the persona must relate to objects and protect the subject" (p. 119), that is, adapt to the outer world while protecting the individuality of the 'subject.' The capacity of the persona to adapt *and* transform is supported by the ego's need both to survive in the outer world yet maintain its integrity and autonomy, a need arising from its archetypal core, its "pure 'I-ness'" (*ibid.*, p. 114). If the ego is strong enough to manage the tension between the need to conform and the need for autonomy, a person's individuality will 'shine through' the way in which the persona 'presents' that person to the world. (We have seen how the ego's autonomy, its 'I-ness,' is lost when the ego identifies with an uncompromising persona.) The persona serves as the ego's 'clothing.' Conscious awareness of the supportive role of the persona as the 'clothing' of an integral ego is evident, for example, when an individual thoughtfully selects an outfit to bolster confidence and poise for an interview or important social event. The individual whose ego maintains its autonomy is aware that he or she is more than the persona or current 'outfit.' A *conscious* choice of appropriate 'clothing' is essential to one's healthy relations with both one's inner and outer worlds.

SUMMARY

- The Persona is the face or 'mask' we each present to the world; it is how we want others to see us and how we like to 'see' ourselves
- The Persona is a functional complex enabling us to communicate with others, adapt to collective expectations, and relate to the external world; it is also archetypal, that is, its formation and function are essential to psychic health and development
- Acceptable traits accrue to the Persona from an early age. Unacceptable traits are denied, repressed, and accrue to the Shadow (see below)
- The ego's unconscious identification with the Persona (a particular 'role') can lead to inflation/deflation of the ego, rigidity of the persona, sacrifice of individuality to collective mores, and inhibition of the personality's natural development
- The Persona will change and adapt as the personality develops to meet the demands of the various steps and stages of life, both outer and inner

SHADOW

When we discussed the formation of the persona, we noted that even very young children are quick to learn how best to present themselves, and behave, in order to win parental approval and treats! The persona enables us to put our desirable traits and so our 'best face forward' in order to communicate with others, adapt to and be accepted by family, community, and culture. What is not desirable is denied and repressed, 'kept under wraps,' in the dark. Jung gave the term *shadow* to anything in the personality that the ego—and the persona as the PR function of the ego—saw as a threat to the public image the individual wants to promote. Jung once wrote: "One could say, with a little exaggeration, that the persona is that which in reality one is not, but which oneself as well as others think one is" (CW9i:221). And we mostly think we *are* how we present ourselves to the world, via the persona, because the ego has a very effective defence mechanism that can keep even a willingly introspective ego 'in the dark' as far as the contents of that ego's shadow are concerned. This means that the contents of the shadow complex remain largely outside the control of the ego simply because the ego is not aware of the extent of this rejected part of the personality. So the ego (that focal point at the centre of the field of consciousness) is nevertheless unconscious of many personality traits that *could* become conscious if the ego could only 'shine its light' in their direction.

ANOTHER METAPHOR

Imagine yourself in a darkened theatre. The stage you face is completely black. A spotlight is switched on and shines a bright, white light on a small area, centre-stage. You start to realise that the brighter the light and the narrower its focus, the more intense the surrounding darkness becomes. You notice a clear demarcation between the bright white of the light and the blackness beyond. Suddenly the circle of spotlight widens. More of the stage is illuminated. As the circle of light expands, the intensity of the light diminishes. The edges of the circle of light become more diffuse, almost grey. You begin to distinguish vague outlines of objects where the softer light now merges with and softens the edges of the darkness.

If we understand the spotlight as the ego, we see that when the ego's focus is narrow (perhaps because of an identification with a somewhat idealised persona image?), there is a clear-cut boundary, a defence against the darkness. Everything is black and white, either/or, admissible or inadmissible. When the ego's focus widens and softens, other objects, personality traits, emotions ... start to show themselves. If the ego is sufficiently resilient and flexible, neither identified with an ideal image of itself nor solely oriented to the outer world, it can work to integrate fragments of the personality relegated to the rubbish heap of the shadow. However disagreeable and difficult this work, it can lead to a growth in consciousness and an enlargement of the conscious personality.

Because a complex, or sub-personality, is unconscious, it does not mean that it ceases to exist. As we saw in Chapter 1, unconscious complexes can exert an unexpected and powerful impact on consciousness, often overwhelming and displacing the ego so that the activated (constellated) sub-personality rather than the conscious personality is in control. Anthony Stevens (1990) points out that:

> The rejected aspects of the developing ego continue to carry a sense of personal identity, and when, from time to time, they impinge on awareness, they are experienced as liabilities: they are tinged with feelings of guilt and unworthiness, and bring fears that one will suffer rejection should they be discovered or exposed. To *own* (or shine a spotlight on) one's shadow is, therefore, a painful, and potentially terrifying, experience – [...] so much so that [...] we *deny* the existence of our shadow and *project* it onto others.

(pp. 43–44)

Projection is not the result of a conscious act of will. Projection 'happens' as an autonomous *defence mechanism* that protects the ego from attack, from facing difficult truths it might not be strong enough to withstand, much less own and integrate into the conscious personality. We fail to see the negative trait in ourselves, only in the other person. And while there is invariably a 'hook' in the other person to activate and catch the projection, it is always the 'other' that is 'bad,' 'dangerous,' 'prejudiced,' etc. We are 'squeaky clean.' It is the other person who needs to change, not us. Here is Jung:

> it is not the conscious subject (ego, I) but the unconscious which does the projecting. Hence one meets with projections, one does not make them. The effect of projection is to isolate the subject from his environment, since instead of a real relation to it there is now only an illusory one. Projections change the world into the replica of one's own unknown face.

(CW9ii:17)

However, if someone were to shine a spotlight on our shadowy rejected traits, we might begin to see that the shadow is often active in subversive, manipulative ways of which we are far from aware: As the good, selfless person I am, I will dog-sit for the neighbours who are on vacation, adjusting my halo on the way to their front door while refusing to acknowledge I want a break from my family, the neighbours' house is a palace with a fully-stocked fridge, and I will be able to have my secret lover over. My family will commend my altruism (I hate dogs) while my manipulative shadow will see to it that all my needs are met. This demonstrates that the ego-complex is unconscious of being controlled by the activity of a shadowy sub-personality of whose existence it is unaware.

Our example of an imaginary character unconsciously intent on getting personal desires fulfilled is objectively fairly innocuous.

But while the shadow is considered a *personal* complex associated with the *personal unconscious* (see below) because its contents are the result of undesirable personal traits, behaviours, memories, powerful affect, etc., that originate in an individual's life experience, like all complexes, the shadow has an archetypal core. The *personal* shadow contains all that the ego rejects as 'bad' and disavows by projecting its own unacknowledged 'badness' onto others; the *archetype* at the core of the shadow is the figure of the Enemy, Predator, Evil Monster, and 'absolute evil' threatening one's personal survival and that of one's family, community, tribe, or nation. It is not difficult to see how shadow projection can lead to enmity, prejudice, conflict, scapegoating, genocide, persecution, and war, and how making it conscious is essential to well-being, peace, and security personally, at the level of family and community, nationally and globally.

The values and traits of the shadow are clearly opposite to those of the persona and *vice versa*; in this way, shadow and persona operate as two sides of the same coin that oppose yet balance and compensate each other. An extraverted, socially sophisticated persona compensates an anti-social shadow; an arrogant, bullying persona is balanced by a timid, under-confident shadow. Shadow and persona 'flank' the ego. Formed as they are through the development of the ego (the ego valuing one—persona—while denying the other—shadow), persona and shadow reflect the polarities of which the ego may be unconscious or partially unconscious. The difficult task of accepting and integrating unconscious elements of persona and shadow into consciousness can, however, result in an enhancement of the personality and an expansion of consciousness. The ego gains an increasing measure of autonomy and individuality: on the one hand, it starts to free itself from the demands of an ideal persona—it can take off its mask; on the other, the ego learns to accept previously repressed shadow qualities and, in doing so, frees itself from the shadow's manipulation of which it had been oblivious. Cited in Murray Stein (1998, p. 123), below is an excerpt from a letter Jung received in which a former patient describes her experience of gaining some degree of autonomy from both persona and shadow:

> *Out of evil, much good has come to me. By keeping quiet, repressing nothing, remaining attentive, and by accepting reality—taking things as they are, and not as I wanted them to be—by doing all this, unusual*

knowledge has come to me, and unusual powers as well [...]. I always thought that when we accepted things they overpowered us in some way or other. This turns out not to be true at all, and it is only by accepting them that one can assume an attitude towards them. So now I intend to play the game of life, being receptive to whatever comes to me, good and bad, sun and shadow forever alternating, and in this way also accepting my own nature with its positive and negative sides. Thus everything becomes more alive to me. What a fool I was! How I tried to force everything to go according to the way I felt it ought to!

Murray Stein comments on the excerpt as follows: This woman has stepped back both from the persona and from splitting persona and shadow into opposites, and she is now simply observing, reflecting on, and accepting her psyche as it comes to her, then sorting, seeing what it was about, and making some choices. She has created a psychological distance between the ego-complex and the persona, as well as between the ego and the shadow. She is no longer possessed on either end of the spectrum.

It is important to remember that, no matter how much work we do to make conscious our relations to those two complexes or sub-personalities so closely tied to the ego (persona and shadow), we are all *always* trailed by our shadows and we all *always* need the mask or 'clothing' of the persona to function in the world. Jung recognised the difficulty of bringing shadow traits to consciousness as a "moral problem that challenges the whole ego-personality, for no one can become conscious of the shadow without considerable moral effort" (CW9ii:14). The shadow is a "moral problem" because we each need the courage to recognise and take moral responsibility for our own quotient of darkness, as well as live our as-yet unlived potential. This applies equally to the dynamics of a relationship, to family dynamics, and the dynamics active in communities, organisations, institutions, and nations. As we have seen, what remains unclaimed and 'in shadow' is invariably projected onto the 'other,' whether that 'other' be a partner, boss, politician, or member of a different religion, culture, race, or ethnic group. Nevertheless, those who are willing and whose psychic constitutions enable them to commit to the task of psychological and spiritual growth might keep the image of the double-faced Janus in mind, regularly turning the ego's discerning eye inward to the shadow, outward to the persona: "One does not become enlightened by imagining figures of light, but by making the darkness conscious" (CW13:335).

Making the darkness of the shadow conscious leads, as we saw in the letter of Jung's patient, to an increase in autonomy and energy for the ego, as a great deal of psychic energy accrues to psychic content that remains active but unconscious, making that energy unavailable to the ego. Also, energy drawn from the psyche's 'quota' of psychic energy in order for the ego's defence mechanisms (repression, denial, projection, etc.) to keep shadow material at bay may be made available to the ego. What lies undeveloped in 'shadow' may also be positive; there is often life-enhancing 'gold' hidden in the shadow. If the persona is identified with the 'victim,' with hopelessness and worthlessness, the shadow will harbour the opposite qualities—agency, competency, a sense of self-worth. This unlived 'shadow' potential, when realised, can only revitalise the ego and transform the individual's inner and outer life. In such a case, a successful therapeutic process enables the development of an ego with sufficient agency—strong, stable, resilient, and curious—to integrate unlived, creative potential into the conscious personality, into life.

Before moving to the final section of this chapter, the personal unconscious, we would like to remind book lovers of the many famous literary works that address the problem of a split between ego/persona and shadow. All present salutary, if extreme, wake-up calls, and provide nuanced studies of underlying psychic and social dynamics. We are sure you will be able to add a long list of literary works, films, TV shows, video games, etc., to the list below. And we must not forget the daily news, which is rife with examples of how the nefarious manipulations of the shadow can upend our best-laid plans and intentions.

EGO vs SHADOW

A few well-known works of literature that explore the ego/persona split with the shadow, most of which suggest that the split is irreparable:

The Strange Case of Dr Jekyll and Mr Hyde (R.L. Stevenson); *William Wilson* (Edgar Allan Poe); *The Portrait of Dorian Gray* (Oscar Wilde); *Faust* (Goethe); *Dr. Faustus* (Christopher Marlowe); *The Double* (Dostoevsky); *The Devil's Elixirs* (E.T.A. Hoffmann); the cult film, *Fight Club*, based on Dostoevsky's *The Double*, which ends in a *conscious* integration of the shadow ... etc., etc.

SUMMARY

- The 'shadow' harbours the undesirable, 'ego-alien' traits incompatible with the persona and ego-ideal, everything we do not want to acknowledge or be. It also harbours desirable, as yet unrealised potential capable of transforming the personality when made conscious
- The shadow opposes the persona, the face we present to the world, the way we want others to 'see' us and the way we want to see ourselves
- Both shadow and persona operate as sub-personalities, complexes imbued with energy and a certain degree of autonomy
- Undesirable shadow traits are projected onto others; we cannot 'own' these traits as a part of our (unconscious) personality
- The personal shadow complex = the 'badness' of *my* personality; the collective or archetypal shadow at the core of the complex = an image of absolute evil
- Two polarities—that of the shadow and that of the person—flank the ego
- Increased consciousness and autonomy of the ego necessitate a conscious differentiation between ego and persona, ego and shadow
- Making conscious and integrating the shadow is a "moral problem" as it entails facing the darkness in one's own personality as present and real

PERSONAL UNCONSCIOUS

Remember the dream Jung had about exploring the different levels of a house that, in the dream, he felt was somehow 'his house'? (See Chapter 2). Jung understood his dream as an invaluable gift which he came to see as presenting an image of the structure of the psyche. This dream occurred early in Jung's career (1909). It became the catalyst and inspiration for his life's work of investigating the nature and dynamics of the unconscious psyche from which ego–consciousness emerges and on which it 'rides.' It focused Jung's interest on the unconscious even before he started to investigate the role of the ego and the phenomenon of consciousness. Jung understood the "lived-in atmosphere" of the salon in the dream to represent 'consciousness.' "The ground floor stood for the first level of the unconscious. [...] the cave, [...] the world of the primitive (instinctual, archaic) man within myself—a world which can scarcely be reached or illuminated by consciousness" (1961/63, p. 160) and which Jung came to designate as the *collective unconscious*, the *impersonal, objective* psyche underlying the (subjective) human psyche.

Jung's emerging model of the psyche started to differ radically from Freud's at this stage. The first level of the two levels of the *un*conscious, the dream's 'ground floor,' Jung called the *personal unconscious,* which basically equates to the *Id,* more or less the entirety of the unconscious in Freud's model. Why the *personal* unconscious? As we have seen in this chapter, *persona* and *shadow* are two complexes or psychic 'organs' that are like antagonistic twins; they form in tandem with the emergence of consciousness in the infant and the development of the ego as the centre of consciousness. The persona enables engagement with the world. The shadow is 'ego-alien.' It becomes the dustbin or repository of all that is incompatible with the persona, one's self-image and the way one wants to be 'seen' by others (e.g., banished is the greed that would belie one's public altruism; suppressed is the rage that would destroy one's self-image as victim, should it be made conscious and realised positively as *agency*, as life-enhancing action.) It is also the *positive* repository of untapped, unrealised potential, of interests and passions denied, of life as yet unlived. We have seen how the ego, though centre of the field of consciousness, is not itself fully conscious of the limitations placed upon its autonomy by its often constricting and manipulative 'off-spring'—persona and shadow. The 'threshold,' then, between conscious and unconscious is not a definitive (black and white) dividing line (as one might hope!): ego-consciousness fades into and merges with psychic content which is either temporarily or permanently 'in shadow' (remember the metaphor of the spotlight: the wider the beam of light, the more its 'edge' becomes diffuse, grey, where it meets the darkened areas of the stage. We saw there were items in shadow that might be identified if the spotlight were focused on them, while in the darkest recesses of the theatre's 'wings' nothing was distinguishable from the darkness.)

Jung often refers to the *shadow complex* as representing the *personal* unconscious in its entirety because it comprises traits that the *ego* rejects, that 'I' reject. These traits and behaviours banished to the shadows result from the ego's ('my') 'collisions' with the environment, that is, from my *personal* experiences *of,* and unique *inner reactions to* my immediate environment (family, community, education, culture, religion, etc.). Although they are considered inadmissible by the ego, they are nevertheless "integral components of the individual personality and therefore could just as well be conscious" (CW9ii:7). There are also other complexes inhabiting the shadowy realm of the personal unconscious: for example, the all-important parental complexes. And then there are other familial complexes that develop through our relationships with siblings and relatives; there are social and cultural complexes that result from individual experience but individual experience *of* shared, collective values, behavioural norms, expectations, systems of education, events that affect a community or group. As Stein writes, "Shared traumas make for shared complexes" (1998, p. 47), and these can be passed from generation to generation at the level of the family, community, ethnicity, or nation.

The concept of the personal unconscious as a psychic 'domain' comprised of potentially disruptive complexes is in many ways daunting. However, rest assured that this, as Jung recognised, "is as true of healthy people as it is of people who are neurotic or psychotic" (Jung quoted in Stevens 1990, p. 31). Here is Jung on the contents and nature of the personal unconscious:

> [E]verything of which I know, but of which I am not at the moment thinking; everything of which I was once conscious but have now forgotten; everything perceived by my senses, but not noted by my conscious mind; everything which, involuntarily and without paying attention to it, I feel, think, remember, want, and do; all the future things which are taking shape in me and will sometime come to consciousness; [...] (CW8:382). Besides these we must include all more or less intentional repressions of painful thoughts and feelings. I call the sum of these contents the 'personal unconscious.'
> (CW8:270)

One of the most powerful characteristics of a complex is its *feeling-tone,* as we saw in Chapter 1. The *feeling-tone,* or affect, is the 'glue' that sticks the two parts of a complex together: the images and memory traces of the original trauma and the complex's archetypal nucleus. When a complex is constellated (when someone pushes one's 'buttons'), "one is as though in the grip of a demon, a force stronger than one's will" (Stein 1998, p. 43). To introduce yet one more metaphor, when a particularly powerful complex is triggered, it can feel as though one has stuck one's finger into an electrical outlet. We might imagine an electrical conduit linking the *personal* complex to its archetypal, instinctual base. With the activation of a complex, we are plugged into a level of primal response—fear for our survival, safety, security, etc. Hence, the extraordinary power of particular complexes to disturb consciousness and disable the ego.

We can now see how the complex serves as the 'dress' or personification of its archetypal core. The new-born's anticipation of being adequately 'mothered' is archetypal, instinctual, innate. It works like a magnet, drawing to it, as a child develops, specific experiences of a particular mother or caretaker, of *feeling* 'safe' or 'unsafe,' etc. These sensations, feelings, and memories 'clothe' the impersonal archetypal imperative in the dress of specific personal experiences to form the 'mother' complex or *imago*. The 'mother' complex is often referred to as the 'mother' *imago,* that is, the sum of the *subjective,* psychic, inner experiences of the child in relation to the mother, *not* an image of the actual mother or even of how she behaves and acts towards the child. Any complex or *imago* can be augmented, modified, and, to an extent, transformed (remember the public face of the ego, the persona, is the psychic organ of *adaptation*). This may happen when a child, for example, experiences *different* examples of 'mothering' through the realisation that other families do things differently, or when a relative or teacher provides qualities of 'mothering' not available from the actual mother. Whether a complex is positive or negative is reflected in the degree to which it enables us to experience a sense of security and trust—in ourselves, in others, and the world—and in our sense of self-worth, self-confidence, aliveness, and agency.

And, yes, despite the bad press complexes get, there *are* positive complexes, and we have those, too!

SUMMARY

- Jung's view of there being two levels to the unconscious, with the top level designated the personal unconscious
- The personal unconscious formed of complexes—positive and negative—developed through 'collisions' with the outer and inner worlds (events—positive and negative; and conflict resulting in trauma at the subjective level)
- Complexes of the personal unconscious as the subjective 'dress' or personification of the archetypes
- Possibility to modify complexes and bring them to consciousness. This transformative process expands the personality and enhances consciousness

⊕

REFERENCES

Edinger, E. (1972) *Ego and Archetype: Individuation and the Religious Function of the Psyche*. Boston, MA: Shambhala.

Humbert, E. G. (1988) *C. G. Jung: The Fundamentals of Theory and Practice*. R. G. Jalbert (Trans.). Wilmette, IL: Chiron Publications.

Jung, C. G. (1953–83) *The Collected Works of C. G. Jung*, 20 vols. W. McGuire, H. Read, M. Fordham, G. Adler (Eds.). R. F. C. Hull (Trans.). London: Routledge & Kegan Paul; Princeton, NJ: Princeton University Press.

Jung, C. G. (1961/63) *Memories, Dreams, Reflections*. Recorded and edited by A. Jaffé. R. and C. Wintston and R. Winston (Trans.). New York: Pantheon Books.

Jung, C. G. (1983) *The Collected Works of C. G. Jung, Supplementary Vol. A: The Zofingia Lectures*. W. McGuire, H. Read, M. Fordham, G. Adler (Eds.). J. van Heurck (Trans.). London: Routledge & Kegan Paul.

Stein, M. (1998) *Jung's Map of the Soul: An Introduction*. Chicago, IL: Open Court.

Stevens, A. (1990) *On Jung*. London: Routledge.

Table 3.1 Ego

TOPIC/ KEYWORDS	LOCATION	DESCRIPTOR
The ego and consciousness	CW6:706 (1921/1923)	"[…] a complex of ideas which constitutes the centre of my field of consciousness and appears to possess a high degree of continuity." Ego as one complex among many.
	CW17:102 *ff* (1928)	Emergence of consciousness; development of ego (sense of 'I') from childhood facilitated through education.
	CW17:169 (1946)	Ego, as "the subject of consciousness [,] comes into existence through the complex interaction between inherited disposition and unconsciously acquired impressions and their attendant phenomena."
Useful condensed discussion of ego	**CW9ii:1–12** (1951)	**Full chapter dedicated to the ego.** The ego as the centre of consciousness, not the centre of the personality (Self); ego as part of the personality and so contained within it. The *somatic* and *psychic* bases of the ego. Ego ('I') develops through 'collisions' with inner & outer worlds.

(Continued)

Table 3.1 (Continued)

TOPIC/ KEYWORDS	LOCATION	DESCRIPTOR
	CW8:387 (1954)	Consciousness may be conceived as an archipelago capable of expansion. Ego-consciousness surrounded by a multitude of little luminosities.
	CW9i:188 (1954)	Differentiation of ego-consciousness from unconscious identity with the mother (archetype).
	CW11:390 *ff* (1954)	The ego's ability to consciously choose self-sacrifice and surrender not only shows that the ego is the object of a moral act, but that it is a "relative quantity which can be subsumed under various supraordinate authorities."
Ego-personality and self-understanding	CW10:491 (1957)	Self-knowledge confused with knowledge of one's conscious ego-personality. "What is commonly called 'self-knowledge' is […] very limited knowledge of what goes on in the human psyche."
The ego's relationship to the unconscious/Self and individuation	CW11:961 (1944)	The necessity of opposites; the ego needs the Self as the Self needs the ego.
	CW8:557 (1948)	A compensatory relationship exists between ego-consciousness and the unconscious. The ego's limited one-sidedness is corrected by "the universal human being in us, whose goal is the ultimate integration of conscious and unconscious […], the assimilation of the ego to a wider personality."
	CW11:391 *ff* (1954)	The ego evolves out of the Self yet is the "exponent" of the Self in consciousness. "The ego stands to the [S]elf as the moved to the mover, or as object to subject." Degree of ego's autonomy versus dependence in relation to the Self. The Self as supraordinate to ego-consciousness.
	CW8:399 (1954)	The organ with which we may apprehend archetypal images—ego-consciousness—"is not only itself a transformation of the original instinctual image, but also its transformer."

(Continued)

Table 3.1 (Continued)

TOPIC/ KEYWORDS	LOCATION	DESCRIPTOR
	CW8:425 *ff* (1954)	The ego preserves its integrity only if it can find a balance between opposing psychological positions. When unconscious contents are successfully integrated into consciousness, wholeness may be achieved, which "has remarkable effects" on ego-consciousness, as both ego-personality and unconscious are transformed (430). Ego-centeredness not equated with individuation (432).
	CW8.430, fn. 128	"Conscious wholeness consists in a successful union of ego and [S]elf, so that both preserve their intrinsic qualities."
	CW14:778 (1955–56)	The Self is both brighter and darker than the ego. "*[T]he experience of the [S]elf is always a defeat for the ego.*" Jung is eager to assert, however, that he in no way underestimates the importance of the ego.
Ego-inflation	CW9ii:45 *ff* (1951)	Two causes of ego-inflation: (1) the ego is assimilated by the Self (45) and (2) the Self becomes assimilated to the ego (47). "In the first case, reality [has] to be protected against an archaic […] dream state; in the second, room must be made for the dream at the expense of the world of consciousness" (47). Psychological health is achieved by maintaining "a balanced state" (47).
	CW8:425 *ff* (1954)	The dangers of the ego being assimilated by the unconscious. Events in Germany (WW2) used as an example. "It is abundantly clear that such an *abaissement du niveau mental*, i.e., the overpowering of the ego by unconscious contents and the consequent identification with a preconscious wholeness, possess a prodigious psychic virulence, or power of contagion, and is capable of the most disastrous results."

(*Continued*)

Table 3.1 (Continued)

TOPIC/ KEYWORDS	LOCATION	DESCRIPTOR
The importance of ego-consciousness/ strong-enough ego	CW7:388 *ff* (1916/1928)	Once the personality has reached a state of heightened consciousness and balance, "nothing more should happen that is not sanctioned by the ego, and when the ego wants something, nothing should be capable of interfering." Such a heightened state of consciousness is consonant with the *mana* personality.
	CW9ii:46 (1951)	"[…] It is of the greatest importance that the ego should be anchored in the world of consciousness and that consciousness should be reinforced by a very precise adaptation."
	CW8:425 *ff* (1954)	"[I]f the structure of the ego-complex is strong enough to withstand their ['unconscious contents'] assault without having its framework fatally dislocated, then assimilation can take place" (430). The ego, however, must relinquish its mistaken belief that it occupies pride of place in the psyche. The ego subordinate to the Self.
"Affect-ego"	CW3:86, fn. 9 (1907)	"Affect-ego" refers to the modification of the ego-complex when impacted by a strongly toned complex.
Ego's relationship to other archetypes	CW7:508 *ff* (1916)	When the ego identifies with either the persona or the anima, the respective archetype will be projected onto real objects in the environment.
Ego and persona	CW7:306 *ff* (1916/1928)	Dangers of the ego identifying with the persona; people believe who they pretend to be.
Ego and Self	CW6:706 (1921/1923)	The ego cannot be equated with the totality of the personality (the Self). Self embraces the ego.
Impact of creativity on the ego; limitations of the ego	CW8:216 (1948) CW15:158 (1950)	Freedom of the ego ends when gripped by complexes. "A person must pay dearly for the divine gift of creative fire." The ego faces danger of depletion, existing at an inferior level, and prone to difficulties.
The role of the ego in Eastern thought	CW11:775 *ff* (1954)	Ego is conceived differently in Eastern thought. The Eastern mind is "less ego-centric." The practice of hatha yoga seeks to extinguish/dissolve the ego.

Table 3.2 Persona

TOPIC/ KEYWORDS	LOCATION	DESCRIPTOR
Persona as archetype	CW7:244 *ff* (1916/1928)	Short essay "The Persona as a Segment of the Collective Psyche." Relationship of Persona to Ego (consciousness) and to the Self (unconscious). Persona and collective psyche; persona and individuality.
Persona as complex	CW6:801 (1921/1923)	Persona as a "functional complex that comes into existence for reasons of adaptation or personal convenience," but in no way equates with individuality.
Persona as function of adaptation; relationship to consciousness and the ego	CW7:507 (1916)	The persona as a "compromise formation between external reality and the individual. [...] it is a function for adapting the individual to the real world." The persona "occupies a place midway between the real world and individuality."
	CW7:312 *ff* (1916/1928)	Tendency of relatively autonomous complex (persona) to direct personification (as a sub-personality) which 'deceives' the ego as to which is the 'true' personality.
Persona as mask/ persona conceals	CW7:244 *ff* (1916/1928)	*Persona* means the mask worn by actors of antiquity. It is the adaptive, collective 'face' that the ego presents to the world. It feigns individuality. One is "simply acting a role through which the collective psyche speaks."
	CW7:305	The persona is a mask designed to make an impression while concealing the true nature of the individual.
	CW9i:221 (1950)	"[T]he persona is that which one in reality is not, but which oneself and others think one is."
	CW9i:43 (1954)	"[T]he face we never show to the world [...] we cover it with the persona, the mask of the actor. But the mirror lies behind the mask and shows the true face."
Persona as a compromise between individual and society	CW7:246 (1916/1928)	The persona is "nothing real," a compromise between individual and society dictating norms. The persona is "a semblance, a two-dimensional reality [...]"
Persona's relationship to individuation	CW7:518 (1906)	The more the ego identifies with the persona, the greater the risk of becoming "de-individualized."

(Continued)

Table 3.2 (Continued)

TOPIC/ KEYWORDS	LOCATION	DESCRIPTOR
	CW7:247 (1916/1928)	Despite its conforming to collective norms, "there is [...] something individual in the peculiar choice and delineation of the persona [...] the unconscious self, one's true individuality, is always present and makes itself felt indirectly if not directly." "The purely personal attitude [of the persona] [...] evokes reactions on the part of the unconscious, and these, together with personal repressions, contain the seeds of individual development in the guise of collective fantasies."
Identification with the persona	CW7:306 (1916/1928)	A suitably constructed persona may lead the ego to identify with the persona, causing the individual to believe they are who they pretend to be.
	CW6:800 (1921/1923)	One who identifies with the persona is referred to as "personal" rather than "individual."
	CW9i:221 (1950)	Every profession has its own characteristic persona. Danger lies in identifying with the persona. Those who do so live exclusively against the background of their own biographies (with no connection to larger psychic reality).
Necessity of persona	CW7:305 (1916/1928)	Society demands that we play a distinct role: "to present an unequivocal face to the world is a matter of practical importance [...]." Achieving anything worthwhile necessitates a level of adaptation.
Compensatory impact of the persona/split between public and private lives	CW7:305 *ff* (1916/1928)	The division between public and private is "bound to have repercussions on the unconscious." The excellence of the outer mask is compensated by the private life. The more perfect the persona, the more irritable the individual becomes behind closed doors. Jung provides the example of "a very venerable personage" he followed for three days, only to realise, on the fourth day, that the shadow side of the persona was projected onto the individual's wife.

(Continued)

Table 3.2 (Continued)

TOPIC/ KEYWORDS	LOCATION	DESCRIPTOR
	CW7:307	The shadow side of an idealised persona: "The social 'strong man' is in his private life often a mere child where his own states of feeling are concerned [...]."
Persona and the anima	CW7:309 *ff* (1916/1928)	The persona (ideal picture of masculinity) is compensated by "feminine weakness." The unconscious attitude is dominated by an undeveloped *anima*. This unconscious aspect of the personality is in danger of being projected onto a female partner.
Undeveloped persona	CW7:318 (1916/1928)	Jung describes the dangers and characteristics of an undeveloped persona. Canadians are a good example! (an assertion to which both authors take exception).
	CW6:804 (1921/1923)	The anima expresses "all those common human qualities which the conscious attitude lacks." (While the persona is the face one presents to the world, the anima mirrors the face that turns towards the unconscious.)
Regressive restoration of the persona	CW7:254 *ff* (1916/1928)	The persona may contract after a catastrophe. Unable to meet the challenge of integrating unconscious contents, one may regress to the comfort of a well-worn persona. This ensures survival but not an experience of the vibrancy of life.
Identification with collective psyche/ dissolution of persona	CW7:260 (1916/1928)	The persona identifies with archetypal energies/images, which leads to inflation or the dissolution of the persona and, in both instances, a loss of individuality.
Dissolution of the persona in analysis	CW7:252 (1916/1928)	When the "false wrappings of the persona" (CW7:269) are dissolved, energy previously invested in the persona activates the unconscious "which is aiming [...] at the creation of a new balance" and which may be achieved if the conscious mind is able to assimilate "the contents produced by the unconscious."

Table 3.3   Shadow

TOPICS/ KEYWORDS	LOCATION	DESCRIPTOR
"The Shadow"— the best description in the CW, first given as a lecture in 1948	CW9ii:13–19 (1951)	The most accessible archetype of *shadow, anima, animus* as contents of shadow **complex** represented in *personal unconscious.* Shadow as "moral problem." Consciousness of personal shadow traits = recognising dark aspects of personality as present and real. This work leads to self-knowledge.
Autonomy/ emotional valence of shadow Projection		Autonomy and emotional nature of shadow, which may possess individual personality. Personal shadow traits = 'ego-alien,' disowned and **projected** onto others. Useful summary of **projection.**
Becoming conscious of personal shadow is a moral problem		Content of **personal shadow (complex)** met in dreams in figure of the same sex. Most intense illusions and projections arise from the anima/animus archetypes, met in dream/ fantasy figures of the opposite sex, not from **archetypal shadow**. (The anima/animus archetypes are further from consciousness than the "moral problem" of the **personal shadow**).
Archetypal shadow equivalent to the "face of absolute evil"		Possible to recognise "relative evil" of one's own nature but "it is a rare and shattering experience […] to gaze into the face of absolute evil" (**archetypal shadow**).
Shadow as the dark side of the personality	CW16:146 (1931)	"Shadow pertains to light as evil to good, and vice versa."
	CW11:131 (1938/1940)	The less we are aware of our shadow, "the blacker and denser it is." Shadow contents may be integrated into the personality if made conscious.
	CW16:470 (1946)	Shadow embodies everything a person has no wish to be.
Shadow projection	CW10:417 *ff* (1945)	An *hysterical dissociation of the personality* seeks to look for everything dark, inferior, and culpable in others. This is an attempt to "jump over" one's shadow. Jung 'diagnoses' Hitler's psychology.
	CW14:203 (1955–56)	We need to own our shadow, i.e., that which is projected onto others is an unconscious factor in ourselves.

(Continued)

Table 3.3 (Continued)

TOPICS/ KEYWORDS	LOCATION	DESCRIPTOR
Confronting/ integrating/ facing shadow	CW7:44 (1917/1926)	The need to reconcile one's relationship with the personal shadow. Its existence cannot be "rationalized into harmlessness."
	CW16:134 (1931)	Recovering inferior aspects of ourselves that have been repressed, lying in shadow, is a gain in itself. Jung describes the withdrawal of shadow projection: "I must have a dark side too if I am to be whole; and by becoming conscious of my shadow I remember once more that I am a human being like any other." Necessity to become conscious of one's own guilt and darkness.
Consciousness of guilt (shadow) as a powerful moral stimulus	CW10:440 (1945)	"Psychological correction" can only be made in consciousness. Without knowledge of the shadow, nothing changes. The concept of the shadow is applied to the "German body-politic" as an example of a collective manifestation of shadow.
	CW16:452 (1946)	Assimilating the shadow is a move towards wholeness, i.e., completion not perfection. It gives the individual a 'body' (connection to instinct and the archaic psyche). It makes undeveloped aspects of personality conscious.
	CW9ii:42 (1951)	Integration of the *personal* shadow is the first stage in analysis without which a recognition of the *archetypal images* of anima/animus would be impossible. Realisation of the shadow is relational in nature.
	CW9i:44 *ff*	Facing the shadow/personal unconscious is an initial step towards wholeness.
	CW14:514 (1955–56)	Confronting shadow is a therapeutic necessity in which both ego and unconscious are transformed. In the end, some 'union' must be sought. If the shadow is repressed, it will continue to accrue energy in the unconscious, and will find ways to express itself.

(Continued)

Table 3.3 (Continued)

TOPICS/ KEYWORDS	LOCATION	DESCRIPTOR
"The Fight with the Shadow"	CW10:444–87 (1946)	The concept of personal shadow is applied to an understanding of collective events. Focusing on Germany in WW2, the nation's attraction to Hitler stems from his capacity to symbolise the nation's shadow. An unacknowledged, collective inferiority is compensated by Hitler's ability to speak to an equally shared desire for order.
Shadow is not entirely negative	CW11:134 (1938/1940)	"If […] the shadow […] were obviously evil, there would be no problem whatever. But the shadow is merely somewhat inferior, primitive, unadapted, and awkward; not wholly bad." It also contains "childish" qualities that may rejuvenate the personality.
'Positive' shadow	CW9ii:423 (1951)	"If it has been believed hitherto that the human shadow was the source of all evil, it can now be ascertained on closer investigation that the unconscious man, that is, his shadow, does not consist only of morally reprehensible tendencies, but also displays a number of good qualities […]."
Shadow and the personal unconscious	CW9ii:261 (1951)	Engagement with the personal unconscious allows us to recognise the shadow; an engagement with the impersonal (collective) unconscious allows us to recognise the archetypal symbol of the Self.
	CW14:128 (1955-56)	The personal unconscious is personified by the shadow.
Shadow in relation to anima and animus	CW9ii:35 (1951)	Recognition of the (personal) shadow is much easier than acknowledgment of the (archetypal) anima/animus. We are prepared to recognise shadow through our education, and most will understand what is meant by the "inferior personality."
Failure to integrate shadow	CW11:131 (1938/1940)	If the shadow is not made conscious, it "is liable to burst forth suddenly in a moment of unawareness."

Table 3.4 Personal Unconscious

TOPICS/ KEYWORDS	LOCATION	DESCRIPTOR
A note on CW7, Two Essays on Analytical Psychology		*CW7, Two Essays on Analytical Psychology, contains "On the Psychology of the Unconscious" and "The Relations between the Ego and the Unconscious" including notes on successive editions. An appendix contains the earliest versions of these essays and of Jung's thinking ("The Structure of the Unconscious" (442–521) and "New Paths in Psychology" (407–41). CW7 enables the reader to trace the evolution of Jung's Analytical Psychology.*
Personal unconscious and collective unconscious; structure of personal unconscious	CW7:442 *ff* (1916)	Jung's differentiation of his view of the contents of the unconscious from Freud's. Jung's concept of the *personal unconscious* may be equated with the entirety of the Freudian unconscious (the *Id*). Contents of the personal unconscious derive from an individual's life experience and psychological factors, including repressed desires, traits, and tendencies unacceptable to consciousness/ego-ideal.
	CW7:218 (1916/1928)	Repressed contents of the personal unconscious may cause a "sense of moral inferiority" indicating the "missing element" ought and *could* be made conscious (is close to consciousness and readily retrievable).
	CW7:103 (1917/1926)	Differentiation of the two levels of the unconscious: the personal and an *impersonal* or *objective/collective unconscious.* The personal unconscious contains lost memories, repressed painful ideas, subliminal perceptions, and contents not yet "ripe for consciousness."
	CW8:321 *ff* (1931)	The three psychic levels described: consciousness, personal unconscious, collective unconscious. "The whole psychic organism corresponds exactly to the body [...] in its development and structure"— psyche/soma correspondence.

(Continued)

Table 3.4 (Continued)

TOPICS/ KEYWORDS	LOCATION	DESCRIPTOR
	CW8:270 (1948)	Instinct and the unconscious; differentiation between unconscious content of a personal and collective (archetypal/instinctual) nature.
	CW8:588 *ff* (1948)	"The Psychological Foundations of Belief in Spirits": 'soul' and 'spirit' in relation to the personal and collective unconscious. Effect of "a complex of the collective unconscious" if it becomes "associated with the ego": state of alienation. Sense of loss if complex associated with ego becomes unconscious (590) or if one 'function' dominates consciousness (588).
	CW11:944 (1948)	Personal unconscious 'rests' on the collective unconscious. Contents of the personal unconscious contrasted to mythological character of contents of the collective unconscious.
Making contents of personal unconscious conscious	CW7.449 *ff* (1916)	Contents of the personal unconscious can be made conscious. The personality is enhanced as a result (450).
	CW7.387 (1916/1928)	Making that which is unconscious conscious minimises the extent to which individuals are possessed by complexes. Contents of the personal unconscious are 'factual contents' as opposed to 'fantasies' of the collective unconscious.
Archetypal material finding expression in the personal unconscious	CW9ii:13 *ff* (1951)	The "most clearly characterized" archetypes are the *shadow, anima, animus* because of their "frequent and disturbing" effect on the personality. *Shadow* is the most accessible as its nature "may be inferred from contents of the personal unconscious."
	CW9ii:42	Integration of the shadow (realisation of the personal unconscious) marks the first stage in the analytic process.

THE STRUCTURE OF THE PSYCHE II

In this chapter, we continue to explore key concepts of Jung's model of the psyche: collective unconscious; archetype and archetypal image; anima and animus; a few of the more familiar *personifications* of the archetypes (archetypal images) as we meet those images in personal dreams and fantasies, in mythology, art, literature, fairy-tale, ritual, religious rite and sacred text, … (the list goes on) … these are images that give symbolic form and expression to the dynamics of the psyche and therefore to the human soul. Last but not least, we discuss the archetype of the Self. As it is impossible to discuss the concept of the collective unconscious without talking about archetypes, these two topics will be addressed together in the first section.

THE ARCHETYPES AND THE COLLECTIVE UNCONSCIOUS

We have finally reached the lowest level of Jung's dream house, the "cave cut into the rock" in which Jung, as dream-ego, discovers thick dust on the floor, "bones and broken pottery, like remains of a primitive culture […] (and) two human skulls, obviously very old and half disintegrated" (1961/63, p. 159). Jung associates the "cave" with a level of being "which can scarcely be reached or illuminated by consciousness" (*ibid.*, p. 160); this level of being he was to designate the *collective* unconscious. Jung always considered his concept of a universal collective unconscious an *hypothesis,* as the collective unconscious (to which he often referred to as the *objective* psyche) is irrepresentable in itself, beyond the reach of consciousness and only partially

DOI: 10.4324/9781315619156-5

discernible through the ways in which its *contents* are perceived by consciousness in the form of *archetypal images, ideas, intuitions, impulses.*

Anthony Stevens (MD, evolutionary psychiatrist, and Jungian analyst) and many others value the hypothesis of the collective unconscious as Jung's most significant contribution to psychology, "a fundamental concept on which the whole science of psychology could be built. Potentially, it is of comparable importance to quantum theory in physics" (1994, p. 47). However, Jung's hypothesis was not well received. It damaged his professional reputation and cost him both professional and personal relationships. The negative reception of Jung's ideas was in part due to his thinking being ahead of that of his time. Members of his profession were still largely proponents of an understanding of the human psyche that regarded the human being, at birth, as a blank slate, a *tabula rasa*; the personality was held to be acquired through life experience and education. The hypothesis of an *im*personal, collective unconscious diametrically opposed the prevailing thinking. Jung was suggesting instead that each human being is born with an innate capacity to develop, physically, psychically, socially, and spiritually as a unique realisation of a species-specific (i.e., human) 'blueprint.' Jung argued that the personality *unfolds*; while it is undoubtedly affected by environmental factors and life experience, it is not acquired through them.

Jung first used the term *primordial images* to designate the 'contents' of the collective unconscious. The term was not new. *Primordial images* had been introduced by Jean-Baptiste Lamarck (d. 1829) to describe a (now long discredited) theory that Jung, by using the term, was accused of promoting: namely, that human beings, and animals, *inherit acquired characteristics*; in other words, "characteristics acquired by individual experience could be passed on genetically to subsequent generations" (*ibid.,* p. 36). Jung first dropped the term *primordial images* in favour of *archetype* in "Instinct and the Unconscious," a paper presented at a symposium at the University of London, July 1919 (CW8:270). It was, however, many years before he could rid himself of accusations of Lamarckianism, partly because he frequently continued to use *both* terms together. The accusations also dogged Jung because of his often rather loose or colourful use of language. When he writes, for example, as late as 1936: "There are as many archetypes as there are typical situations in life. Endless repetition has *engraved* (emphasis added) these experiences into our psychic constitution [...]" (CW9i:99), his detractors had a field day. First, the idea that *every* typical situation in life constitutes an archetype invites the conflation of the *personal* with the *archetypal/collective* ("our psychic constitution"). The statement that repetition over thousands of years *engraves* "typical situations" onto the human mind suggests the *inherited acquired characteristics* of Lamarckian theory. Jung did, however, also write in the same paragraph that archetypes are "*forms without content,* representing merely the possibility of a certain type of perception and action," (*ibid.*), for anyone paying attention!

Were there other ideas 'in the air' before or around the time that Jung developed his archetypal hypothesis? Well, yes. Jung writes that:

> Mythological research calls them (i.e., archetypal images) 'motifs;' in the psychology of primitives they correspond to Lévy-Bruhl's concept of "représentations collectives," and in the field of comparative religion, Hubert and Mauss identify "categories of the imagination." Adolf Bastian long ago called them "elementary" or "primordial thoughts." From these references it should be clear enough that my idea of the archetype— literally a pre-existent form—does not stand alone but is something that is recognized and named in other fields of knowledge.
>
> (CW9i:89)

We might add the work in the field of linguistics of Noam Chomsky who held that the brain of every child contains innate language acquisition capabilities which enable facility with language; and that language contains *deep structures* Chomsky considered to be universal, so that all languages "prove reducible to the universal grammar (i.e., archetype) on which all individual grammars are based" (Stevens 1990, p. 49). In the following pages, we cite analogous ideas evident in ethology, the study of animal behaviour in the wild.

Before we look more closely at Jung's hypothesis of the collective unconscious, a note in praise of adjectives:

NOUN OR ADJECTIVE? As we all know, nouns name, denote objects, point to 'things,' places, etc. that are concrete, knowable, touchable ... When we talk about psychic factors, we are not talking about concrete things or even 'entities,' so the use of nouns can be misleading. This is especially true when we talk about aspects of psyche that can at best be *inferred* because they can't be experienced directly by ego-consciousness. Enter the archetype! Yes, a noun! Jung talks of 'the archetype' as being irrepresentable, beyond the reach of consciousness. Only through extensive study of a huge number of *archetypal images* that *can* reach consciousness may we glimpse the countless possibilities of representation of the hypothetical *archetype-as-such*. So we encourage the use of adjectives, wherever possible, when speaking of psychic dynamics. This isn't always possible, of course, but adjectives do remind us that the closest we can get to 'psyche' is by meticulously describing our subjective experiences of psychic processes; we can't pin psyche to a specimen board.

In the box below is a concise yet all-embracing overview of Jung's hypothesis which emphasises how critical to psychic and physical health—in fact, to life—is the relationship of consciousness to the collective unconscious 'base' on which it rests and depends. It was written shortly before Jung's death in 1961.

Consciousness is phylogenetically (i.e., in the development of the human species) and ontogenetically (i.e., in the development of the individual) a secondary phenomenon. It is time this obvious fact were grasped at last. Just as the body has an anatomical prehistory of millions of years, so also does the psychic system. And just as the human body today represents in each of its parts the result of this evolution, and everywhere still shows traces of its earlier stages—so the same may be said of the psyche. Consciousness began its evolution from an animal-like state which seems to us unconscious, and the same process of differentiation is repeated in every child. The psyche of the child in its preconscious state is anything but a *tabula rasa* (i.e., blank slate); it is already preformed in a recognizably individual way, and is moreover equipped with all specifically human instincts, as well as with the *a priori* foundations of the higher functions (i.e., of consciousness).

On this complicated base, the ego arises. Throughout life, the ego is sustained by this base. When the base does not function, stasis ensues [...]. Its life and its reality are of vital importance. Compared to it, even the external world is secondary, for what does the world matter if the endogenous (i.e., originating from within) impulse to grasp it and manipulate it is lacking? In the long run, no conscious will can ever replace the life instinct. This instinct comes to us from within, as a compulsion or will or command, and if—as has more or less been done from time immemorial—we give it the name of a personal daimon, we are at least aptly expressing the psychological situation. And if, by employing the concept of the archetype, we attempt to define a little more closely the point at which the daimon grips us, we have not abolished anything, only approached closer to the source of life (1961/63, pp. 348–49).

In the boxed quotation above, Jung links psyche and soma, pointing to the indivisibility of the psychical and the physiological. He repeatedly reaffirms the inseparability of psyche and soma in his discussion of archetypes which, he argues, shape the typical, species-specific development of the lives of all creatures, animals and human beings alike, and all organic matter. In the following statement, Jung defines the biological role of the *archetype* with reference to the innate organising principles evident in animals:

[The term archetype] is not meant to denote an inherited idea, but rather an inherited mode of functioning, corresponding to the inborn way in which the chick emerges from the egg, the bird builds its nest, a certain kind of wasp stings the motor ganglion of the caterpillar, and eels find their way to the Bermudas. In other words, it is a 'pattern of behaviour.' This aspect of the archetype, the purely biological one, is the proper concern of scientific psychology.

(CW18:1228)

Research by ethologists, who study animal behaviour, and anthropologists corroborate Jung's statements. We would do well to remember that we are, after all, primates! Elsewhere, Jung maintains that instinctual modes of functioning are dynamic, energic, and *teleological,* that is, they serve a purpose (e.g., to get the chick out of the egg!), which is arguably to ensure primal imperatives are fulfilled: survival and propagation of the species (eels to the Bermudas to mate):

[...] instincts are impersonal, universally distributed, hereditary factors of a dynamic or motivating character, which very often fail so completely to reach consciousness that modern psychotherapy is faced with the task of helping the patient to become conscious of them. Moreover, the instincts are not vague and indefinite by nature, but are specifically formed motive forces which, long before there is any consciousness, and in spite of any degree of consciousness later on, pursue their inherent goals. *Consequently, they form very close analogies to the archetypes, so close, in fact, that there is good reason for supposing that the archetypes are the unconscious images of the instincts themselves, in other words, that they are **patterns of instinctual behaviour**.*

(CW9i:91, emphasis added)

Here Jung describes instinct and archetype as working together; elsewhere, he speaks of instinct and archetype working together "as correspondences" (CW8:406), the archetype giving shape and form to the instinct; the dynamism of the instinct infusing the form, image, or pattern of behaviour of the archetype with motive force. In the previous quotation, we saw how the 'dance' of instinct and archetype appears in the outer world in the behaviour of animals. Jung also writes, "the archetypes are simply the forms that the instincts assume. From the living fountain of instinct flows everything that is creative; hence the unconscious [...] is the very source of the creative impulse" (*ibid.*:339). But what about our *subjective* experience of the dynamism of an archetype? Jung speaks of the archetypal image that presents to consciousness via a dream, vision, or fantasy, as having "a distinctly numinous character which can only be described as 'spiritual,' if 'magical' is too strong a word" (*ibid.*:405):

> [...] when looked at from the inside, that is, from within the realm of the subjective psyche [...] the archetype presents itself as numinous (i.e., fascinating, forceful, awe-inspiring), that is, it appears as an *experience* of fundamental importance. Whenever it clothes itself in the appropriate symbols (which is not always the case), it seizes hold of the individual in a startling way, creating a condition amounting almost to possession, the consequences of which may be incalculable. It is for this reason that the archetype is so important in the psychology of religion.
>
> (CW18:1229)

The psychology of religion? Jung talks of the powerful effect of an archetype as

> unambiguous. It can be healing or destructive, but never indifferent [...]. This aspect deserves the epithet 'spiritual' above all else. It not infrequently happens that the archetype appears in the form of a *spirit* in dreams or fantasy-products [...]. There is a mystical aura about its numinosity, and it has a corresponding effect upon the emotions. It mobilizes philosophical and religious convictions [...] [and] draws the subject under

its spell [...] [bringing] with it a depth and fulness of meaning that was unthinkable before [...]. The essential content of all mythologies and all religions and all 'isms' is archetypal.

(CW8:405-06)

The numinosity of the archetypal image and the dynamism of instinct make them—instinct and 'spirit'—"the most polar opposites imaginable, as can easily be seen when one compares a man who is ruled by his instinctual drives with a man who is seized by the spirit" (*ibid*.:406). Yet, as previously quoted, "the archetypes are simply the forms which the instincts assume" (*ibid*.:339)! We noted in Chapter 1 that analytical psychology was once referred to as Complex Psychology. Might it not also be appropriately dubbed a Psychology of Paradox?

Jung's evaluation of instinct and spirit (archetype) is that they

subsist side by side as reflections in our own minds of the opposition that underlies all psychic energy. Man finds himself simultaneously driven to act and free to reflect. This contrariety [...] has no moral significance, for instinct is not in itself bad any more than spirit is good. Both can be both.

(*ibid*.)

The psyche, as the body, functions as a self-regulatory system that seeks balance, homeostasis. An archetypal image, however, has the power to fascinate, inspire awe or fear. It is a disruptive force whether its effect be positive, negative, healing, or destructive. In itself it simply *is*. Its impact on consciousness is determined by the conscious attitude.

Jung writes that "an archetypal content (i.e., undifferentiated, paradoxical, disturbing) expresses itself, first and foremost, in metaphors" (CW9i:267). This leaves it up to the discerning ego to *interpret* the metaphors! A daunting but necessary task which reminds us, once again, of the importance of an ego-consciousness strong enough *to* interpret the enigmatic images of the archetypal unconscious; this means an ego-consciousness that has integrated some of the personal shadow and developed an awareness of the *reality* of the objective psyche—the collective unconscious. An ego that is resilient and flexible is best able to *hold the tension of opposites* between its own standpoint and that of the powerful (often seductive!) impact of the archetypal image in order to restore homeostasis and maintain freedom of will. This is possible not through assimilation, adaptation, denial, or suppression but by the emergence of a new attitude that 'transcends' the original polarisation. "In terms of energy," Jung argues, "polarity means a potential, and wherever a potential exists there is the possibility of a current, a flow of events, for the tension of opposites strives for balance" (*ibid.*:426). (We will discuss, in the following chapter, Jung's concept of the Transcendent Function of the Psyche.) Elsewhere, Jung states that the "problems of life are fundamentally insoluble. They must be so, for they express the necessary polarity inherent in every self-regulating system. They can never be solved, but only outgrown (i.e., transcended)" (CW13:18).

Now we come to a particularly difficult concept but one which completes Jung's picture of the relationship of consciousness to the personal unconscious, collective unconscious, instinct, and archetype. Here again is Jung. (We are quoting extensively from Jung's later, carefully revised essay, "On the Nature of the Psyche" in CW8 because, although difficult, it provides perhaps the most comprehensive synthesis of his life's work of empirical, experiential investigation of the 'nature of the psyche'. In this 1946 essay, Jung finally clearly differentiates between the irrepresentable *archetype-as-such* and the archetypal image, and introduces the concept of the *psychoid* nature of the archetype):

> Psychic processes [...] behave like a scale along which consciousness 'slides.' At one moment it finds itself in the vicinity of instinct, and falls under its influence; at another, it slides along to the other end where spirit predominates and even assimilates the instinctual processes most opposed to it. These counter-positions, so fruitful of illusion, are by no means symptoms of the abnormal; [...] they form the twin poles of that psychic one-sidedness which is typical of the normal (individual).
>
> (CW8:408)

We have already seen how the psyche is characterised by opposites and counter-positions—in our discussion of typology, with thinking opposing feeling, intuition opposing sensation, introversion opposing extraversion; in the opposition of persona and shadow, conscious and unconscious. We noted that the inevitable one-sidedness,—should the ego identify with one pole of a pair of opposites to the exclusion of the other,—may be 'corrected' through a conscious realisation of the pole that remains 'in shadow' or unconscious. We saw that this 'work' enhances both consciousness and the personality in the process: "there is no consciousness without discrimination of opposites" (CW9i:178). But we were talking about making conscious contents of the *personal unconscious*. When it comes to contents of the *collective unconscious*, the task involves "the conscious realization of the archetype's *effects* (authors' emphasis) upon the conscious contents (i.e., on ego-consciousness)" (CW8:413).

How does the activation of an archetype, which is *irrepresentable to consciousness*, have an effect on ego-consciousness? How does that 'work'? What does the scale or spectrum on which Jung maps the psyche look like? What follows is *not* a diagram devised by Jung but the authors' (very basic) attempt at one, inspired by Murray Stein. We hope you find it helpful to your understanding of Jung's concept of the relationship of the different 'levels' of the unconscious to each other, and to psyche (consciousness):

Psyche/field of consciousness

Instinct (psychoid (c.uncs. **(p.uncs. (cs(EGO)cs) p.uncs)** c.uncs) psychoid) archetype

>>>>>>>>>>   <<<<<<<<<<

INFRA–RED   ULTRA–VIOLET
the biological instinctual psyche   *the psychic ultra-violet archetype*

Imagine the *brackets* () between the categories above (instinct, psychoid, etc.) as the points where a series of concentric circles intersect the Infra-Red/Ultra-Violet colour spectrum, and the spectrum as the diameter cutting through all the circles. You will see that Ego is at the centre. The field of consciousness, of which Ego is the centre, surrounds ego on all sides. Then comes the circle of the personal unconscious, and the collective unconscious. Jung reminds us that the contents of the collective unconscious are inaccessible by consciousness unless and until they enter the personal unconscious through dream or fantasy, emotion, impulse, etc., that is, through an archetypal image. The next circle is labelled *psychoid*. Jung explains his use of the term 'psychoid' (a term borrowed from his former supervisor at the Bürgholzli, Zürich, Eugene Bleuler), in the following way: "unconscious is not simply the unknown, it is rather the *unknown psychic*; and this we define on the one hand as all those things in us which, if they came to consciousness, would presumably differ in no respect from the known psychic contents, with the addition, on the other hand, of the psychoid system, of which nothing is known directly" (CW8:382). The "psychoid functions [...] are not capable of consciousness" (*ibid.*); we only have indirect, partial knowledge of them through those archetypal images that reach and impact consciousness. How does this happen? Murray Stein (1998) gives us an excellent explanation of Jung's idea of how the different levels of the unconscious relate to each other and, finally, to consciousness. We quote him in full:

> The psychoid boundary defines the gray area between the potentially knowable and the totally unknowable—the potentially controllable and the wholly uncontrollable—aspects of human functioning. This is not a sharp boundary but rather an area of transformation. The *psychoid* thresholds show an effect that Jung calls 'psychization': non-psychic information becomes *psychized,* passing from the unknowable into the unknown (the unconscious psyche) and then moving toward the known (ego-consciousness). The human psychic apparatus, in short, shows a capacity to *psychize* material from the somatic and spiritual poles of non-psychic reality.
>
> (p. 98)

Our illustration, above, is an admittedly inadequate attempt to illustrate the line Stein asks us to imagine. Below is Stein's commentary on that imaginary line:

> This line is attached to archetype on one end and to instinct at the other. It passes information and data through the psychoid realm into the collective and then into the personal unconscious. From there these contents make their way into consciousness. Instinctual perceptions and archetypal representations are the data of actual psychic experience, not the instincts and archetypes in themselves. Neither of the ends of the spectrum can be experienced directly, for neither is psychic. At the ends, the psyche fades into matter and spirit. And what are experienced as archetypal images "are very varied structures which all point back to one essentially 'irrepresentable' basic form." (*ibid.,* p. 102).

Notice Jung's designation of the *archetype* as ultra-violet. Instinct is, understandably, infra-red, pure instinctuality. However, 'archetype' = red (instinct) + blue (spirit) which together = violet. This suggests that archetype and instinct are indeed, as we earlier quoted Jung as saying, "correspondences," working "side by side." "As information passes through the psychoid area, it becomes psychized and transformed into psyche (i.e., images, ideas, impulses apprehensible by consciousness)," Stein writes, coming to an all-important and thought-provoking conclusion: "In the psyche, matter and spirit meet" (*ibid.,* p. 103).

Final word from Jung on the instinct/archetype, matter/spirit question:

Since psyche and matter are contained in one and the same world, and moreover are in continuous contact with one another and ultimately rest on irrepresentable, transcendental factors, it is not only possible but fairly probable, even, that psyche and matter are two different aspects of one and the same thing. [...] there is probably no alternative now but to describe their (i.e., the archetypes') nature, in accordance with their chiefest effect, as 'spirit,' [...] If so, the position of the archetype would be located beyond the psychic sphere, analogous to the position of physiological instinct, which is immediately rooted in the stuff of the organism and, with its psychoid nature, forms the bridge to matter in general. In archetypal conceptions (i.e., images) and instinctual perceptions, spirit and matter confront one another on the psychic plane. Matter and spirit both appear in the psychic realm as distinctive qualities of conscious contents. The ultimate nature of both is transcendental, that is, irrepresentable, since the psyche and its contents are the only reality which is given to us *without a medium* (CW8:420).

We return, now, to less heady spheres.

Instinct and archetype may well be described as the *architects of the natural, species-specific unfolding of the stages (infancy, childhood, adolescence, ...) of human life.*

The archetypal heritage with which each of us is born [...] presupposes the natural life cycle of humanity: being mothered and fathered, exploring the environment, playing in the peer group, meeting the challenges of puberty and adolescence, being initiated into the adult group, establishing a place in the social hierarchy, accomplishing courtship and marriage, child-bearing, hunting, gathering and fighting, participating in religious rituals and ceremonials, assuming the responsibilities of advanced maturity, old age and the preparations for death.

(Stevens 1990, pp. 60–1)

We can see how instinct and archetype are indivisible in the course of every human life, replete, as each life is, with a plethora of individual yet typically human experiences. For example, somatic, physiological developments in the body at puberty lead to the awakening of sexuality that is actualised according to archetypal patterns of behaviour: the desire for sexual intimacy and a partner, for independence from one's parents, for a place for oneself in the world, for purpose and meaning, etc. The motive forces of instinct and archetype orchestrate the individual's journey through life, as well as the personal rituals and patterns of social engagement that shape life on a day-to-day basis. Ubiquitous. Invisible. Except in their impact on consciousness and the homeostasis of the psyche.

Before we move to a discussion of *anima* and *animus* … "it would be an unpardonable sin of omission […]to overlook the *feeling-value* of the archetype" (CW8:411)!

It is very easy (and generally more comfortable!) to focus on archetypes as "mere images and forget that they are living entities that make up a great part of the human psyche" (CW18:596). This is to deny the *feeling-value* or numinosity of the archetype so it becomes a mere word. That word or designation may then be linked to endless mythological, artistic, political, religious, cultural "representations, and so the process of limitless substitution begins" (*ibid.*)—'this' = 'that' *ad infinitum*. The 'word' or 'image' then becomes meaningless. Yet the numinosity of archetypes

> is and remains a fact. It represents the *value* of an archetypal event. This emotional value must be kept in mind and allowed for throughout the whole intellectual process of interpretation. The risk of losing it is great, because thinking and feeling are so diametrically opposed that thinking abolishes feeling-values and *vice versa. Psychology is the only science that has to take the factor of value (feeling) into account, since it forms the link between psychic events on the one hand, and meaning and life on the other.*
>
> (*ibid.*, emphasis added)

An archetypal image is never a "mere piece of indifferent information," (*ibid.*:588) a word, "it is a piece of life, an image connected with

the living individual by the bridge of emotion. [...] [T]he archetype is living matter. It is not limitlessly exchangeable but always
belongs to the economy of a living individual, from which it cannot be detached and used arbitrarily for different ends. It cannot be
explained in just any way, but only in the one that is indicated by that
particular individual," (*ibid.*:589) that is, by the one who has experienced the inspiring, alarming, enlightening, mystifying archetypal
'event.'

Elsewhere, in "On the Nature of the Psyche," Jung links 'numinosity' to 'luminosity' in a useful discussion of the relation between the
archetypal unconscious and the very earliest inklings of consciousness in the preconscious infant:

> As we know from direct experience, the light of consciousness has many
> degrees of brightness, and the ego-complex many gradations of empha-
> sis. On the animal [...] level there is a mere 'luminosity,' differing hardly
> at all from the glancing fragments of a dissociated ego. Here, as on the
> infantile level, consciousness is not a unity, being as yet uncentred by a
> firmly-knit ego-complex, and just flickering into life here and there wher-
> ever outer or inner events, instincts, and affects happen to call it awake.
> At this stage it is still like a chain of islands or an archipelago. Nor is it
> a fully integrated whole even at the higher and highest stages; rather,
> it is capable of indefinite expansion. Gleaming islands, indeed whole
> continents, can still add themselves to our modern consciousness [...].
> Therefore we would do well to think of ego-consciousness as being sur-
> rounded by a multitude of little luminosities.
>
> (CW8:387)

These "little luminosities" are potential accretions to consciousness.
Jung goes on to describe the light of the "luminosities" still unat-
tached to the ego-complex as *scintillae* that are "germinal luminosities
shining forth from the darkness of the unconscious" (*ibid.*:389). It is,
then, the numinous, *scintillating,* emotional energy of the archetypal
image that alone can bridge the gap between the conscious ego and
as yet unrealised potential—the "luminosities" in the depths of the
unconscious, which, if made conscious, may enhance the personality
and life of the individual. The archetypal image, therefore, provides
a link between the ego (the 'I') and the core of one's individuality ('me'), the vital centre of the whole personality (conscious and
unconscious), which Jung called the Self—a concept we discuss later
in this chapter.

⊕

Just one more thought!:

We have been presented with a variety of 'descriptors' concerning the nature and dynamics of the archetype, archetypal image, unconscious (personal and collective), and the psychic system as a whole: negative, positive, compensatory, complementary, polar opposites, tension of opposites, unity of opposites, correspondences, counter-positions, etc. At times, this might seem confusing, even contradictory. If archetype and instinct constitute the "most polar opposites imaginable," why does Jung write that "the archetypes are simply the forms which the instincts assume" (CW8:339)?

What do we mean by 'opposites,' really?

It's a funny thing about opposites: they often turn out to be two sides of the same coin, not irreconcilable at all. The English poet Samuel Taylor Coleridge argued that there is no such thing as true opposition, simply polarities of a single force or power that *look like* opposites. So it seems that only those so-called 'pairs of opposites' that share an essential commonality (i.e., are polarities or radically different aspects of the same thing) may be sensibly opposed. A lobster cannot be opposed to a theorem, unless we can discover in what way each is like the other. What we think of as opposites may, then, more usefully be called 'extremes'—as hot and cold are extremes of temperature.

And here is Jung: "True opposites are never incommensurables; if they were they could never unite. All contrariety notwithstanding, they do show a constant propensity to union [...]. Opposites are extreme qualities in any state, by virtue of which that state is perceived to be real, for they form a potential. The psyche is made up of processes whose energy springs from the equilibration of all kinds of opposites" (CW8:406-07).

Given that Jung describes the psyche as made up of "processes whose energy springs from the equilibration of all kinds of opposites," it is perhaps surprising that there is only one entry in the Index to the *Collected Works* for *bipolarity of the archetype*. It takes us to CW12, where we find a brief but very useful commentary by

Jung on an image from one of the unicorn tapestries, *The Hunt of the Unicorn*. Referring to the horn of the unicorn, Jung writes:

> The horn as an emblem of vigour and strength has a masculine character, but at the same time it is a cup, which, as a receptacle, is feminine. So we are dealing here with a 'uniting symbol' that expresses the bipolarity of the archetype.

(CW12:553)

While the word *bipolarity* tends to constellate either/or thinking, Jung's commentary illustrates the *synthetic* or *synthesising* role of the archetypal *image* as a "uniting symbol" which both *contains* and "expresses the bipolarity of the archetype." It is well to remember the complexity of the archetypal image as "uniting symbol" when we meet it in dreams, fantasies, and visions, in art, mythology, literature, in social, political, and cultural spheres.

We find the same complexity whenever an archetypal image is constellated. If we take the perhaps over-determined 'mother' archetype, we see at once that where there is a mother there is, or was, or will be, a child. We have a dyad; mother and child are "correspondences," to borrow from Jung. They belong together and define each other, each bringing the other into being, as it were. In the archetypal image of the mother–child dyad, we witness a "uniting symbol" that expresses the bipolarity of the archetype: the infra-red of instinct, the ultra-violet of spirit. When circumstances are "good enough" (to borrow D. W. Winnicott's [1971/2017] term), there occurs an intricate dance of instinct and spirit as biological and emotional needs are met through physical nurture and care, on the one hand, and love, holding, containment, on the other. The lived experience of the mother–child relationship as it progresses will, of course, shape the mother *complex* that develops around the archetypal nucleus. Personified archetypes reveal—and contain—their inherent, irreducible polarity in the configuration of their images: mother/child, *puer*—eternal boy/*senex*—old man, tyrant/victim, maiden/crone, hero/villain, etc. You cannot have one without the other. We meet such 'pairings' in countless folk- and fairy-tales, myth, literature and art, in history, in current affairs.

⊕

SUMMARY

- The reception of Jung's hypothesis of the collective unconscious, and complementary theories in other fields of which Jung was aware; Jung's early use of the term *primordial image*; and accusations of Lamarckianism
- A late summary, by Jung, of his hypothesis of the collective unconscious in relation to consciousness before moving into a discussion of the nature of the archetype
- The biological pole of the archetype; instincts as "specifically formed motive forces"; and instinct and archetype as "correspondences" such that Jung refers to the archetypes as *patterns of instinctual behaviour*
- The powerful numinosity of the archetypal image; the dynamism of the instinct
- The psyche as a self-regulatory system that seeks balance or homeostasis
- Jung's concept of the *psychoid* nature of the archetype; how the archetype, though irrepresentable to consciousness, has an effect on ego-consciousness
- Murray Stein's helpful explanation of Jung's hypothesis of how 'data' from the irrepresentable (instinct/archetype or spirit) is passed through the *psychoid* realm to the collective unconscious, then to the personal unconscious, and finally to consciousness. Irrepresentable data in this way becomes *psychized* and eventually accessible by consciousness via instinctual perceptions and archetypal images
- How instinct and archetype shape the unfolding 'programme' of human life
- The *feeling-value* of the archetype; the link that Jung makes between the *numinosity* of the archetype and *luminosity*. Jung saw "little luminosities" or *scintillae* in the deep unconscious as potential accretions to consciousness, carried to consciousness by the numinosity of the archetypal image
- Finally, a brief discussion of opposites, opposing pairs in the psyche. An example of how polarities—in this case, masculine and feminine principles—may be united in the image was found in Jung's commentary on the "unifying symbol" of the unicorn horn in a Medieval tapestry. We found a unifying symbol of both poles of the archetype (instinct and spirit) in the archetypal image of the mother–child dyad

$\oplus$

ANIMA AND ANIMUS

After Jung's break with Freud in 1912, following the publication of *Symbols of Transformation* (CW5), Jung felt "I had to make it on my own" (1961/63, p. 206). An intense period followed (1913–17)—the *creative illness* in which Jung struggled to understand the images and visions arising from the unconscious. He recorded the images and, in order to "seize hold of the fantasies" (*ibid.,* p. 181), dialogued with the inner figures that presented themselves through Active Imagination (see Chapter 5), a technique to activate unconscious content that he developed and used in his work with patients.

Throughout this process, Jung questioned what he was *really* doing, "Certainly this has nothing to do with science. But then what is it?" The answer came in the form of an inner voice:

> 'It is art.' I was astonished. It had never entered my head that what I was writing had any connection with art. Then I thought, 'Perhaps my unconscious is forming a personality that is not me, but which is insisting on coming through to expression.' I knew for a certainty that the voice had come from a woman.
>
> (*ibid.,* p. 185)

Jung concluded that this inner voice was that of the 'soul.' He writes: "I began to speculate on the reasons why the name *anima* was given to the soul. Why was it thought of as feminine? Later I came to see that this inner feminine figure plays a typical, or archetypal, role in the unconscious of a man, and I called her the *anima*. The corresponding figure in the unconscious of woman I called the *animus*" (*ibid.,* p. 186). Here Jung introduces what has become the 'conventional'—and controversial!—understanding of anima and animus; he also speaks of the anima as the archetype of life, the face or mouthpiece of the unconscious, "communicating the images of the unconscious to the conscious mind" (*ibid.*).

Jung wrote extensively on the anima, much less so on the animus, leaving that area of research to his wife, Emma (née Rauschenbach), who was herself an analyst and author of *Anima and Animus* (1957), and, with Marie-Louis von Franz, *The Grail Legend* (1960/98). Jung was aware of his own masculine bias, which is why he encouraged—arguably to various degrees—his wife, Esther Harding, and Toni Wolff to pursue and publish their own research (Saban 2019; Clay 2016; Savage-Healy 2017). Jung's earliest writings on the anima are to be found in CW6, Chapter XI, ("Definitions"), published in 1921. At that time, he had not yet clarified his thinking on the *shadow*, so you will not find an entry for shadow in Chapter XI. *Anima* is discussed under "Soul" and "Soul-Image," rather than as a separate category. In 1921, 'psyche' was still generally equated with 'mind,' so Jung is careful to clarify his use of the term 'psyche' and distinguish between 'psyche' and 'soul.' (In Greek, psyche and soul are synonyms; psyche is also the Greek word for butterfly, the life-cycle of which— not unlike the human life-cycle—involves a number of stages and transformations):

> By psyche I understand the totality of all psychic processes, conscious as well as unconscious. By soul, [...] I understand a clearly demarcated functional complex that can best be described as a 'personality.'
>
> (CW6:797)

PSYCHE? SOUL?

The editors of the edition of the CW that we are using point to a problem of translation in CW12:9n. "The translation of the German word *Seele* (soul) presents almost insuperable difficulties [...] because it combines the two words 'psyche' and 'soul' in a way not altogether familiar to the English reader." Throughout the CW, 'psyche' is generally used to designate the totality of *all* psychic processes, conscious and unconscious. 'Soul' "refers to a 'functional complex' or partial personality and never to the whole psyche. It is often applied to anima and animus" (soul-image). "This conception of the soul is more primitive than the Christian one [...] (which) refers to 'the transcendental energy in man' and 'the spiritual part of man considered in its moral aspect or in relation to God' (OED)." 'Soul' refers to "a psychic (phenomenological) fact of a highly numinous character." Jung's early use of 'soul' often designates an autonomous, split-off psychic 'part-soul,' fragment or complex; 'soul' or 'soul-image' is often used for *anima*. In later writings, Jung used *anima* for the inner psychological figure, and 'soul' to refer to the movement, dynamics, depth, and plurality of the psyche—and an individual's experience thereof.

In CW6, under Definition 48, SOUL, Jung places both *persona* and *anima*. He understands *anima* and *persona* as compensatory: *anima* describes an inner attitude or relation to the inner object (i.e., the unconscious), in contrast to the *outward-facing persona*. Here are a few (early) statements about anima and animus from CW6 that may appear to some a little too formulaic.

- "If the persona is intellectual, the anima will quite certainly be sentimental. The complementary character of the anima also affects the sexual character [...]. A very feminine woman has a masculine soul, and a very masculine man has a feminine soul. This contrast is due to the fact that a man is not in all things wholly masculine, but also has certain feminine traits" (CW6:804)
- A man's "anima contains all those fallible human qualities his persona lacks" (*ibid.*)
- "If, therefore, we speak of the *anima* of a man, we must logically speak of the *animus* of a woman, if we are to give the soul of a woman its right name" (*ibid.*:805)
- "Whereas logic and objectivity are usually the predominant features of a man's outer attitude, [...] in the case of a woman it is feeling. But the soul is the other way round: inwardly it is the man who feels, and the woman who reflects" (*ibid.*)
- "With men the anima is usually personified by the unconscious as a woman; with women the animus is personified as a man" (*ibid.*:808)
- "For a man, a woman is best fitted to be the real bearer of his soul-image, because of the feminine quality of his soul; for a woman it will be a man" (*ibid.*:809)

It is not difficult to see why Jung's early conception of what he termed the *contrasexual archetype* provoked, and continues to provoke, considerable controversy. Attitudes have changed radically since Jung's introduction of his ideas, certainly since his death in 1961, and it is helpful to realise that the Switzerland in which Jung was born and lived his whole life was extremely conservative. Women did not have the vote during his lifetime (it was granted in a referendum in 1971); the women maintained the household; the men went to work; and as late as the 1990s, a husband's written permission was sometimes still required for his wife to take a job outside the home. It is therefore not surprising that Jung's early ideas about anima and animus were heavily influenced by prescriptive cultural gender roles. We must also remember what Jung himself said when he was working on psychological typology (see Chapter 2), namely, that we cannot escape our own 'personal equation,' our subjectivity, our psychology: "My life is what I have done, my scientific work; the one is inseparable from the other. The work is an expression of my inner development" (1961/63, p. 211). Jung was exceptional but he was no exception!

There has, however, been considerable work done to update Jung's fundamental concepts in the light of changes in cultural attitudes towards gender and gender roles. Before we continue with the development of Jung's thinking on the contrasexual archetype, in the box below is a statement from "On the Brink of Momentous Change," a chapter in Claire Douglas's *The Woman in the Mirror: Analytical Psychology and the Feminine* (1990), which provided, at the time, a thorough review of work to date on the 'rehabilitation' of Jung's contrasexual archetype.

> The use of the terms animus and anima as pejoratives and as limitations on the range of individual behavior must stop, as must any consideration of the feminine as inferior to the masculine, or vice-versa. Jung's descriptions of the animus and anima need to be seen as specific to his personality, to his era and its attitudes about the sexes. [...] The classical usage of writers limiting themselves to what Jung wrote is too strict, too tidy, and too simple; it is not appropriate for real people leading complex lives. [...] [T]he use of the concepts [...] as a model remains of value, particularly in the exploration and expression of the 'other' (one manifestation of which is the contrasexual), and the hold this 'other' may have on us all through its varieties of projection and possession. It remains useful as a way of talking about [...] the impingement of culture on self-development. [...] This must be defined individually. Each manifestation of animus and anima—its strengths and weaknesses— are as idiosyncratic as each individual personality. The archetypes of animus and anima remain unconscious and incapable of full delineation. Examination of their images—which change with culture, with the growth and development of consciousness, and with individual needs—enriches and deepens our understanding of ourselves (pp. 200–01).

In an essay written in 1925, "Marriage as a Psychological Relationship," Jung makes no further mention of the anima/animus in a compensatory relationship to the persona, and speaks of anima and animus as inborn images. This description is perhaps familiar but while it clarifies the *function* of anima and animus, it is nevertheless controversial:

> Every man carries within him the eternal image of woman, not the image of this or that particular woman, but a definite feminine image. This image is fundamentally unconscious, an hereditary factor of primordial origin [...] or 'archetype' [...] in short, an inherited system of psychic adaptation. [...] The same is true of woman: she too has her inborn image of man. [...] Woman has no anima, no soul, but she has an *animus*. The anima has an erotic, emotional character, the animus a rationalizing one. Hence most of what men say about feminine eroticism, and particularly about the emotional life of women, is derived from their own anima projections and distorted accordingly. On the other hand, the astonishing assumptions and fantasies that women make about men come from the activity of the animus, who produces an inexhaustible supply of illogical arguments and false explanations.
>
> (CW17:338)

(We will return to the statement that a woman has no anima—no soul?—later!) In this same essay, Jung writes of marriage as a 'container' in which the development of consciousness may unfold, with each partner's relationship to anima/animus transformed. 'Falling in love' has mostly to do with 'falling in love' with the unconscious anima/animus image as it is projected onto one's partner. The often surreal arguments that erupt (in any emotionally-charged relationship) 'happen,' not between two reasonably conscious adults but between adults who are "relating to *images* of the other sex rather than to actual people. The [...] images housed in the unconscious of each gender [...] are primordial and relatively unchanged by historical and cultural circumstance [...] (and) repeat their portraits in individual human psyches from generation to generation" (Stein 1998, p. 141).

How can one's relationship to anima/animus be made conscious ... and transformative? The powerful emotion that characterises the contrasexual inner images engenders hate as well as love. Love and hate are extremes and an *enantiodromia* can easily occur: one may 'flip' into (i.e., become) its opposite—love turns to hate, hate to love. Fear of this happening often causes people to walk away from arguments, talk of ending the relationship, etc. Transformation, however, comes by working through and realising differences; this, in turn, enables one to 'see' the other as he or she *is*. It then becomes possible to engage in the painful but rewarding process of first recognising, then starting to withdraw, the projection of the *image* that has been placed onto the other. Differentiating one's *own inner image* from one's image of one's partner marks the beginning of a conscious relationship with anima/animus and a better relationship with one's partner. This more conscious relationship with one's inner self does not happen overnight! One is 'in it'—or on the path of individuation (see Chapter 5)—for the long haul. Jung writes:

> What we can discover about them (i.e., anima and animus) from the conscious side is so slight as to be almost imperceptible. It is only when we throw light into the dark depths of the psyche and explore the strange and tortuous paths of human fate that it gradually becomes clear to us how immense is the influence wielded by these two factors that complement our conscious life.
>
> (CW9ii:41)

So we work to identify and withdraw projections; question our assumptions; query our beliefs; "dismember the illusory world of unconscious fantasy; […] experience most profoundly the heights and depths of one's own mental universe, [and disable] the iron chain of stimulus-response sequences. Dungeons and dragons, myths and fairy-tales, romantic excess and sarcastic recriminations are all a part of the world woven in our psychic interiors by the anima/us" (Stein 1998, p. 141). Very few reach the final stage (the *marriage quaternio*—see below), other than mystics, yoga masters, shamans, and others like them, but much is to be gained in the attempt: "Personality, as the complete realization of our whole being, is an unattainable ideal. But unattainability is no argument against the ideal, for ideals are only signposts, never the goal" (CW17:291). Jung's summary of the process follows:

> Recapitulating, I should like to emphasize that the integration of the shadow, or the realization of the personal unconscious, marks the first stage in the analytic process, and that without it a recognition of anima and animus is impossible. The shadow can be realized only through a relation to a partner, and anima and animus only through a relation to a partner of the opposite sex, because only in such a relation do their projections become operative. The recognition of the anima gives rise, in a man, to a triad, one third of which is transcendent: the masculine subject, the opposing feminine subject, and the transcendent anima. With a woman the situation is reversed. The

> missing fourth element that would make the triad a quaternity is, in a man, the archetype of the Wise Old Man, [...] and in a woman the Chthonic Mother. These four constitute a half immanent and half transcendent quaternity, an archetype which I have called the *marriage quaternio*. The marriage quaternio provides a schema not only for the [S]elf but also for the structure of primitive society with its cross-cousin marriage, marriage classes, and division of settlements into quarters. The [S]elf, on the other hand, is a God-image, or at least cannot be distinguished from one. Of this the early Christian spirit was not ignorant, otherwise Clement of Alexandria could never have said that he who knows himself knows God (CW9ii:42).

The image of the *marriage quaternio* brings us to an image of the Self, which we discuss next. This is a symbol of wholeness, completion, of a *coniunctio*, a 'marriage' or resolution of opposites. The Wise Old Man and the Chthonic Mother, sky and earth, spirit and instinct, personify the essential opposition in the Self, the creative tension of opposites that generates life and creativity in all their myriad manifestations.

Before we move on to a discussion of the archetype of the Self, we back-track for a moment to discuss Jung's often strong descriptions of anima and animus as manifested in life. It is easy to become confused or lulled (depending, perhaps, on your 'type'!) by Jung's language, especially when he is writing about an "experience" of something as elusive and enigmatic as anima and animus. He does warn his reader:

> The empirical reality summed up under the concept of the anima forms an extremely dramatic content of the unconscious. It is possible to describe this content in rational, scientific language, but in this way one entirely fails to express its living character. Therefore, in describing the living processes of the psyche, I deliberately and consciously give preference to a dramatic, mythological way of thinking and speaking, because this is not only more expressive but also more exact than an abstract scientific terminology, which is wont to toy with the notion that its theoretic formulations may one fine day be resolved in algebraic equations.
>
> (CW9ii:25)

If, however, you read Jung carefully, you will find that he inserts what we might call 'corrections' every so often. In "The Syzygy: Anima and Animus," he provides an extravagant image of the *projection-making factor* that he attributes to the anima, likening the anima to Maya, the "Spinning Woman" of Taoist thought, "who creates illusion by her dancing" (*ibid.*:20). Yet shortly afterwards, he writes, "The projection-making factor is the anima, *or rather the unconscious as represented by the anima* (author's emphasis). [...] She is not a product of the conscious, but a spontaneous product of the unconscious" (*ibid.*:26).

One of the complaints lodged against Jung is his linking of the anima to Eros and feminine traits (Eros was actually a *male* god in the Greek pantheon), and the animus to Logos and masculine traits which, in turn, links both to gender and gender roles. However, Jung does make it clear that he is using Eros and Logos to distinguish the psychological differences he finds between men and women:

> [The animus] corresponds to the paternal Logos just as the anima corresponds to the maternal Eros. But I do not wish or intend to give these two intuitive concepts too specific a definition. I use Eros and Logos merely as conceptual aids to describe the fact that woman's consciousness is characterized more by the connective quality of Eros than by the discrimination and cognition associated with Logos. In men, Eros, the function of relationship, is usually less developed than Logos. In women, on the other hand, Eros is an expression of their true nature, while their Logos is often only a regrettable accident. It gives rise to misunderstandings and annoying interpretations in the family circle and among friends.
>
> (*ibid.*:29)

"Regrettable accident," and the lengthy harangue which follows, is an example of Jung's often negative view of the animus! However, this view is tempered by what he has to say about the positive aspect of the animus:

> (The animus) expresses not only conventional opinion but—equally—what we call 'spirit,' philosophical or religious ideas in particular, or rather the attitude resulting from them. Thus the animus is a psychopomp, a mediator between the conscious and the unconscious and a personification of the latter. Just as the anima becomes, through integration, the Eros of consciousness, so the animus becomes a Logos; and in the same way that the anima gives relationship and relatedness to a man's consciousness, the animus gives to woman's consciousness a capacity for reflection, deliberation, and self-knowledge.
>
> (*ibid.*:33)

Emma Jung, from her own experience of making the animus conscious, confirms her husband's comments, writing that the process "makes possible the development of a spiritual attitude which sets us free from the limitation and imprisonment of a narrowly personal standpoint [...] to raise ourselves out of our personal troubles to suprapersonal thoughts and feelings, which, by comparison, make our misfortunes seem trivial and unimportant" (1957, p. 40).

And Jung describes a man "with a finely differentiated Eros [...] [as having] a great capacity for friendship, which often creates ties of astonishing tenderness between men and may even rescue friendship between the sexes from the limbo of the impossible. He may have good taste and an aesthetic sense [...] (and) be supremely gifted as a teacher because of his almost feminine insight and tact" (CW9i:164).

A note to the reader: whenever we think, talk, write, or read about archetypal dynamics, those dynamics may well become activated *in us* and affect us accordingly. This is not right or wrong; it simply *is* but we need to reflect on what is happening both in the text, and in us. Reflecting on a shift in language or tone (in the text, in us) may perhaps help us better understand what Jung is saying, as well as the mixed, often strong, response to Jung's ideas in general, and his concept of the contrasexual archetype in particular.

This returns us to the controversial (surprising?) suggestion that woman does not have an anima and, consequently, no soul! And therefore to the question of the usefulness of Jung's terms: anima and animus. Despite Jung's often problematic language and the challenge, to 21st-century ears, of his thinking about gender, masculine and feminine principles, Logos and Eros, etc., Jung's theory of anima/ animus works. Earlier in this section, we quoted Claire Douglas's (1990) view that Jung's concept of anima/animus is of value "in the exploration and expression of the 'other' (one manifestation of which is the contrasexual), [...] [for understanding] varieties of projection and possession [...] [and] as a way of talking about [...] the impingement of culture on self-development" (p. 200). Stevens (1990) argues for the retention of both terms, anima and animus: "At its most basic, the archetype represents the psychic equivalent of the physical contrasexual features present in all men and women [...] and it is no inert vestige: it is a dynamic system which plays an indispensable social role in mediating life between the sexes and an equally vital symbolic role in the psychic life of the individual" (p. 226). It is 'otherness,' in whatever form it takes, that generates energy and the possibility of transformation. Stevens reminds us that "Sexuality is every bit as much concerned with pleasure and with bonding as it is with procreation" (*ibid.,* p. 229); so it has a lot to do with play and, therefore, with creativity. It is also operative throughout the lifespan, with people 'falling in love' from infancy to old age, from adolescent crushes on someone of the same sex to the blessing of new love in one's 80s, perhaps. All relationship is to an 'other,' and an emotionally-charged relationship activates the contrasexual archetype in whatever form that takes.

Stevens makes the important point that "Archetypal imperatives are not absolute: experience transforms them into modes compatible with the living circumstances of the individual. Thus, the unmarried man or childless woman is not doomed to a life of emotional sterility or frustration: other archetypal possibilities are always available if they but put themselves in the way of experiencing them" (*ibid.*, p. 230). Any deeply emotional relationship is fertile ground for the individuation process and psychological growth because one partner projects onto the other, "and actively seeks in him or her, the unactualized or inadequately incarnated archetypal potential [...] of the Self" (*ibid.*). So anima/animus draw us towards the inner world, serving as bridge and guide to one's individuality and the spiritual heights and chthonic depths of the psyche. This process shifts the *active centre* of the psyche from its base in the ego to the centre of the psyche as a whole, and so into conscious relation with the Self that "not only contains the deposit and totality of all past life, but is also a point of departure, the fertile soil from which all future life will spring" (CW7:303).

A final note on Jung's use of the word *syzygy*, anima + animus. *Syzygy* means 'to yoke together' (Edinger 1996, p. 28), as oxen are yoked or 'coupled' together. In his later writing on the contrasexual archetype, Jung saw anima/animus as inseparable, 'yoked together,' a pair: "the syzygy motif [...] expresses the fact that a masculine element is always paired with a feminine one" (CW9i:134) and *vice versa*; "Together they form [...] the divine syzygy" (CW9ii:41); "the One is never separated from the Other" (CW9i:194). (Might, then, a term incorporating the notion of the syzygy better serve as a soul-term?). Although "[w]hen projected, the anima always has a feminine form with definite characteristics," Jung argues that "[t]his empirical finding *does not mean that the archetype is constituted like that in itself*" (*ibid.*:142, emphasis added). (Perhaps the anima might not be so feminine after all!). He warns: "It is a well-nigh hopeless undertaking to tear a single archetype out of the living tissue of the psyche" (*ibid.*:302), insisting on the inseparability of anima/animus:

> The discriminating intellect naturally keeps on trying to establish their singleness of meaning and thus misses the essential point; for [...] the one thing consistent with their nature is their *manifold meaning*, their almost limitless wealth of reference, which makes any unilateral formulation impossible.
>
> (*ibid.*:80)

A BIT OF FUN

Marie-Louise von Franz (1964/90) links the stages in the development of anima and animus (i.e., how the conscious ego *experiences itself* as a result of its *conscious recognition* of these archetypal images) to mythological and religious figures, in the case of the anima. With the animus, she likens the stages to qualities of masculinity rather than to specific figures. Below is a list of figures, from art and sacred text, that represent the stages of development of the anima, and a list of characteristics representing the developmental stages of the animus. You are invited to supply your own ideas of which figures (pop stars, leaders, heroes, 'gods') most accurately represent these stages:

Anima Development

EVE—purely biological, instinctual relations

HELEN—a romantic, aesthetic level still characterised by sexual elements

VIRGIN MARY—who raises love (eros) to the heights of spiritual devotion

SAPIENTIA/SOPHIA—wisdom transcending the most bold and most pure (von Franz argues that in the psychic development of modern man this stage is rarely reached. The Mona Lisa comes nearest to such a wisdom anima)

Animus Development

The animus first appears in the form of pure physical power—an athlete, Tarzan

In the 2nd stage, he possesses initiative and the capacity for planned action/a romantic hero

3rd stage—animus becomes the 'word'—intellect, spirit, inspirational leader

4th stage—he is the incarnation of meaning. The animus (like the anima) becomes a mediator of religious experience whereby life acquires new meaning

SUMMARY

- Jung's 'discovery' of the *anima* during his 'confrontation with the unconscious'
- Translation difficulties with the German word *Seele* which combines both 'psyche' and 'soul' in its meaning
- Jung's early definitions of anima and animus, noting their controversial reception
- Introducing Douglas's book on post-Jungian revisions to the concept of anima/animus
- Jung's summary of the process of withdrawing anima/animus projections from a partner and developing the personality through consciousness of the projected image as an *inner* image (anima/animus)
- Jung's argument for a "dramatic, mythological way of thinking and speaking" when describing the "living processes of the psyche"
- More of what Jung wrote on anima and animus, noting problematic language
- The relevance of the concept of the contrasexual archetype. Jung's controversial statement: "Woman has no anima, no soul, but she has an *animus*"; the problematic use of *anima* as a soul-term
- Jung's late thoughts on anima/animus as "divine *syzygy*"
- And "A Bit of Fun"—a chance to put faces to the ever-shapeshifting personifications of anima and animus that we meet in dreams, fantasies, myth, literature, film ... and life

VERY BRIEF NOTES ON A FEW FAMILIAR PERSONIFIED ARCHETYPES (BOXED EDITION)

The Hero

Jung on Myth: "Myths are original revelations of the preconscious psyche, involuntary statements about unconscious psychic happenings, and anything but allegories of physical processes (i.e., the diurnal passage of the sun.). Myths, on the contrary, have a vital meaning. Not merely do they represent, they *are* the psychic life of the primitive tribe, which immediately falls to pieces and decays when it loses its mythological heritage, like a man who has lost his soul. A tribe's mythology is its living religion, whose loss is always and everywhere, even among the civilized, a moral catastrophe" (CW9i:261) … which begs the question: does the loss of a common, shared mythology underlie the divisive, rootless quality of 21st-century Western culture?

And on Fairy-tales: "In myths and fairy-tales, as in dreams, the psyche tells its own story, and the interplay of the archetypes is revealed in its natural setting as 'formation, transformation/the eternal Mind's eternal recreation'" (CW9i:400). Marie-Louise von Franz differentiates fairy-tales from myth: "Fairy-tales are the purest and simplest expression of collective unconscious psychic processes. [...] They represent the archetypes in their simplest, barest and most concise form" (1970/78, p. 1), that is, without the overlay of cultural material that we find in myth.

The Hero

- "The finest of all symbols of libido (psychic energy) is the human figure, conceived as a demon or hero" (CW5:251). For "human figure" perhaps read 'heroic aspect of the ego.' Hero myths and fairy-tales concern the process of psychological development (individuation), many focusing on a *portion* of that journey. Note the polarity (or complementarity) of "demon or hero." The archetypal image of the hero, like any personification of an archetype, will be equivocal, dual, complex, especially in relation to its 'shadow' or 'dark brother'—the demon or villain.
- "The heroes (of myth) are usually wanderers, and wandering is a symbol of longing, of the restless urge which never finds its object, of nostalgia for the lost mother. [...] [The hero] is first and foremost a self-representation of the longing of the unconscious, of its unquenched and unquenchable desire for the light of consciousness. But consciousness, continually in danger of being led astray by its own light and of becoming a rootless will o' the wisp, longs for the healing power of nature, for the deep wells of being and for unconscious communion with life in all its countless forms" (CW5:299). This suggests that the individuation process is the unseen author of myth (and fairy-tale); it also describes the push in the psyche for a union of opposites between conscious and unconscious.
- Jung describes "the almost worldwide myth of the typical deed of the hero. He journeys by ship, fights the sea monster, is

swallowed, struggles against being bitten and crushed to death, and having arrived inside the 'whale-dragon,' seeks the vital organ, which he proceeds to cut off or otherwise destroy. Often the monster is killed by the hero lighting a fire inside him—that is to say, in the very womb of death he secretly creates life, the rising sun. Thus the fish dies and drifts to land, where with the help of a bird the hero once more sees the light of day. [...] This ascent signifies rebirth, the bringing forth of life from the mother, and the ultimate conquest of death [...]. It is easy to see what the battle with the sea monster means: it is the attempt to free the ego-consciousness from the deadly grip of the unconscious. The making of a fire in the monster's belly suggests as much, for it is a piece of apotropaic magic (i.e., with the power to avert evil influence) aimed at dispelling the darkness of unconsciousness. The rescue of the hero is at the same time a sunrise, the triumph of consciousness" (CW5:338).

- We can see how this myth portrays one stage in the process of individuation, the birth of the hero from the unconscious or from an infantile attachment to the 'mother.' Other myths detail the struggle with the shadow, the confrontation with the anima/us (god/goddess), the hero's attainment of supernatural powers/spiritual knowledge, etc., returning with the ability to bestow a boon on his community.

The Wise Old Man

- In "The Syzygy: Anima and Animus," Jung links the archetype of the Wise Old Man with that of the Chthonic (Earth) Mother. Both images are personifications of the deeper layers of the unconscious encountered after work with the personal shadow and a withdrawal of anima/us projections have been achieved. The Wise Old Man and Chthonic Earth Mother would seem to represent perhaps the deepest differentiation of the Self—as One—first into two (themselves) and then into the multiplicity of archetypes that populate the collective unconscious. Jung: "Reality consists of a multiplicity of things. But one is not a number. The first number is two and with it multiplicity and reality begin" (CW14:659).

- Jung: the Wise Old Man personifies, in "a numinous personality, the embodiment of an archetype, [...] the 'spirit' in myth and folklore" (CW9ii:362).

- Von Franz: "The Wise Old Man is the wisdom of the unconscious, the archetype of the spirit, which gives that undirected *élan vital* of the young hero—the life drive in the unconscious—an opportunity to move in the right direction, toward where it could help to correct some wrong things in the collective consciousness" (1997, p. 30).

- Jung: "The old man always appears when the hero is in a hopeless and desperate situation from which only profound reflection or a lucky idea—in other words, a spiritual function or an endopsychic automatism of some kind—can extricate him. [...] Often the old man in fairy-tales asks questions like Who? Why? Whence? and Whither? for the purpose of inducing self-reflection and mobilizing the moral forces, and more often still he gives the necessary magical talisman, the unexpected and improbable power to succeed, which is one of the peculiarities of the unified personality in good or bad alike. But the intervention of the old man—the spontaneous objectivation of the archetype—would seem to be equally indispensable, since the conscious will by itself is hardly ever capable of uniting the personality to the point where it acquires this extraordinary power to succeed. For that, not only in fairy-tales but in life generally, the objective intervention of the archetype is needed" (CW9i:401-04).

- Like all archetypes, the Wise Old Man is dual in nature. Jung speaks of the 'lower' aspect of the Wise Old Man as "having a magical and nefarious significance" (*ibid.*). He often has "an ambiguous elfin character [...]: in certain of his forms, to be good incarnate and in others an aspect of evil. Then again, he is the wicked magician who, from sheer egoism, does evil for evil's sake" (*ibid.*). He will often assume the "guise of an evil-doer" though effecting good, which "hints at a secret inner relation of evil to good and vice versa" (*ibid.*:417).

The Mother

- "The qualities associated with it (the Mother archetype) are maternal solicitude and sympathy; the magic authority of the female; the wisdom and spiritual exaltation that transcends reason; any helpful instinct or impulse; all that is benign, all that cherishes and sustains, that fosters growth and fertility. The place of magic transformation and rebirth, together with the under-world and its inhabitants are presided over by the Mother. On the negative side the mother archetype may connote anything secret, hidden, dark; the abyss, the world of the dead, anything that devours, seduces, and poisons, that is terrifying and ines-capable like fate" (CW9i:158). A vivid portrait of both the Good Mother and the Terrible Mother—both a Fairy God-Mother and the Baba Yaga of Russian tales, or the Witch in the Gingerbread House in "Hansel and Gretel."

- "Like any other archetype, the mother archetype appears under an almost infinite variety of aspects. [...] Mythology offers many variations of the mother archetype, as for instance the mother who reappears as the maiden in the myth of Demeter and Kore; or the mother who is also the beloved, as in the Cybele-Attis myth. Other symbols of the mother in a figurative sense appear in things representing the goal of our longing for redemption, such as Paradise, the Kingdom of God, the Heavenly Jerusalem. Many things arousing devotion or feelings of awe, as for instance the Church, university, city or country, heaven, earth, the woods, the sea or any still waters, matter even, the underworld and the moon, can be mother-symbols. The archetype is often associ-ated with things and places standing for fertility and fruitfulness: the cornucopia, a ploughed field, a garden. It can be attached to a rock, a cave, a tree, a spring, a deep well, or to various ves-sels such as the baptismal font, or to vessel-shaped flowers like the rose or the lotus. Because of the protection it implies, the magic circle or mandala can be a form of mother archetype. Hollow objects such as ovens and cooking vessels are associ-ated with the mother archetype, and, of course, the uterus, *yoni*, and anything of a like shape. Added to this list there are many animals, such as the cow, hare, and helpful animals in general" (CW9i:156). Well! Not always so easy to spot!

- "An ambivalent aspect (of the Mother archetype) is seen in the goddesses of fate—Moira, Graeae, Norns. Evil symbols are the witch, the dragon (or any devouring and entwining animal, such as a large fish or a serpent), the grave, the sarcopha-gus, deep water, death, nightmares and bogies (Lilith, etc.)" (*ibid.*:157).

- The Chthonic Earth Mother is the personification in myth and fairy-tale of the unconscious, the underworld. Unconsciously identified with the Chthonic Mother, or still 'in the mother,' the heroic ego must differentiate from 'mother' (security, dependency, etc.) in order to connect with spirit (animus) and acquire the ego strength necessary to enable her to recognise and relate to the positive 'face' of the Chthonic Mother. Again, the story of individuation.

The Child Archetype

- Jung: "The child motif represents the pre-conscious, childhood aspect of the collective psyche" (CW9i:161), i.e., the original, unconscious, and instinctive state out of which modern human consciousness has evolved and on which the life of every newborn baby rests and depends. The birth of a child-god or child-hero serves "the purpose of bringing the image of childhood, and everything connected with it, again and again before the eyes of the conscious mind so that the link with the original condition may not be broken" (*ibid.*:162).
- One of the functions of the archetype, when it erupts into consciousness in the image of the child "is to compensate or correct, in a meaningful manner, the inevitable one-sidedness and extravagances of the conscious mind" (*ibid.*:163). "[T]he more differentiated consciousness becomes, the greater the danger of (humankind's) severance from the root-condition and of deviating further [...] from the laws and roots of (our) being" (*ibid.*).
- The child archetype has to do with the past, and connecting back (to ancestral history, beginnings, origins) but it also has to do with futurity. The child is the as yet unrealised future, the next generation. So it is both provocative and conservative, demanding change and the new while pointing to past, forgotten values that need to be redeemed.
- In the dreams and psychology of the individual, "'the child' paves the way for a future change of personality" (*ibid.*:164).

- The child motif "signifies no more than a possibility" (CW9i:165), an anticipation of something evolving towards independence and conscious realisation. "The motifs of 'insignificance,' exposure, abandonment, danger, etc., (i.e., the conditions of the child's birth), show how precarious is the psychic possibility of wholeness, that is, the enormous difficulties to be met with in attaining [the] 'highest good'" (ibid.).
- The child-god's or child-hero's task is "to overcome the monster of darkness: [...] the long hoped-for and expected triumph of consciousness over the unconscious" (ibid.:167), of light over darkness. However, if the collective consciousness is trapped in a conflict situation, the 'child' bears "no resemblance to the conscious factors [and] is therefore easily overlooked and falls back into unconsciousness" (ibid.:170).
- The 'child' "is born out of the womb of the unconscious, begotten out of the depths of human nature; [...] it is a personification of vital forces quite outside the limited range of our conscious mind; of ways and possibilities of which our one-sided conscious mind knows nothing: a wholeness which embraces the very depths of Nature. It represents the strongest, the most ineluctable urge in every being, namely the urge to realize itself, [...] an incarnation of the *inability to do otherwise*" (ibid.). We need to watch for the manifestation of the child archetype in one of its myriad forms, as it "is extremely variable and assumes all manner of shapes, such as the jewel, the pearl, the flower, the chalice, the golden egg, the quaternity, the golden ball, and so on" (ibid.:270).

The *Puer Aeternus* (Eternal Boy)

- The term *puer aeternus* was introduced by Ovid (43 BC–17/18 AD) in his description of the young Dionysus as a beautiful, virginal *eternal boy* who passes for a maiden when he hides the horns with which he was born.
- Dionysus is both masculine and feminine; he is a wanderer in lonely places; he is a nature god, a vegetation deity, associated

with the vine and the culture of grapes; he carries a staff (the phallic *thyrsis*) and inherits from his father (Zeus) a powerful phallic character and so, with Pan and Hermes, is often understood as a figure for an instinctual, primordial dynamism, the "creative divinity" for which the phallus frequently stands (CW5:183).

- The *puer aeternus* is one way in which the child archetype manifests. "The 'child' is all that is abandoned and exposed and at the same time divinely powerful,' the insignificant, dubious beginning, and the triumphal end. The 'eternal child' in man is an indescribable experience, an incongruity, a handicap, and a divine prerogative; an imponderable that determines the ultimate worth or worthlessness of a personality" (CW9i:300).

- *Puer* calls into being *senex* (old man). They may pose as opposites but need to work as complementaries. Youth, spontaneity, creativity, flight from reality (the *puer*) needs the gravitas, the historicity of the *senex* to ground himself in life. Again, we have an archetypal configuration, *puer-senex*, in need of a compensatory rather than an openly oppositional relationship. The boy-man configuration, which appears as an image on a Theban case, is identified by Jung as relating to "a Phoenician cult of father and son" in which phallic energy (creative libido) was passed from father to son (CW5:184). This suggests "the boy who is born from the maturity of the adult man, and not the unconscious child we would like to remain" (CW11:742).

- For further reading, see von Franz (2000), Hillman et al. (1987), and Yeoman (1998)

THE SELF

As Jung was emerging from his *creative illness* towards the end of the First World War, he started every morning to sketch a mandala corresponding to his "inner situation at the time. With the help of these drawings I could observe my psychic transformations from day to day" (1961/63, p. 195). Jung drew countless mandalas between 1918 and 1920, asking himself what might be the goal of this process that he felt compelled to continue. He began to realise that what the mandala symbolised "corresponds to the microcosmic nature of the psyche," and, evoking Goethe's *Faust,* Jung characterised the dynamic process of the psyche as continuous "Formation, Transformation, Eternal Mind's eternal recreation. And that is the [S]elf, the wholeness of the personality, which if all goes well is harmonious, but which cannot tolerate self-deceptions. [...] It is the exponent of all paths. It is the path to the center, to individuation. [...] There is no linear evolution; there is only a circumambulation of the [S]elf" (*ibid.,* p. 196). A few years later, in 1927, Jung had a dream that confirmed, for him, his ideas about the 'centre' of the psyche, the Self. Here is the dream:

> I found myself in a dirty, sooty city. It was night, and winter, and dark, and raining. I was in Liverpool. With a number of Swiss—say, half a dozen—I walked through the dark streets. I had the feeling that there we were coming from the harbor, and that the real city was actually up above, on the cliffs. We climbed up there. It reminded me of Basel, where the market is down below and then you go up through the Totengässchen ('Alley of the Dead'), which leads to a plateau above and so to the Petersplatz and the Peterskirche. When we reached the plateau, we found a broad square dimly illuminated by street lights, into which many streets converged. The various quarters of the city were arranged radially around the square. In the center was a round pool, and in the middle of it a small island. While everything round about was obscured by rain, fog, smoke, and dimly lit darkness, the little island blazed with sunlight. On it stood a single tree, a magnolia, in a shower of reddish blossoms. It was as though the tree stood in the sunlight and were at the same time the source of light. My companions commented on the abominable weather, and obviously did not see the tree. They spoke of another Swiss who was living in Liverpool, and expressed surprise that he should have settled here. I was carried away by the beauty of the flowering tree and the sunlit island, and thought, 'I know very well why he has settled here.' Then I awoke.
>
> On one detail [...] I must add a supplementary comment: the individual quarters of the city were themselves arranged radially around a central point. This point formed a small open square illuminated by a larger street lamp, and constituted a small replica of the island. I knew that the 'other Swiss' lived in the vicinity of one of these secondary centers.
>
> (*ibid.,* p. 198)

Jung understood from his dream that what he called the Self "is the principle and archetype of orientation and meaning. Therein lies its healing function" (*ibid.,* p. 199).

Because the role of ego-consciousness is to differentiate, separate into units, and understand, it is "well-nigh impossible" (to pinch Jung's expression!) to move beyond the idea that the Self is, if not a 'thing,' then surely a reasonably consistent 'entity,' by virtue of the fact that it is equated with wholeness and unity. This returns us to Jung's recognition (which bears repeating) that "Reality consists of a multiplicity of things. But one is not a number; the first number is two, and with it multiplicity and reality begin" (CW14:659). Elsewhere, he writes that "the striving for unity is opposed by a possibly even stronger tendency to create multiplicity, so that even in strictly monotheistic religions like Christianity the polytheistic tendency cannot be suppressed" (CW5:149). We need only to consider Dante's *Divine Comedy,* Milton's *Paradise Lost,* and the paintings of Brueghel, to be reminded of the multitudes of angels and saints, demons and sinners that populate the Christian imagination. Yet Jung argues that, when it comes to the psyche, "we lack all knowledge of the unconscious psyche and pursue the cult of consciousness to the exclusion of all else. Our true religion is a monotheism of consciousness, a possession by it, coupled with a fanatical denial of the existence of fragmentary autonomous systems" (CW13:51).

Those "fragmentary autonomous systems" of the psyche we meet, personified, in mythology, folk- and fairy-tale, literature, art, film, on Oxford Street, in relationships. So while Jung uses the concept of the Self to signify an organising, ordering principle in the psyche, it is a principle, nevertheless, that is characterised by multiplicity, and signifies an irreducible source of creativity. It is both the One and the Many, the All of what is known, knowable, and unknowable. It is, therefore, transcendent (of consciousness), 'Other,' *numinous,* and consequently can only present itself to consciousness *empirically,* i.e., symbolically. We might say these empirical symbols proffer to consciousness *intimations* of the Self. Such symbols appear in a multitude of forms: as images of the God-head, cosmic order (the mandala), divine and earthly totality (circles, squares, mathematics), fantastical beings, gods and god-like beings, exceptional human beings (priests, kings and queens, leaders, revered elders), as well as the myriad creatures that make earth, air, and water their home, the exquisite symmetry of plant-life, the miracle of the proportions and functioning of the human body and of all living beings. Jung adds to this catalogue of empirical representations, the Self as the union of opposites:

> When it (i.e., the Self) represents a *complexio oppositorum,* a union of opposites, it can also appear as a united duality, in the form, for instance, of *tao* as the interplay of *yang* and *yin,* or of the hostile brothers, or of the hero and his adversary (arch-enemy, dragon), Faust and Mephistopheles, etc. Empirically, therefore, the self appears as a play of light and shadow,

although conceived as a totality and unity in which the opposites are united. Since such a concept is irrepresentable [...] it is transcendental on this account also. It would, logically considered, be a vain speculation were it not for the fact that it designates symbols of unity that are found to occur empirically. [*Remember the 'unifying symbol' of the unicorn's horn earlier in this chapter.*]

(CW6:790)

While Jung takes great pains to ground his concept of the Self in empirical symbolic evidence ranging from sacred text and mythology to the dreams and lived experience of his patients, his comments in an interview with Miguel Serrano are helpful in reminding us that the Self is an hypothesis, a postulate of a creative, ordering principle operative beyond the reach of consciousness: the archetype of archetypes. Seranno (1966/77) records Jung in an interview in Locarno, Switzerland, February, 1959:

So far, I have found no stable or definite centre in the unconscious and I don't believe such a centre exists. I believe that the thing which I call the Self is an ideal centre, equi-distant between the Ego and the Unconscious, and it is probably equivalent to the maximum natural expression of individuality, in a state of fulfilment or totality. As nature aspires to express itself, so does man, and the Self is that dream of totality. It is therefore an ideal centre, something created.

(p. 50)

Commentaries on the hypothesis of the Self are to be found throughout *The Collected Works,* from "Definitions" in CW6 (1921) to *Aion: Researches into the Phenomenology of the Self* (CW9ii, 1951) which is devoted to the subject. In the first four short chapters of *Aion,* Jung provides a review of key concepts: ego, shadow, the *syzygy*—anima/animus, and Self, reminding his reader that shadow, syzygy, and Self "are psychic factors of which an adequate picture can be formed only on the basis of a fairly thorough experience of them. Just as these concepts arose out of an experience of reality, so they can be elucidated only by further experience. Philosophical criticism will find everything to object to in them unless it begins by recognizing that they are concerned with *facts,* and that the 'concept' is simply an abbreviated description or definition of these facts" (CW9ii:63). If Jung's concepts, particularly that of the Self, remain opaque to you, don't dismiss them; keep them in the back of your mind for when an experience that might be just around the corner cracks open their opacity for you in an "Aha" moment! As Jung argues, the intellect alone works with any science except psychology because science utilises sense-perception and thinking, while "[e]very psychic process has a value quality attached to it, namely its feeling-tone. This indicates the degree to which the subject is *affected* by the process or how much it means to him (in so far as the process reaches consciousness at all). It is through the 'affect' that the subject becomes involved and so comes to feel the whole weight of reality. [...] In psychology one possesses nothing unless one has experienced it in reality" (*ibid*.:61). Why such emphasis on "affect"? "The feeling-value [...] determines in large measure the role which the (assimilated unconscious) content will play in the psychic economy. That is to say, the affective value gives the measure of the intensity of an idea, and the intensity in its turn expresses that idea's energic tension, its effective potential" (*ibid*.:53).

We have learnt from Jung that, in the work of acquiring self-knowledge and thereby enhancing the personality, first comes awareness and integration of shadow content—complexes, followed by conscious differentiation of the syzygy—anima/animus. When the syzygy's manifestation in consciousness as 'personalities' has been realised as an inner image and their projection onto others withdrawn, anima/animus provide a 'bridge' to the deeper levels of the unconscious psyche, to the Self. Each stage of this process (which may take some a lifetime if they engage in it at all) will have affected ego-consciousness with the dynamism, numinosity, and feeling-tone of the complexes and archetypal images confronted. Jung writes that "the more numerous and the more significant the unconscious contents which are assimilated to the ego, the closer the approximation of the ego to the [S]elf, even though this approximation must be a never-ending process" (*ibid*.:44). The closer to the Self, the more the assimilation of previously unconscious content "augments not only the area of the field of consciousness but also the importance of the ego, especially when, as usually happens, the ego lacks any critical approach to the unconscious. In that case it is easily overpowered and becomes identical with the contents that have been assimilated" (*ibid*.:43). When this happens, and the *ego is assimilated by the Self*, there occurs an inflation of the ego, and one 'becomes' the god or star whose numinous image has fascinated and possessed one's imagination:

> The image of wholeness then remains in the unconscious, so that on the one hand the ego shares the archaic nature of the unconscious and on the other finds itself in the psychically relative space-time continuum

that is characteristic of the unconscious as such. Both these qualities are numinous and hence have an unlimited determining effect on ego-consciousness, which is differentiated, i.e., separated, from the unconscious and moreover exists in an absolute space and an absolute time. [...] Under the control of an unconscious factor, [the ego's] adaptation is disturbed and the way opened for all sorts of possible accidents.

(*ibid.*:45)

Remember the myth of Icarus!

An inflation of the ego also results, Jung tells us, should the Self become *assimilated to the ego,* despite the fact that this is the opposite of the condition described above. When the Self is assimilated to the ego, "[t]he world of consciousness must be levelled down in favour of the reality of the unconscious. [...] [T]he presumption of the ego can only be damped down by moral defeat. This is necessary, because otherwise one will never attain that median degree of modesty which is essential for the maintenance of a balanced state (i.e., homeostasis)" (*ibid.*:47). In order to prevent—or correct—an inflation of the ego:

A critical line of demarcation [needs to be] drawn between it and the unconscious figures. But this act of discrimination yields practical results only if it succeeds in fixing reasonable boundaries to the ego and in granting the figures of the unconscious [...] relative autonomy and reality [of a psychic nature]. [...] One cannot dispose of [psychic] facts by declaring them unreal. [...] This condition [of inflation] should not be interpreted as one of conscious self-aggrandizement. Such is far from being the rule. In general we are not directly conscious of this condition at all, but can at best infer its existence indirectly from the symptoms. [...] A clear symptom of this is our growing disinclination to take note of the reactions of the environment and pay heed to them (i.e., the reactions of family, friends and colleagues to our insufferable behaviour!).

(*ibid.*:44)

This leads us to conclude that both ego and Self play essential roles in the process of individuation and the growth of consciousness. The ego needs experience of the Self in order to become whole; the Self needs the vessel of the ego in order for its contents to be realised in the world, that is, made conscious. There is a compensatory relationship between conscious and unconscious, ego and Self, that seems to operate both in the interests of the homeostasis of the psyche and in furthering its development towards wholeness (or as close to that ideal as is possible). It is, then, advisable, as Jung writes, to relate the contradictory manifestations of the unconscious causally to the conscious attitude, at least to some degree. But consciousness should not be overrated either, for experience provides too many incontrovertible proofs of the autonomy of unconscious compensatory processes for us to seek the origin of these antinomies only in the conscious mind. Between the conscious and the unconscious there is a kind of 'uncertainty relationship,' because the observer is inseparable from the observed and always disturbs it by the act of observation. In other words, exact observation of the unconscious prejudices observation of the conscious and vice versa.

(ibid.:355)

Another way of understanding this is to say that the face or attitude with which ego-consciousness approaches the Self can affect the way in which the Self presents itself to consciousness—and, of course, *vice versa*. This is wonderfully illustrated in Goethe's (1749–1832) *Faust*. When Mephistopheles (the devil) first appears to Faust, it is in such an abominable, threatening animal form that Faust is terrified—but duly chastened—such that Mephistopheles leaves and returns in the guise of a travelling scholar.

In the final chapter of *Aion,* Jung elaborates the enormous variety of symbols in which the Self may present to consciousness. A short list was cited earlier in the present chapter, and, adding to that, Jung cites gemstones, buildings such as churches and castles, vessels and containers, city plans, wheels, mountains, lakes, plants such as the tree and the rose, and the phallus. The numinosity of each may, of course, range from the divine to the diabolical, depending, perhaps, on the attitude of consciousness and the Self's role in compensating a one-sided conscious attitude. Jung writes: "Thus the [S]elf can appear in all shapes from the highest to the lowest, inasmuch as these transcend the scope of the ego personality [...]" (CW9ii:356). The remainder of the chapter presents Jung's diagrammatic elaboration of the hypothetical structure and dynamic of the Self, based on the symbols used to represent the Self in Gnosticism, astrology, and alchemy. The diagram maps hypothetical developmental levels in the Self. "Each level," as Murray Stein writes, "is built of a quaternary, and each of them represents complexity and wholeness at that level. The image of the four quaternities, which are stacked in an order that ascends from material to spiritual poles on a continuum, expresses totality and wholeness" (1998, p. 161). To explore this particular thread of Jung's thinking, head to CW9ii:358-420.

⊕

SUMMARY

- Jung's dream that confirmed his intuitive sense of a principle of orientation and meaning at the core of the psyche
- The multiplicity of the unconscious psyche. Archetypal content and fragmentary autonomous systems personified in myth, art, and relationship
- The Self as a *complexio oppositorum* and also a united duality. Image of unicorn horn which serves as symbol that unites the 'opposites' of masculine and feminine
- Comments to Miguel Serrano: the Self as an ideal centre, something created
- Psychology is to be understood not solely intellectually but experientially, as the unconscious in its compensatory role to consciousness is 'real'—it happens to one
- Meaning and value reside in how consciousness is affected by unconscious content
- The dangers of the confrontation between ego and the Self: assimilation of the ego by the unconscious; assimilation of the unconscious by the ego. Consequences and a corrective explored
- Compensatory relationship of ego and Self operates to achieve homeostasis in the psychic system and to promote the development of consciousness

REFERENCES

Clay, Catrine. (2016) *Labyrinths: Emma Jung, her Marriage to Carl and the Early Years of Psychoanalysis*. London: William Collins.

Douglas, C. (1990) *The Woman in the Mirror: Analytical Psychology and the Feminine*. Boston, MA: Sigo Press.

Edinger, E. F. (1996) *The Aion Lectures: Exploring the Self in C. G. Jung's Aion*. Toronto: Inner City Books.

Hillman, J. et al. (1987) *Puer Papers*. Irving, TX: Spring Publications.

Jung, C. G. (1953–83) *The Collected Works of C. G. Jung*, 20 vols. W. McGuire, H. Read, M. Fordham, G. Adler (Eds.). R. F. C. Hull (Trans.). London: Routledge & Kegan Paul; Princeton, NJ: Princeton University Press.

Jung, C. G. (1961/63) *Memories, Dreams, Reflections*. Recorded and edited by A. Jaffé. R. and C. Winston (Trans.). New York: Pantheon Books.

Jung, E. (1957) *Animus and Anima*. New York: Analytical Psychology Club of New York.

Jung, E. and von Franz, M. L. (1960/1998) *The Grail Legend*. A. Dykes (Trans.). Princeton, NJ: Princeton University Press.

Saban, M. (2019) *'Two Souls Alas': Jung's Two Personalities and the Making of Analytical Psychology*. Asheville, NC: Chiron Publications.

Savage-Healy, N. (2017) *Toni Wolff and C. G. Jung: A Collaboration*. Los Angeles, CA: Tiberius Press.

Seranno, M. (1966/77) *C. G. Jung and Hermann Hesse: A Record of Two Friendships*. London: Routledge & Kegan Paul.

Stein, M. (1998) *Jung's Map of the Soul: An Introduction*. Chicago, IL: Open Court.

Stevens, A. (1990) *On Jung*. London: Routledge.

Stevens, A. (1994) *Archetype Revisited: An Updated History of the Self*. London: Brunner-Routledge.

Von Franz, M. L. (1964/90) "The Process of Individuation" in C. G. Jung (Ed.), *Man and His Symbols*. London: Arkana.

Von Franz, M. L. (1970/78) *The Interpretation of Fairy Tales*. Irving, TX: Spring Publications.

Von Franz, M. L. (1997) *Archetypal Patterns in Fairy Tales*. Toronto: Inner city Books.

Von Franz, M. L. (2000) *The Problem of the Puer Aeternus*. Toronto: Inner City Books.

Winnicott, D. W. (1971/2017) *Playing and Reality*. London: Routledge.

Yeoman, A. (1998) *Now or Neverland: Peter Pan and the Myth of Eternal Youth*. Toronto: Inner City Books.

Table 4.1 Collective Unconscious and Archetypes

TOPIC/ KEYWORDS	LOCATION	DESCRIPTOR
The Relations Between the Ego and the Unconscious, Chapter 1: The Personal and the Collective Unconscious	CW7:202–20 (1916/1928)	Collective unconscious extends Freud's notion of unconscious, equivalent of Jung's personal unconscious. Dream images that point beyond analysand's personal circumstances indicate impersonal, inherited thought categories, or archetypes.
On the Psychology of the Unconscious, Chapter 5: The Personal and the Collective (or Transpersonal) Unconscious	CW7:97–120 (1917/1926)	Role of collective unconscious in interpreting transference. Proof for existence of collective unconscious found in ancient myths and religions. Robert Mayer's discovery of conservation of energy is an archetypal idea.

(Continued)

Table 4.1 (Continued)

TOPIC/ KEYWORDS	LOCATION	DESCRIPTOR
"The Role of the Unconscious"	CW10:1–48 (1918)	Distinction made between personal and collective unconscious. Unconscious possesses a compensatory function and capacity to produce symbols.
"The Structure of the Psyche"	CW8:283–342 (1931)	Knowledge of myth required to understand dreams as products of the collective unconscious. Evidence for collective unconscious found in clinical cases, world religions (archetypal images).
The Tavistock Lectures, Lecture II	CW18:74–144 (1935)	Collective unconscious comprised of archetypes with a mythological character that belong to all humanity. Archetypes reflect history of the human brain; constellation in social groups. Unconscious engaged via word association tests, dream analysis, and active imagination.
"The Concept of the Collective Unconscious"	CW9i:87–110 (1936/1937)	Collective unconscious is universal, impersonal level of psychic functioning containing pre-existing thought forms that shape psychic material (archetypes). Relation of archetypes and instincts. Evidence for collective unconscious provided. Case of man's vision of solar phallus presented as 'proof' of collective unconscious.
"Archetypes of the Collective Unconscious"	CW9i:1–86 (1954)	Deeper level of the unconscious. Collective unconscious manifests as universal, archaic images finding expression in dreams, religion, mythology, and fairy-tales. Personified archetypes discussed, including shadow and anima/animus. Possession by an archetype may lead to psychosis. Therapeutic process pioneered by Jung to work with archetypal material makes aspects of archetypes as conscious as possible, integrating contents into consciousness.
Collective unconscious and its relationship to consciousness	CW8:403 (1954)	Ego-consciousness depends on (1) collective consciousness and (2) archetypes. Archetypes irrational, ignored at our peril. Individual suspended in "unbridgeable gulf" between the two.

(Continued)

Table 4.1 (Continued)

TOPIC/ KEYWORDS	LOCATION	DESCRIPTOR
Relationship between personal and collective unconscious	CW12:38 (1944/1952)	Contents of personal and collective unconscious are interconnected (particularly in the case of the shadow).
	CW12:81 (1944) CW9i:314 (1951)	Personal unconscious must be dealt with first before facing contents of collective unconscious. Impersonal psyche (collective unconscious) expresses itself through the personal unconscious.
	CW9i:3 (1954)	Personal unconscious rests on collective unconscious. Latter constitutes a "common psychic substrate of a suprapersonal nature."
Transpersonal/ Suprapersonal	CW7:103 (1917/1926) CW10:13 (1918) CW8:311 (1931)	Collective unconscious detached from anything personal and common to all humanity. "Collective" and "transpersonal" used interchangeably. Suprapersonal unconscious is source of creativity.
Absolute unconscious	CW18:84 (1935)	"Absolute unconscious" operates independently of conscious mind.
Not a *tabula rasa*	CW9i:88 *ff* (1936/1937)	Child's mind is not a *tabula rasa*. Brain has its history. In the basic structure of the mind, traces of archaic inheritance will be found. Collective unconscious not individually acquired; owes its existence to heredity. Identical in all individuals (90).
Numinosity	CW8:405 *ff* (1954)	Archetypes have numinous and spiritual character.
Contents of the collective unconscious/ archetypes/ mythology/ instincts	CW7:219 *ff* (1916/1928)	Archetypes (previously referred to as primordial images) denote inherited thought patterns, not inherited ideas. Impersonal inherited categories remain in relatively active state (220).
	CW7:520	Collective unconscious comprised of subliminal perceptions, vestiges, and combinations in symbolic form. Most important contents are primordial images (archetypes) and instincts.
	CW7:101 *ff* (1917/1926)	Archetypes as inherited possibilities of human imagination. Expression of mythical ideas and impressions of ever-repeated typical experiences. Numinosity of archetypes and potential influence (including possession) when constellated.

(*Continued*)

Table 4.1 (Continued)

TOPIC/ KEYWORDS	LOCATION	DESCRIPTOR
	CW7:118 (1917/1926)	Collective unconscious comprised of "residues of ancestral life." 'Content' of archetypes not filled out; "they are forms not personally experienced."
	CW7:151	Collective unconscious: repository of man's experience and the prior condition of this experience. An image of the world which has taken aeons to form. Archetypes crystallise in course of time; typical images of "dominant laws and principles" occurring regularly throughout life.
	CW10:14 (1918)	Archetypes give form to acquired content. As part of inherited brain structure, they are source of symbols and myth-motifs in all parts of the world.
	CW6:746 *ff* (1921/1923)	Primordial images as "mnemic deposits," imprints, or engrams. Ideas that are the underlying principle of all experience (750). Inherited organisation of psychic energy and an ingrained system.
	CW8:325 *ff* (1931)	Collective unconscious may be studied via (1) mythology and (2) individual analysis. Mythology as projection of collective unconscious. Archetypes may be understood biologically, as dangerous situations that have left imprint.
	CW8:339	Collective unconscious: "The deposit of all human experience right back to its remotest beginnings [...] the totality of all archetypes."
	CW8:342	"The collective unconscious contains the whole spiritual heritage of mankind's evolution, born anew in the brain structure of every individual [...] The unconscious [...] is the source of the instinctual forces of the psyche and of the forms or categories that regulate them [...] [i.e.] archetypes."
	CW18:80 (1935)	Connection between archetypes and mythic motifs; several named (hero, dragon, *nekyia*, etc.).
	CW10:395 (1936)	Archetypes are like riverbeds into which individual experience flows
	CW8:280 *ff* (1948)	Archetypes as typical, recurring modes of apprehension with distinct uniformity. Collective unconscious as sum of instinct and archetype.

(Continued)

Table 4.1   (Continued)

TOPIC/ KEYWORDS	LOCATION	DESCRIPTOR
	CW11:222, fn. 2 (1948)	Archetypes comparable to invisible presence of crystal lattice in saturated solution. Recognised only by their effects on consciousness.
	CW11:944	Images in deeper unconscious possess mythological character. They "coincide with those widespread primordial ideas which underlie the myths." Found in all myths and legends, regardless of differences in cultural "dress" (particulars).
	CW18:1158 (1948)	Based on clinical experience, typical dream/fantasy motifs that recur in myths (archetypes). Not inherited ideas, but equivalent to "patterns of behaviour" in biology. Archetypes as mode of psychic behaviour and "irrepresentable." They organise psychic content so that it falls within typical configurations. Associations and representations will differ depending on context, but basic pattern remains the same.
	CW9i:261 *ff*	Perhaps Jung's most concise statement on connection between archetypes, collective unconscious, and myth. Child archetype described and examples from myth and legend provided.
	CW11:845 (1953)	Archetypes as "dynamic organs of the psyche" and "instinctual complexes."
Archetype and instinct	CW8:339 *ff* (1931)	Archetypes described as "the forms which the instincts assume."
	CW9i:91 *ff* (1936/1937)	Archetypes: "unconscious images of instincts themselves" and "patterns of instinctual behaviour."
	CW8:277 (1948)	Archetypes are "the *instinct's perception of itself*, or the self-portrait of the instinct […]."
	CW8:281 *ff*	Impossible to know which comes first, instinct or archetype. Both aspects of same vital activity. Interconnected nature of archetypes and instincts.
	CW8:404 *ff* (1954)	Archetype (spirit) and instinct indivisible; extreme opposites share aspects of the other (406).
	CW8:413 *ff*	Instinct and archetype (spirit) located at opposites ends of colour spectrum.

(Continued)

Table 4.1 (Continued)

TOPIC/ KEYWORDS	LOCATION	DESCRIPTOR
	CW8:423	Archetypes fall into two categories: instinctual and archetypal. The first includes natural impulses; the second, dominants emerging as universal ideas.
	CW9i:714 (1955) CW10:10 *ff* (1957)	Archetype as a frequently occurring, formal aspect of instinct. (Archetypal) image expresses nature of instinctive impulses concretely. Example of yucca moth given.
Precursor to archetypal hypothesis	CW10:14 (1918)	Archetypes—innate possibilities of ideas and *a priori*—condition for fantasy production—similar to Kantian categories.
	CW9i:89 (1936/1937) CW8:353 (1954)	Henri Hubert, Marcel Mauss, and Adolf Bastian as precursors to concept of archetype. Adolf Bastian and *elementary ideas.* Wilhelm Wundt rejects idea of common psychic heritage.
	CW9i:5 (1954)	Philo Judaeus, Dionysus the Areopagite, St. Augustine, Plato, and Lucien Lévy-Bruhl.
Personified archetypes	CW7:185 (1917/1926) CW8:336 *ff* (1931)	'Definite' archetypes described: shadow, wise old man, anima/animus, mother, and child. Common experiences and roles create most powerful archetypes (i.e., mother, father). Complexes developing from experience of archetypal roles expressed in religious and political life (337).
	CW9i:80 (1954)	Distinction between personified archetypes and *archetypes of transformation.* Latter are not personalities, but "typical situations, places, ways, and means that symbolize the kind of transformation in question."
Bipolarity of archetypes	CW9i:413 (1948) CW12:553 (1954)	All archetypes have positive and negative side; ambivalence Archetypal image of unicorn's horn as synthesis of opposites
Archetype and symbol	CW5.344 (1912/1952)	Symbols are grounded in archetypes. Symbols act as "transformers" that "convert libido from a 'lower' into a 'higher' form."

(Continued)

Table 4.1 (Continued)

TOPIC/ KEYWORDS	LOCATION	DESCRIPTOR
Psychoid archetype	CW9ii:40 (1951)	Archetypes are factors transcending consciousness and beyond the reach of perception.
	CW8:417 *ff* (1954)	Archetype-as-such is irrepresentable psychoid factor at ultra-violet end of psychic spectrum. Real nature of archetype cannot be made fully conscious. Psychoid nature extends from spirit to include matter (420).
Archetypal image	CW15:11 (1934)	New archetypal images arise when previous ones, representing an outworn worldview, collapse.
	CW11:845 (1953)	Archetypes as universally inherited forms having no specific content. Content only appears when shaped by personal circumstances of individuals.
	CW9i:155 (1953)	Archetype itself is an *a priori* possibility of representation that is purely formal. Representations not inherited, only the forms/templates.
	CW8:417 *ff* (1954)	Archetype itself is irrepresentable. Perception of archetypes made possible through archetypal images. Archetype as such is psychoid; archetypal images perceived by consciousness represent variations on a central theme. Archetypes emerge into consciousness as *ideas* and *images* (435).
	CW10:10 *ff* (1957)	Adaptability of primordial patterns (archetypes); archetypal forms 'remould' to maintain their dynamism.
	CW18:1589 (1956–57)	Archetypal image likened to portrait of unknown man in a gallery, i.e., of unknown archetype.
	CW18:1686 (1956–57)	Autonomous life of archetypes revealed through continuous transformations of archetypal images.
Necessity of engaging/ integrating contents of the collective unconscious	CW7:387 (1916/1928)	Unconscious is first met in contents of personal unconscious, and then "in the fantasies of the collective unconscious." Getting to deeper level enables engagement with roots of complexes.

(*Continued*)

Table 4.1 (Continued)

TOPIC/ KEYWORDS	LOCATION	DESCRIPTOR
Developing a conscious relationship to the collective unconscious	CW7:159 (1917/1926)	Deleterious impact of unconscious images (e.g., animal imagery) curtailed "through man's conscious attitude towards the collective unconscious." *Transcendent function* as method through which rapprochement of conscious and unconscious may be achieved.
	CW8:410 (1954)	Integrating archetypal material is an ethical problem of greatest magnitude. Individuals who do this take responsibility for their predicaments.
	CW9i:44 (1954)	Collective unconscious must be approached with 'open' attitude.
Projection and constellation of archetypes Possession	CW7:152 *ff* (1917/1926)	Danger of psychic infection when archetypal content is projected and not withdrawn. Necessity of recognising when projection has occurred, and ego's responsibility to face projected content.
	CW10:395 *ff* (1936)	If left unchecked, archetypes constellated at level of collective can lead to mass-mindedness.
	CW9i:97 *ff* (1936/1937)	Rise of National Socialism attributed to the constellation of an archetype (Wotan).
	CW12:38 *ff* (1944/1952)	Activated archetypes may have uncanny influence on consciousness. Those possessed by archetype identify with archetypal content. If one fails to understand how energies must be consciously lived, archetypal themes are lived concretely.
	CW9i: 82 *ff* (1954)	When archetypal images not made conscious, danger of succumbing to fascinating influence of archetypes. Where predisposition to psychosis exists, archetypes escape from conscious control and become independent, possessing individual.
Evidence for the collective unconscious	CW8:317–21 (1931)	Case of man's vision of solar phallus illustrates universality of mythological/ archetypal motifs.
	CW9i:92 (1936/1937)	Critiques of hypothesis of the collective unconscious. Jung asserts there is substantial evidence "showing the autochthonous revival of mythological motifs" to support his hypothesis.

(*Continued*)

Table 4.1 (Continued)

TOPIC/ KEYWORDS	LOCATION	DESCRIPTOR
Creativity and the collective unconscious/ archetypes	CW6:323 (1921/1923)	Creativity stems from collective unconscious.
	CW8:339 (1931)	Unconscious not merely "conditioned by history, but the very source of the creative impulse."
	CW15:128 *ff* (1931)	Constellation of archetype brings emotional intensity due to transpersonal nature of contents. Linked to experiences, art and creative process.

Table 4.2 Anima/Animus

TOPIC/ KEYWORDS	LOCATION	DESCRIPTOR
Defining anima and animus	CW6:808 *ff* (1921/1923)	Soul-images produced by the unconscious. As persona denotes outer attitude, inner attitude of the unconscious is represented by "definite [personified images] with corresponding qualities." In men, anima personified by the unconscious as a woman; in women, vice versa. When individuals identify with persona, projections of soul-image projected onto suitable hook in world. This object, usually a person of the opposite sex, becomes the subject of intense emotions (love, hate, fear) and always provokes strong emotional reactions. Intense, oscillating feelings usually denote issues in adaptation. A more conscious relationship develops when projections withdrawn.
"Anima and Animus"	CW7:296–340 (1916/1928)	'Typical' traits of masculinity and femininity are described. To achieve individuation, man must disidentify from persona and anima, navigating tension between the two.
"The Syzygy: Anima and Animus"	CW9ii:20–42 (1951)	Children shaped by early experiences of parent of the opposite sex to create specific father and mother imagos. Certain aspects of anima/animus will forever remain unknown. Realisation of the shadow is doorway to integration of anima/animus.

(*Continued*)

Table 4.2 (Continued)

TOPIC/ KEYWORDS	LOCATION	DESCRIPTOR
"Concerning the Archetypes, with Specific Reference to the Anima Concept"	CW9i:111–47 (1954)	Duality of masculine/feminine represented in syzygy symbolism (symbols of connection, especially between opposites) and have their source in one's parental images (experiences). Anima images are prone to projection and are central to comprehending a psychology of masculinity.
"Animus and Anima"	CW13:57-63 (1957)	Parallels to anima/animus in Chinese culture illustrated. In women, animus denotes an inferior Logos while the anima expresses an inferior Eros in men. Anima is a personification of the unconscious in general and a bridge between conscious and unconscious. East sees consciousness as an effect of the anima, whereas West understands the unconscious as a derivative of consciousness.
"The Psychological Aspects of the Kore"	CW9i:306-83 (1951)	The Kore figure, when constellated in man, represents the anima and in women, the Self.
"Woman in Europe"	CW10:236-75 (1927)	Women post World War I, stimulated by the animus, compelled to challenge stereotypes.
Animus as the image of masculinity in women	CW7:336 (1916/1928)	Animus "is the deposit […] of all woman's ancestral experience of man, he is also a creative and procreative being."
	CW17:338 (1931)	Women possess an image of *men* in general, whereas men possess an image of a particular *woman*.
	CW9ii:29 *ff* (1951)	Jung details animus/anima possession. Also Jung's infamous comment "often the man has the feeling" that only seduction, a beating, or rape will break grip of animus possession.
	CW9ii:33	Positive aspects of the animus (i.e., as spirit and psychopomp) further elaborated.
Anima as the image of the feminine in man	CW17:338 *ff* (1931)	Every man carries within an eternal and definite image of woman, an accumulation of all ancestral experiences and impressions of femininity.

(*Continued*)

Table 4.2 (Continued)

TOPIC/ KEYWORDS	LOCATION	DESCRIPTOR
	CW9ii:24 (1951)	There is in man an image not only of the mother but an imprint of other feminine encounters and roles (daughter, sister, beloved, etc.). Every mother and beloved carries this ageless image, which corresponds to the deepest reality in man. Anima has positive and negative aspects.
Manifestations of anima in culture and society	CW9i:516 (1939)	Archetypal nature of anima is explored through suspected case of cryptomnesia. Anima is amplified, and manifestations of image in other texts elaborated.
Function of the anima/animus	CW7:336 (1916/1928)	Facilitates relations with the unconscious.
Anima/animus as bridge	CW13:62 (1957)	Anima as both a personification of the unconscious and bridge to enable ego to relate to the unconscious.
Anima/animus as soul	CW6.803 *ff* (1921/1923)	Anima as soul.
	CW16:522 (1946)	'Soul,' which gathers to ego-consciousness during individuation, takes on a feminine character in men and masculine character in women. Anima desires to reconcile and unite while animus discerns and discriminates.
	CW9i:57 *ff* (1954)	Anima is not the soul in a dogmatic sense, but a natural archetype summing up all statements of the unconscious. Anima represents what is spontaneous in psychic life. It is something that lives and makes us live.
Impact of the anima on a masculine psyche	CW16:521 (1946)	Anima may influence and distort man's understanding. Anima has "a predilection for everything that is unconscious, dark, equivocal, and unrelated in woman [...]."
	CW9i:144 *ff* (1954)	Anima may intensify, exaggerate, falsify, and mythologise all emotional relations. When constellated, can impact man's character.
Impact of the animus on a female psyche	CW16:521 (1946)	Animus in women formed of spontaneous, hasty opinions which exercise a powerful influence. Animus is projected upon "intellectuals" and all kinds of "heroes."

(Continued)

Table 4.2 (Continued)

TOPIC/ KEYWORDS	LOCATION	DESCRIPTOR
Anima and the persona	CW6:803 *ff* (1921/1923)	Character of the anima complementary to that of the persona.
Four stages of the anima	CW16:361 (1946)	Four stages of anima development explored: Eve, Helen of Troy, the Virgin Mary, and Sophia.
Anima/animus projection/ integration	CW7:317 (1916/1928)	In marriage, man's wife has to take on magical role of the mother. Marriages based on this dynamic are "permanently on the brink of explosion from internal tension."
	CW7:336 *ff*	Coming to terms with animus involves learning to critically assess opinions and knee-jerk reactions by investigating their origins, delving more deeply into their background.
	CW7:374	Integration of anima entails transforming it from autonomous complex to a function of relationship between conscious and unconscious. Anima becomes "a psychological function of an intuitive nature […]."
	CW17:338 (1931)	Images of anima/animus are projected onto the person of the beloved, giving rise to intense and opposing emotions.
	CW9ii:30 (1951)	"[W]hen animus and anima meet, the animus draws his sword of power and the anima ejects her poison of illusion and seduction. The outcome need not always be negative, since the two are equally likely to fall in love (a special instance of love at first sight)."
	CW9ii:33	When integrated, anima becomes the Eros of consciousness and animus a Logos. Anima provides relationship and relatedness; animus facilitates reflection, deliberation, and self-knowledge.
	CW9ii:58	One must come to grips with anima/animus "problem" to achieve more holistic understanding of oneself, facilitating higher union of opposites (*coniunctio oppositorum*) between conscious and unconscious.
	CW9i:61 (1954)	Relations with anima a "test of courage," facing psychic facts that have been projected but never conscious.

(Continued)

Table 4.2 (Continued)

TOPIC/ KEYWORDS	LOCATION	DESCRIPTOR
Autonomous nature	CW9ii:40 *ff* (1951)	Anima/animus may behave like "systems split off from the personality, or like part souls."
Anima and stages of life	CW9i:146 *ff* (1954)	After mid-life, permanent loss of the anima may result in "a diminution of vitality, flexibility, and human kindness."
Anima/animus possession	CW7:337 (1916/1928)	Woman possessed by her animus runs risk of losing adapted feminine persona. Same holds true for men who are anima-possessed.
	CW9ii:29 (1951)	Anima-possessed men may be transformed into the "animus of their own anima." With women it is a question of *power*. No logic can shake her when animus-possessed.

Table 4.3   The Self

TOPIC/ KEYWORDS	LOCATION	DESCRIPTOR
Defining the Self	CW6:789 *ff* (1921/1923)	Concept pronouncing the unity of the personality. Self has both conscious and unconscious aspects and finds expression in the figure of the "supraordinate personality," which possesses a distinct numinosity.
	CW11:232 *ff* (1948)	Psychic totality of the individual. Anything perceived as greater totality than oneself may become symbol of Self. Symbols of Self that omit shadow/dark side of psyche are not representative of a totality. Christ figure lacks darkness of spirit so not a symbol of totality.
	CW11:391 *ff*	Self an *a priori* existent. Ego stands to Self as moved to mover.
	CW9i:248 *ff* (1950)	A psychic totality and centre that includes the ego. The character of the Self as a personality in Khidr legend.
"The Self"	CW9ii:43–67 (1951)	Relationship between the Self, ego, and instincts elaborated. Equilibrium between the Self (unconscious) and ego (conscious) is the ultimate goal. Difficulties achieving this balance are presented.

(*Continued*)

Table 4.3 (Continued)

TOPIC/ KEYWORDS	LOCATION	DESCRIPTOR
"Christ, a symbol of the Self"	CW9ii:68–126 (1951)	Christ both a God-image and exemplifies Self, but is incomplete as a symbol as fails to include inferior aspects of the personality. A symbol must unite opposites—good and evil, conscious and unconscious.
"The Symbol of the Self"	CW12:323–31 (1944/1952)	Central symbol—the world clock (a mandala)—in a dream series (of physicist Wolfgang Pauli) is analysed in detail. Psychological process whereby the unconscious circulates around a centre (Self)—which attracts disparate elements—is elucidated.
Individuation and the Self	CW7:266 *ff* (1916/1928) CW11:745 (1952)	Goal of the individuation is becoming one's own [S]elf, i.e., embracing one's innermost uniqueness. Self as image of the goal of life produced unconsciously, irrespective of our awareness. Realisation of wholeness may occur without our consent and knowledge.
Self as God-image	CW7:303 *ff* (1916/1928) CW11:231 *ff* (1948)	Self embraces our whole living organism; is soil from which future life springs. Self and immortality. Self and God-image are indistinguishable concepts. Self-realisation amounts to God's incarnation (233).
Numinosity of the Self	CW18:1567 (1954)	Self as an archetype represents numinous wholeness, expressible only through symbols (e.g., mandala, tree, etc.). Realisation of Self nearly always connected with feelings of timelessness, "eternity," or immortality.
Self as sum total of conscious and unconscious **Coniunctio/union of opposites**	CW5:576 (1912/1952) CW13:226 (1942)	Self is a *coincidentia oppositorum* (a coming together of opposites) and therefore includes light and dark simultaneously. Self and individuation expressed as a relational union: "[…] the self which includes me includes many others also, for the unconscious that is 'conceived in our mind' does not belong to me and is not peculiar to me, but is everywhere. It is the quintessence of the individual and at the same time the collective."
Self in relation to a tension of opposites	CW12:20 *ff* (1944/1952)	Self seeks to capture the indeterminable nature of psychological wholeness (conscious and unconscious).

(Continued)

Table 4.3 (Continued)

TOPIC/ KEYWORDS	LOCATION	DESCRIPTOR
	CW12:247	Self is a union of opposites *par excellence* (22). Self as borderline concept similar to Kant's *Ding an sich*. No limits to the Self, entirely unknowable (psychoid).
	CW16:400 (1946b)	End goal [of individuation] is an idea that can never be attained. Even united personality will still experience tension of opposites.
Self as wholeness/ totality	CW16:474	Self, as "uniting symbol," is both ego and non-ego, subjective and objective, individual and collective.
	CW9i:653 (1950)	Self is androgynous, both masculine and feminine.
	CW9ii:123 (1951)	Realisation of Self leads to suspension between opposites, "and to an approximate state of wholeness that lacks perfection."
	CW18:1672 (1956–1957)	Self as a borderline concept designating the unknown totality of humanity. A myriad of symbols, therefore, can represent the concept.
Symbolic expressions of the Self	CW12:20 *ff* (1944/1952)	Representations of Self may be found across all cultures and religions.
	CW16:378 *ff* (1946b)	Divine child as a symbol of Self, which is supported by analysis of noteworthy case with abundant representations of Self.
	CW16:474	Self appears in dreams and spontaneous fantasies. Finds visual expression in mandalas occurring in dreams, drawings, and paintings. Integration of Self is usually a problem arising in the second half of life.
	CW9i:278 (1951)	Self can be expressed "by roundness, the circle or sphere, or else by the quaternity as another form of wholeness."
	CW9ii:297 (1951)	Synthesis of conscious and unconscious leads to an experience of totality. In alchemy, this is expressed through the symbol of the uroboros.
	CW9ii:351 *ff*	Self revealed in geometrical and arithmetical symbols, gods or godlike beings, princes, priests, historical personalities, dearly loved, successful family members.

(Continued)

Table 4.3 (Continued)

TOPIC/ KEYWORDS	LOCATION	DESCRIPTOR
		Self is a *complexio oppositorum*, symbolised in circle contrasted with the square, the quaternity contrasted with the 3 + 1, good and evil, male and female, old and young, large and small (355). Self may take the form of animals, plants, and inorganic products (356).
	CW14:776 (1955–56)	Alchemical statements on the lapis describe the Self. Other representations point to theme of union of opposites.
	CW10:635 (1958)	Plurality of UFOs as projection of psychic images of wholeness, i.e., God-images, images of Self.
Relationship between the ego and the Self	CW11:961 (1944)	Ego needs Self and vice versa.
	CW16:400 (1946b)	Self referred to as an "objective" ego.
	CW16:474	Union of ego with unconscious (personified as anima) produces a new personality compounded of both. New personality is not a third thing midway between conscious and unconscious, but both.
	CW8:557 (1948)	One-sidedness of conscious life is compensated by the universal human being in us, whose goal is the assimilation of the ego to a wider personality (Self).
	CW9ii:9 (1951)	Ego is subordinate to Self, related to Self as a part to the whole. Self may act upon the ego like an *objective occurrence*, bringing into question individual free will.
	CW9ii:257	Self is comparable to an all-encompassing atmosphere with no definite limits within which ego is contained.
	CW9ii:297	Self constitutes the creation of a wider personality whose centre does not coincide with the ego and, in reality, thwarts ego-tendencies.
	CW8:430 (1954)	Once individuation process vitalised, risk exists of ego identifying with Self, leading to potential inflation.
	CW14:778 (1955–56)	Self reaches out beyond the ego-personality and has a numinous power. Experience of the Self is always defeat of the ego. Ego may defend itself and, when ultimately defeated, can still affirm its existence (e.g., Job's encounter with Yahweh).

(Continued)

Table 4.3 (Continued)

TOPIC/ KEYWORDS	LOCATION	DESCRIPTOR
Integration/ humanisation of the Self	CW11:400 (1954)	Integration entails becoming more conscious of selfish aims, forming more objective picture of our nature. This is an act of self-recollection—a gathering together of the scattered aspects of ourselves, coming to terms with who we are with view of achieving greater consciousness. Self drives us towards this difficult task; it demands a sacrifice by sacrificing itself.
Self as the new centre of the personality	CW12:44 (1944/1952)	Self as new centre of the psyche, and also the circumference, embracing conscious and unconscious.
	CW16:219 *ff* (1946a)	A new centre of the personality superior to the ego.
Dark side of the Self	CW9ii:79 (1951)	In Christ image, other half of the Self appears in the Antichrist (symbolising its darker aspects).
	CW9ii:116 *ff*	The Self is not exclusively 'good.' As a totality, it must include light and dark, a *mysterium coniunctionis*.

THE DYNAMICS OF THE PSYCHE

In this chapter, we introduce a number of Jung's original contributions to our understanding of the dynamics of the psyche and ways of working with the contents of the unconscious: Active Imagination, the Transcendent Function, Individuation, Synchronicity, Dreams, and Transference/Counter-Transference. Dreams and Transference/Counter-Transference are clearly not aspects of psychological theory and therapeutic work that originate with Jung; nevertheless, Jung's contributions to both are significant.

ACTIVE IMAGINATION

One of the 'seeds,' perhaps, that led to Jung's development of a technique to facilitate conscious engagement with images and figures of the unconscious, and that he was later to call Active Imagination, may well have been planted at the time he was working on his doctoral dissertation, "On the Psychology and Pathology of So-Called Occult Phenomena" (CW1:1-150). The focus of the dissertation was Jung's study of his 15-year-old cousin, Hélène Preiswerk, a medium who was able to contact and converse with 'spirits.' Jung attended her séances, observing and recording his cousin's 'performances.' He was struck by her insistence on the 'reality' of the spirits with whom she conversed: "I see them before me, I can touch them. I speak to them about everything I wish as naturally as I'm talking to you (i.e., Jung)" (ibid.:43); and by the way in which she was able to 'let go' and surrender to a trance state. Jung thought it was conceivable that his cousin's 'spirits' might be "new character formations, or attempts of the future personality to break through" (ibid.:136).

DOI: 10.4324/9781315619156-6

Jung also grew up experiencing his mother as having two distinct personalities, No. 1 and No. 2. Mother No. 1 "had a hearty animal warmth, cooked wonderfully, and was most companionable and pleasant. She was very stout, and a ready listener" (1961/63, p. 48). Mother No. 2 was the polar opposite: "unexpectedly powerful: a somber, imposing figure possessed of unassailable authority—and no bones about it" (*ibid.*). This 'second personality' "emerged only now and then, but each time it was unexpected and frightening. She would then speak as if talking to herself, but what she said was aimed at me and usually struck to the core of my being" (*ibid.*, p. 49). Jung, too, from an early age, experienced himself as having the same "archaic nature" (*ibid.*, p. 50):

> The play and counterplay between personalities No. 1 and No. 2, which has run through my whole life, has nothing do with a 'split' or dissociation in the ordinary medical sense. On the contrary, it is played out in every individual. In my life No. 2 has been of prime importance, and I have always tried to make room for anything that wanted to come to me from within. He is a typical figure, but he is perceived only by the very few. Most people's conscious understanding is not sufficient to realize that he is also what they are.
>
> (*ibid.*, p. 45)

In his 'autobiography,' Jung describes how, during his *creative illness* after his break with Freud in 1913, he was flooded with dreams and fantasy images from the unconscious. In order to try to ground himself, he started to practise and develop a way of working with these inner figures; this technique he would call active imagination and utilise in his therapeutic work with patients:

> In order to seize hold of the fantasies, I frequently imagined a steep descent. I even made several attempts to get to the very bottom. The first time I reached, as it were, a depth of about a thousand feet; the next time I found myself at the edge of a cosmic abyss. It was like a voyage to the moon, or a descent into empty space. First came the image of a crater, and I had the feeling that I was in the land of the dead. The atmosphere was that of the other world. Near the steep slope of a rock I caught sight of two figures, an old man with a white beard and a beautiful young girl. I summoned up my courage and approached them as though they were real people, and

listened attentively to what they told me. The old man explained that he was Elijah, and that gave me a shock. But the girl staggered me even more, for she called herself Salome! She was blind. What a strange couple: Salome and Elijah. But Elijah assured me that he and Salome had belonged together from all eternity, which completely astounded me. They had a black serpent living with them which displayed an unmistakable fondness for me. I stuck close to Elijah because he seemed to be the most reasonable of the three, and to have a clear intelligence. Of Salome I was distinctly suspicious. Elijah and I had a long conversation which, however, I did not understand (1961/63, p. 181).

In a subsequent experience, "another figure rose out of the unconscious," (*ibid., p.* 182), whom Jung named Philemon: "It was he who taught me psychic objectivity, the reality of the psyche. [...] He confronted me in an objective manner, and I understood that there is something in me which can say things that I do not know and do not intend, things which may even be directed against me" (*ibid., p.* 183). In order to 'fix' in consciousness images he did not understand, and explore their possible significance from every conceivable perspective, Jung drew and painted, as well as recorded them. When using active imagination therapeutically in his work with patients, he would often suggest they sculpt, draw, paint, carve, and even dance their images in order to bring them closer to consciousness.

The essential thing is to differentiate oneself from these unconscious contents by personifying them, and at the same time to bring them into relationship with consciousness. That is the technique for stripping them of their power. It is not too difficult to personify them, as they always possess a certain degree of autonomy, a separate identity of their own. Their autonomy is a most uncomfortable thing to reconcile oneself to, and yet the very fact that the unconscious presents itself in that way gives us the best means of handling it.

(*ibid.*, p. 187)

Jung was insistent that the images and figures encountered through active imagination be taken very seriously and submitted to a rigorous process of both emotional and intellectual understanding; in other words, the 'work' following an encounter involves translating the essentially mythological imagery of the unconscious into the language of consciousness. As early as 1912, in "The Theory of Psychoanalysis" (a series of lectures originally delivered at Fordham University, New York), Jung emphasises the need for an *active,* purposeful approach to fantasy images. When treated rationally, they will surely be dismissed as irrelevant nonsense and fall back into the unconscious. Jung uses a colourful metaphor to describe the intrinsic value of inner images: "They are sunken treasures which can only be recovered by a diver; in other words the patient, contrary to his wont, must now deliberately turn his attention to his inner life. Where formerly he dreamed, he must now think, consciously and intentionally" (CW4:418).

CW14, *Mysterium Coniunctionus*, is the last book Jung wrote. It took him from 1941 to 1954 to complete and he finished it in his 80th year. It gives us Jung's final thoughts on an interest he pursued from 1929 to the end of his life, namely, the significance of the symbolism of alchemy and the alchemical *opus* for depth psychology, analytical psychology in particular. In CW14, Jung provides a lengthy, detailed description of the technique of active imagination. The excerpt in the box below describes the first stage in the process of active imagination and concerns "the personality's coming to terms with its own background, the shadow" (CW14:707). Jung provides a psychological interpretation of the stages in the alchemical 'procedure' necessary to effect a union of opposites—in this case, between ego and shadow; later in the individuation process, between ego and Self, as the Self presents itself to consciousness first through the mediating figures of anima/animus. It is essential for anyone engaging in the process of active imagination to have some degree of self-knowledge through the integration of personal unconscious content (shadow/complexes) into consciousness. One needs an ego strong enough to maintain its standpoint in the face of autonomous, numinous unconscious content:

> [Active imagination can] take place spontaneously or be artificially induced. In the latter case, you choose a dream, or [...] fantasy-image [...] [or] a bad mood as a starting-point, and then try to find out what sort of fantasy-image [...] expresses this mood. You then fix this image in the mind by concentrating your attention. Usually it will alter, [...] [as] contemplating it animates it. The alterations must

be carefully noted down [...], for they reflect the psychic processes in the unconscious background, which appear in the form of images consisting of conscious memory material. In this way conscious and unconscious are united [...]. A chain of fantasy ideas develops and gradually takes on a dramatic character: the passive process becomes an action. At first it consists of projected figures, [...] observed like scenes in the theatre. In other words, you dream with open eyes. [...] [If you simply] enjoy this interior entertainment and leave it at that [...] there is no real progress but only endless variations on the same theme [...]. [However,] [i]f the observer understands that his own drama is being performed on this inner stage, he cannot remain indifferent to the plot and its dénouement. He will notice [...] that [the actors] all have some purposeful relationship to his conscious situation, that he is being addressed by the unconscious, and that *it* causes these fantasy-images to appear before him. He therefore feels compelled [...] to take part in the play and, instead of just sitting in a theatre, really have it out with his alter ego. For nothing in us ever remains quite uncontradicted, and consciousness can take up no position which will not call up, somewhere in the dark corners of the psyche, a negation or a compensatory effect, approval or resentment. This process of coming to terms with the Other in us is well worth while, because in this way we get to know aspects of our nature which we would not allow anybody else to show us and which we ourselves would never have admitted. It is very important to fix this whole procedure in writing [...], for you then have ocular evidence that will effectively counteract the ever-ready tendency to self-deception. A running commentary is absolutely necessary in dealing with the shadow, [...] [to fix] its actuality [...] [and] to gain a positive insight into the complex nature of one's own personality (CW14:706).

Jung realised, from when he first started to work with his fantasies and let the unconscious 'lead' the process, that he was activating

[t]he same psychic material which is the stuff of psychosis and is found in the insane. This is the fund of unconscious images which fatally confuse the mental patient. But it is also the matrix of a mythopoeic imagination which has vanished from our rational age. Though such imagination is present everywhere, it is both tabooed and dreaded, so that it even appears to be a risky experiment or a questionable adventure to entrust oneself to the uncertain path that leads into the depths

> of the unconscious. It is considered the path of error, of equivocation and misunderstanding.
>
> (1961/63, p. 181)

It is with good reason that Jung did not use active imagination as a therapeutic tool with all his patients, but looked for clear indications that the method suited the individual. However, when active imagination is 'working,' dream material often becomes scarce: the fantasy images "anticipate the dreams," and their "creative form has great advantages over dream-material" (CW18:399) as their immediacy tends to speed up the analytic process. Being able to practise active imagination effectively also enables the patient to become less dependent on the analyst, as analysing one's own dreams is next to impossible, while active imagination is not.

THE TRANSCENDENT FUNCTION

This topic brings us back, once again, to the inescapable problem of opposites! We have, however, been talking about opposites when discussing Active Imagination, as that procedure involves, again, the opposition of conscious and unconscious: the ego actively 'meeting' contents of the unconscious, working to give them form and understanding, and then integrating their content and meaning into consciousness.

In his essay, "The Transcendent Function," Jung speaks of the compensatory and complementary relation of the unconscious to consciousness, and of the intensity which psychic material needs to attain in order to remain above the threshold of consciousness. Contents lacking the necessary 'threshold intensity' fall into or have always belonged to the unconscious which:

> [c]ontains not only all the forgotten material of the individual's own past (personal unconscious), but all the inherited behaviour traces constituting the structure of the mind (collective unconscious) [...] (Also) the unconscious contains all the fantasy combinations which have not yet attained the threshold intensity, but which in the course of time and under suitable conditions will enter the light of consciousness.
>
> (CW8:132)

The psyche is a dynamic system, characterised by opposition and compensation. The functions of consciousness are, for the most part, directed towards adaptation in the outer world; unwelcome intrusions from the unconscious are repressed, and this dynamic establishes the opposition between conscious and unconscious. We can see, then, how the unconscious is often in a *compensatory* relationship to the inevitable one-sidedness of the conscious attitude, and *vice versa*. The development of the personality, however, is achieved through the enhancement or expansion of consciousness. Personality develops through conflict between the one-sided stance of the ego-consciousness and the inexorable imperative of the unconscious, the Self, towards growth and wholeness. As a result, the conscious attitude of the ego is repeatedly challenged by new, often disturbing content from the unconscious which may present in the form of dreams, fantasies, doubts, neurotic behaviour, and external accident. The *tension* inherent in the ensuing conflict needs to be held (that is, suffered) until an alternative attitude and 'way forward' presents itself. Resolution of conflict results from neither a fundamental lessening in value of either of the two poles of the conflict nor the assimilation of one by the other. In other words, ego finds itself suspended—'crucified'—between two opposing positions: the conscious stance to which it is clinging and the demands of the unconscious. This is the condition for an activation of the Transcendent Function. As Jung explains:

> The confrontation of two positions (consciousness and previously unconscious material) generates a tension charged with energy and creates a living, third thing—not a logical still-birth in accordance with the principle *tertium non datur* ('the third not given') but a movement out of the suspension between opposites, a living birth that leads to a new level of being, a new situation.
>
> (*ibid.*:189)

Opposites cannot be resolved purely rationally, but only by "some new thing arising between them which, although different from both, yet has the power to take up their energies in equal measure as an expression of both and of neither. Such an expression cannot be contrived by reason, it can only be created through living" (CW6:169) or by the creation of a 'living symbol,' a new possibility. Because the problem cannot be resolved by the ego, only by the dynamic process of the unconscious (i.e., the 'transcendent function'), the 'new,' or 'third thing' that emerges is "of an irrational nature, which the conscious mind neither expects nor understands. It presents itself in a form that is neither a straight 'yes' nor a straight 'no,' [...]. For the conscious mind knows nothing beyond the opposites and, as a result, has no knowledge of the thing that unites them" (CW8:285). The 'third thing,' or "new configuration is a nascent whole; it is on the way to wholeness, at least in so far as it excels in 'wholeness' the conscious mind when torn by opposites and surpasses it in completeness. For this reason all uniting symbols have a redemptive significance" (*ibid*.). Whether the 'third thing' is a new attitude or understanding, or a 'creative formulation' such as a work of art or a significant motif or figure within a work of art, it is most certainly a symbol, that "best possible expression for a complex fact not yet clearly apprehended by consciousness" (CW6:148). This establishes the transcendent function as both a bridging and a transformative function *par excellence* (Table 5.2).

Before we take a moment to discuss Jung's thinking about the symbol, we need to ask the question: How does all this happen? What makes the 'third thing' appear? If the ego can hold the opposites in parity (as equals), without being pulled to favour one at the expense of the other, the following occurs:

> [...] when there is full parity of the opposites, attested by the ego's absolute participation in both, this necessarily leads to a suspension of the will, for the will can no longer operate when every motive has an equally strong counter-motive. Since life cannot tolerate a standstill, a damming up of vital energy results, and this would lead to an insupportable condition did not the tension of opposites produce a new, uniting function that transcends them. This function arises quite naturally from the regression of libido (psychic energy) caused by the blockage. All progress having been rendered temporarily impossible by the total division of the will, the libido streams backwards, as it were, to its source. In other words, the neutralization and inactivity of consciousness bring about an activity of the unconscious, where all the differentiated functions have their common, archaic root, and where all contents exist in a state of promiscuity [...]. From the activity of the unconscious there now emerges a new content, constellated by thesis and antithesis in equal measure and standing in a compensatory relation to both. It thus forms the middle ground on which the opposites can be united. If, for instance, we conceive the opposition to be sensuality versus spirituality, then the mediatory content born out of the unconscious provides a welcome means of expression for the spiritual thesis, because of its rich spiritual associations, and also for the sensual antithesis, because of its sensuous imagery.
>
> (CW6:824-25)

THE SYMBOL

- Jung is clear to distinguish a sign (pointing to something specific) from a symbol: "A symbol always supposes that the chosen expression is the best possible description or formulation of a relatively unknown fact, which is none the less known to exist or is postulated as existing" (CW6:814). (Given developments in the field of Semiotics since his death, Jung would no doubt be revisiting his terms, were he alive today.)
- "Since every scientific theory contains an hypothesis, and is therefore an anticipatory description of something still essentially unknown, it is a symbol. [...] every psychological expression is a symbol if we assume that it states or signifies something more and other than itself which eludes our present knowledge" (*ibid.*:817).
- "Whether a thing is a symbol or not depends chiefly on the attitude of the observing consciousness; for instance, on whether it regards a given fact not merely as such but also as an expression of something unknown" (*ibid.*:818).
- "The attitude that takes a given phenomenon as symbolic may be called, for short, the *symbolic attitude*. [...] [I]t is the outcome of a definite view of the world which *assigns meaning* to events, whether great or small, and attaches to this meaning a greater value than to bare facts" (*ibid.*:819).
- "A symbol really lives only when it is the best and highest expression for something divined but not yet known to the observer" (*ibid.*).
- "The living symbol formulates an essential unconscious factor, [...]. (To have a social or cultural effect) it must embrace what is common to a large group [...]. This can never be what is most differentiated, the highest attainable [...]. The common factor must be something that is still so primitive that its ubiquity cannot be doubted. Only when the symbol embraces that and expresses it in the highest possible form is it of general efficacy. Here lies the potency of the living, social symbol and its redeeming power" (*ibid.*:820).
- "Only the passionate yearning of a highly developed mind, for which the traditional symbol is no longer the unified expression of the rational and the irrational, of the highest and the lowest, can create a new symbol. But precisely because the new symbol is born of man's highest spiritual aspirations and must at the same time spring from the deepest roots of his being, it cannot

be a one-sided product of the most highly differentiated mental functions but must derive equally from the lowest and most primitive levels of the psyche" (*ibid.*:823-24).

- "The raw material shaped by thesis and antithesis, and in the shaping of which the opposites are united, is the living symbol." Jung provides examples of the "process of symbol-formation" in the "conflicts experienced by the founders of religion during their initiation period, e.g., the struggle between Jesus and Satan, [...] or the regeneration of Faust through the pact with the devil" (*ibid.*:828-29).

From what we have so far learnt about the transcendent function and symbols, and as we look ahead to our discussion of the process of individuation, the goal of which is wholeness, we can begin to see how integral symbols and the psyche's capacity to create symbols are to the development of each one of us. Symbols of wholeness are ubiquitous. This fact alone gives credence to Jung's hypothesis of an innate pattern and dynamic of development towards wholeness in the human psyche simply because these same symbols are generated by and emerge from the depths of the human psyche, the collective unconscious.

Jung raises a question in the Prefatory Note to his essay, "The Transcendent Function": How does one come to terms in practice with the unconscious? at the same time reminding his reader that "the unconscious is not this thing or that; it is the Unknown as it immediately affects us" (CW8, pp. 67–68). The answer, of course, is through the Transcendent Function, often with the aid of Active Imagination to activate the "production of those contents of the unconscious which lie, as it were, immediately below the threshold of consciousness and, when intensified, are the most likely to irrupt spontaneously into the conscious mind" (*ibid.*). The Transcendent Function itself, Jung writes,

does not proceed without aim and purpose, but leads to the revelation of the essential man. It is in the first place a purely natural process, which may in some cases pursue its course without the knowledge or assistance of the individual, and can sometimes forcibly accomplish itself in the face of opposition (i.e., from ego-consciousness). The meaning and purpose of the process is the realization, in all its aspects, of the personality originally hidden away in the embryonic germ-plasm; the production and unfolding of the original, potential wholeness. The symbols used by the unconscious to this end are the same as those which mankind has always used to express wholeness, completeness, and perfection: symbols, as a rule, of the quaternity and the circle. For these reasons I have termed this the *individuation process.*

(CW7:186)

Jung's reference to the Transcendent Function's being able to "pursue its course without the knowledge or assistance of the individual" points to this complex function as 'the way of the psyche' at all levels, the dynamic that propels content from the deeper levels of the unconscious to the point at which it is accessible by consciousness. The Transcendent Function describes the essential dynamism that is indivisible from the process and pattern of Individuation and, for that matter, life itself.

INDIVIDUATION

We have seen how the Transcendent Function transforms unconscious content through the generation of a unifying symbol; it enhances consciousness by moving the ego out of a position of conflict and 'stuckness,' and into one of possibility. It is a natural dynamic of the psychic system, innate, a given, and, from the beginning to the end of the individual life span, it enables the enhancement of consciousness and the psyche's movement towards wholeness. The Transcendent Function, then, appears to be the mover and shaker behind and in partnership with the process of Individuation, that imperative in the unconscious psyche of every individual to evolve towards wholeness and the development and fulfilment of the personality. For, as Jung clarifies:

Conscious and unconscious do not make a whole when one of them is suppressed and injured by the other. If they must contend, let it at least be a fair fight with equal rights on both sides. Both are aspects of life. Consciousness should defend its reason and protect itself, and the chaotic life of the unconscious should be given the chance of having its way too—as much of it as we can stand. This means open conflict and open collaboration at once. That, evidently, is the way human life should be. It is the old game of hammer and anvil: between them the patient iron is forged into an indestructible whole, an 'individual.'

(CW9i:522)

"The unconscious," Jung writes, "has a Janus-face: on one side its contents point back to a preconscious, prehistoric world of instinct, while on the other side it potentially anticipates the future—precisely because of the instinctive readiness for action of the factors that determine man's fate" (*ibid.*:498). The process of individuation, perhaps not surprisingly, demands of the ego that it, too, be Janus-faced—that it look both towards the outer and the inner world, the past and the future. This is because the goal of the process of individuation appears to be the achievement of personality—in other words, the achievement of *individuality*. To 'step into one's shoes' or 'own' one's individuality has nothing to do with individualism. Quite the opposite. One face of individuality has to do with 'unhooking' from collective expectations and iden-tifications. The other is focused on the realisation and integration of one's 'individuality,' which means "embracing (one's) innermost, last, and incomparable uniqueness, it also implies becoming one's own self. We could therefore translate individuation as 'coming to selfhood' or 'self-realization'" (CW7:266):

> The aim of individuation is nothing less than to divest the self of the false wrappings of the persona on the one hand, and of the suggestive power of primordial images (archetypes) on the other.
>
> (CW9i:269)

Step 1: Divesting oneself of the "false wrappings of the persona." This means challenging one's assumptions and values—are they mine? are they my parents'? have they simply been uncritically absorbed?— and dissolving identifications with outer, collective mores; question-ing the roles one has, perhaps, unthinkingly assumed because of familial and societal expectations, etc. Saying 'No'! "Individuation is a process by which a man (or woman) becomes the definite, unique being he (or she) in fact is. In so doing he (or she) does not become 'selfish' in the ordinary sense of the word, but is merely fulfilling the peculiarity of his (or her) nature, and this [...] is vastly different from egotism or individualism" (*ibid.*:267). Facing and integrating shadow content goes hand-in-hand with challenging the persona, the 'face' we present to the world. Rejected values and traits, unful-filled desire, unlived potential, rage, jealousy, and a host of 'ego-alien' factors hide in the shadow. But, as the magician, Prospero, at the end of Shakespeare's *The Tempest*, recognises the purportedly 'monstrous' Caliban as part of himself—"This thing of darkness I acknowledge mine" (1984 [originally written 1610—1611])—so, too, recognition and integration of shadow material are essential to the process of individuation (whether Shakespeare adopts a colonial or anti-colonial mindset is up for debate).

Step 2 involves confrontation with the deeper collective unconscious and the archetypal images. The danger is that one may become overwhelmed, fascinated and even possessed by the numinosity of archetypal images to the point of assuming or identifying with the power of the god-like figure that haunts one's dreams. Preserving the autonomy of the ego in the face of powerful, affective intrusions from the unconscious is essential, or the ego once again becomes part of a 'collective' and individuality is lost. Ego-consciousness needs to differentiate itself from the suggestive power of archetypal images while integrating as much as possible of their content into consciousness, as it needs to maintain its individuality in the face of the inner and the outer collective.

We have seen, in the first two sections of this chapter, that individuation may be enhanced or accelerated by the technique of active imagination in engaging the transcendent function. We have also seen that the process of analysis can support and promote the individuation process. But, if the individuation process, like the transcendent function, is an innate imperative, surely it operates without the need for active imagination and therapy? Is one's contented and wise old grandmother, knitting and nodding in a chair by the open fire, with a wealth of life experience, as individuated as the person who has had years of analysis—or not? A good question. Jung writes: "There are natural transformation processes which simply happen to us, whether we like it or not, and whether we know it or not. These processes develop considerable psychic effects, which would be sufficient in themselves to make any thoughtful person ask himself what really happened to him" (CW9i:234). "In so far as (individuation) runs its course unconsciously as it has from time immemorial, it means no more than the acorn becomes an oak, the calf a cow, and the child an adult" (CW11:460). "Natural transformation processes announce themselves mainly in dreams" (CW9i:234), for example, in imagery which symbolises transformation and rebirth, or in the form of an authoritative inner voice. "This 'other being' is the other person in ourselves—that larger and greater personality maturing within us, whom we have already met as the inner friend of the soul" (*ibid.*:235). Dream images of a child also herald a transformation, as "the 'child' paves the way for a future change of personality. In the individuation process, it anticipates the figure that comes from the synthesis of conscious and unconscious elements in the personality. It is therefore a symbol which unites the opposites; a mediator, bringer of healing, that is, one who makes whole" (*ibid.*:278).

While the process of individuation may run its course naturally, *un*consciously, "if the individuation process is made conscious, consciousness must confront the unconscious and a balance between the opposites must be found. As this is not possible through logic, one is dependent on *symbols* which make the irrational union of opposites possible. They are produced spontaneously by the unconscious and are amplified by the conscious mind. The central symbols of this process describe the [S]elf, which is man's totality, consisting on the one hand of that which is conscious to him, and on the other hand of the contents of the unconscious. The [S]elf is the [...] whole man, whose symbols are the divine child and its synonyms" (CW11:755). Jung continues:

> The difference between the 'natural' individuation process, [...] and the one which is consciously realized, is tremendous. In the first case consciousness nowhere intervenes; the end remains as dark as the beginning. In the second case so much darkness comes to light that the personality is permeated with light, and consciousness necessarily gains in scope and insight. The encounter between conscious and unconscious has to ensure that the light which shines in the darkness is not only comprehended by the darkness, but comprehends it.
>
> (*ibid.*:756)

While individuation stresses the development of the psychological *individual,* as distinct from one identified with collective, 'mass' psychology, this does not mean that to individuate is to condemn oneself to social alienation. Anything that thwarts the natural unfolding of the individuation process risks stunting the development of the individual, and this also means inhibiting the individual's participation in society. "As an individual is not just a single, separate being, but by his very existence presupposes a collective relationship, it follows that the process of individuation must lead to more intense and broader collective relationships and not to isolation" (CW6:758). Consequently, "[i]ndividuation does not shut one out from the world, but gathers the world to oneself" (CW8:432).

However, the hero of myth whose journey takes him to the heights and to the depths in search of greater knowledge is often shunned on his return to his community. He has changed. He is different. Nobody recognises him. We are reminded of Odysseus who returns to his kingdom, Ithaca, in the guise of a beggar, after a 20-year journey of self-discovery that took him to the depths of Hades; the only person who does recognise him is his old nurse from childhood, and she knows he is Odysseus by the scar on his thigh from a wound he suffered during his youth. There is a price to pay for individuation. "Individuation cuts one off from personal conformity and hence from collectivity. [...] He (the returning individuated hero) must offer a ransom in place of himself, that is, he must bring forth values which are an equivalent substitute for his absence in the collective personal sphere" (CW18:1095):

> Individuation remains a pose so long as no positive values are created. Whoever is not creative enough must re-establish collective conformity with a group of his own choice, otherwise he remains an empty waster and windbag. Whoever creates *unacknowledged* values belongs to the contemned, and he has himself to blame for this, because society has a right to expect *realizable* values. For the existing society is always of absolute importance as the point of transition through which all world development passes, and it demands the highest collaborative achievement from every individual.
>
> (*ibid.*:1098)

So the hero returns home with a boon—the *greater* knowledge acquired through the process of self-knowledge. Like Nietzsche's Zarathustra, one must come down from the mountain-top and teach in the market-place, for individuation is both "an internal, subjective process of integration, and [...] an indispensable process of objective relationship" (CW16:448) with one's community.

SYNCHRONICITY

Jung refers, throughout his writings, to what he considers to be a general lack of awareness of the *fact* of unconscious processes. We might imagine a boundary or membrane between conscious and the unconscious that is more or less permeable, depending on the psychic constitution of the individual. Certainly, Jung's own 'membrane' appears to have been extremely permeable, beginning with his early experiences of his mother's, and his own, No. 1 and No. 2 personalities; the séances led by his mediumistic cousin,

Hélène Preiswerk; a number of inexplicable paranormal occurrences throughout his life (1961/63); and his life-long exploration of the border country between conscious and unconscious, psychic and non-psychic, and the relationship of psyche to soma, spirit to matter, and manifest to transcendent. As the scientific principle of causality (cause and effect) failed him in his research into these matters, Jung sought "another kind of principle altogether" to explain the *acausal* relationship of factors that were as much a part of the same psychophysiological system, and certainly part of the same world, as those that could be explained by causality. This led him to develop his Theory of Synchronicity:

> My researches into the psychology of unconscious processes long ago compelled me to look around for another principle of explanation, since the causality principle seemed to me insufficient to explain certain remarkable manifestations of the unconscious. I found that there are psychic parallelisms which simply cannot be related to each other causally, but must be connected by another kind of principle altogether. This connection seemed to lie essentially in the relative simultaneity of the events, hence the term 'synchronistic.' (CW15:81). (Originally delivered as the principal address at the Memorial service for sinologist Richard Wilhelm, March 1930.)

Jung's intuition of an underlying unity to all things had previously led to his archetypal hypothesis of the Self. With the theory of synchronicity, Murray Stein points out, Jung extended the "theory of the [S]elf into cosmology, (as) synchronicity speaks of the profound hidden order and unity among all that exists" (1998, p. 200), an idea expressed in the term *unus mundus* (unitary world), which Jung adopted from the Medieval alchemists.

Jung first used the term 'synchronistic' in the passage quoted above in 1930, and the notion of a unitary reality underlying all things is mentioned throughout his earlier work, yet he did not publish anything comprehensive on his theory of synchronicity until 1952 (*Synchronicity: An Acausal Connecting Principle,* CW8, although a short lecture, "On Synchronicity" had been published the previous year). Two years later, *On the Nature of the Psyche,* originally published in 1947, was revised and augmented with a supplement that included Jung's recent thinking on the theory of synchronicity and linked it to his archetypal hypothesis. In early 1955, when he revised Chapter 2 of *Synchronicity* for inclusion in the *Collected Works,* Jung wrote to Michael Fordham explaining the reason for publishing his work on synchronicity as his growing concern about science's "blind and dangerous belief in the security of the scientific Trinity (time, space, causality)" (Jung 1953/75, p. 216):

> Funny how few people can draw the inevitable conclusion from causality being of statistical nature, that it must suffer exceptions. You can arbitrarily dismiss them as indispensable parts of the real world, if you like averages better than random facts. The latter are facts none the less and cannot be treated as non-existent. Moreover, since the real man is always an individual and unique event and as such merely "random," you have to label the whole of mankind in its essentials as "valueless." But on the other hand, only the individual carries life and consciousness of life, which seems to me rather a significant fact not to be lightly dismissed at least not by the physician.
>
> (*ibid.*)

Jung's work on synchronicity was interdisciplinary; he worked as empirically and scientifically as possible, and consequently valued his relationship with Albert Einstein and a number of other physicists; he also worked closely with quantum physicist Wolfgang Pauli. Jung's collaboration and correspondence with eminent contemporary physicists enabled him to recognise parallels between "the deepest patterns of the psyche (archetypal images) and the processes and patterns evident in the physical world and studied by physicists" (Stein 1998, p. 209), who were discovering "events and processes for which there are no causal explanations, only statistical probabilities" (*ibid.*, p. 205). Jung writes:

> Although I have been led by purely psychological considerations to doubt the exclusively psychic nature of the archetypes, psychology sees itself obliged to revise its 'only psychic' assumptions in the light of the physical findings too. [...] the relative or partial identity of psyche and physical continuum is of the greatest importance theoretically, because it brings with it a tremendous simplification by bridging over the seeming incommensurability between the physical world and the psychic, not of course in any concrete way, but from the physical side by means of mathematical equations, and from the psychological side by means of empirically derived postulates—archetypes—whose content, if any, cannot be represented to the mind.
>
> (CW8:440)

Grounds that support the hypothesis of a 'non-psychic' (psychoid) aspect of the archetype, Jung argues, are "supplied by the phenomena of synchronicity, which are associated with the activity of unconscious operators and have hitherto been regarded, or repudiated, as 'telepathy,' etc." (*ibid.*). The ESP (extra-sensory perception) experiments of J.B. Rhines of Duke University, Florida, which Jung followed with interest, also "provided a statistical basis for evaluating the phenomenon of synchronicity, and at the same time have pointed out the important part played by the psychic factor" (CW8:863).

So what *is* it, this theory of synchronicity?

Here is Jung:

The problem of synchronicity has puzzled me for a long time, ever since the middle twenties (1920s), when I was investigating the phenomena of the collective unconscious and kept on coming across connections which I simply could not explain as chance groupings or 'runs.' What I found were 'coincidences' which were connected so meaningfully that their 'chance' concurrence would represent a degree of improbability that would have to be expressed by an astronomical figure (CW8:843).

My example concerns a young woman patient who, in spite of efforts made on both sides, proved to be psychologically inaccessible. The difficulty lay in the fact that she always knew better about everything. Her excellent education had provided her with a weapon ideally suited to this purpose, namely a highly polished Cartesian rationalism with an impeccably 'geometrical' idea of reality. After several fruitless attempts to sweeten her rationalism with a somewhat more human understanding, I had to confine myself to the hope that something unexpected and irrational would turn up, something that would burst the intellectual retort into which she had sealed herself. Well, I was sitting opposite her one day, with my back to the window, listening to her flow of rhetoric. She had had an impressive dream the night before, in which someone had given her a golden scarab—a costly piece of jewellery. While she was still telling me this dream, I heard something behind me gently tapping on the window. I turned round and saw that it was a fairly large flying insect that was knocking against the window-pane from outside in the obvious effort to get into the dark room. This seemed to me very strange. I opened the window immediately and caught the insect in the air as it flew in. It was a scarabaeid beetle, or common rose-chafer, whose gold-green colour most nearly resembles that of a golden scarab. I handed the beetle to my patient with the words, "Here is your scarab." This experience punctured the desired hole in her rationalism and broke the ice of her intellectual resistance. The treatment could now be continued with satisfactory results (CW8:982).

Jung writes that the incident of the scarab is just one amongst innumerable examples of meaningful coincidence recorded by many others. These examples also include anything attributed to clairvoyance, telepathy, etc., "from Swedenborg's well-attested vision of the great fire in Stockholm to the recent report by Air Marshal Sir Victor Goddard about the dream of an unknown officer, which predicted the subsequent accident to Goddard's plane" (*ibid.*:983), all phenomena that Jung groups under three categories (see following box):

Jung's Three Categories of Synchronistic Occurrences:

1 The coincidence of a psychic state in the observer with a simultaneous, objective, external event that corresponds to the psychic state or content (e.g., the scarab), where there is no evidence of a causal connection between the psychic state and the external event, and where, considering the psychic relativity of space and time, such a connection is not even conceivable.

2 The coincidence of a psychic state with a corresponding (more of less simultaneous) external event taking place outside the observer's field of perception, i.e., at a distance, and only verifiable afterwards (e.g., the Stockholm fire).

3 The coincidence of a psychic state with a corresponding, not yet existent future event that is distant in time and can likewise only be verified afterwards (CW8:984).

A personal example:

I was in my early thirties, living in Canada; all my family lived in England. One night I dreamt of a great aunt on my father's side of the family, Aunt Beat. I was in her tiny cottage in the village near which I grew up. In the dream, I was very conscious of the familiar smells, textures of her very Victorian tendency to layer cloth on cloth on her dining table, and the dimness of the light through the small windows set deep into the thick, cob walls. Aunt Beat was not there. I knew she had died. In the morning, I received a call from my mother. The first thing I said to her was, "I know, Aunt Beat has died." "Yes,"

> my mother said, "she died this morning." My mother did not ask me how I knew—she had herself experienced many synchronistic occurrences and had also, on occasion, found herself in our 16th-century farmhouse kitchen as it was when occupied by its inhabitants of the 1500s. It is conceivable that the dream occurred at the time Aunt Beat died, given the time difference between Toronto and England; this I shall never know but I do know that she died very close to the time I found myself in her cottage (Ann Yeoman).

Jung's definition of synchronicity in terms of the type of experiences cited above is of "the simultaneous occurrence of a certain psychic state with one or more external events which appear as meaningful parallels to the momentary subjective state" (CW8:850). He defines *simultaneous* as "the falling together in time" of events (psychic and physical), and argues that this means "it (an occurrence of synchronicity) is a modality without a cause, an 'acausal orderedness'" (*ibid.*:965). Jung then sees the necessity of a wider definition of synchronicity to include the archetypal background of synchronistic events in general, rather than the more narrow appreciation of a *particular* synchronistic occurrence. He talks of a *general acausal orderedness* (*ibid.*), and writes:

> How could an event remote in space and time produce a corresponding psychic image when the transmission of energy necessary for this is not even thinkable? However incomprehensible it may appear, we are finally compelled to assume that there is in the unconscious something like an *a priori* knowledge or an 'immediacy' of events which lacks any causal basis.
>
> (*ibid.*:856)

So we know what we don't know we know... deep in the unconscious. Murray Stein writes: "It is this notion that takes Jung into the furthest reaches of his speculations about the unity of psyche and world. If we know things that are beyond our conscious possibility of knowing, there is also an unknown knower in us, an aspect of the psyche that transcends the categories of time and space and is simultaneously present here and there, now and then. This would be the [S]elf" (1998, p. 212).

Towards the end of his life, Jung looked to the psychological meaning of numbers to answer some of the questions raised by the 'fact' of synchronistic occurrences. We have seen how we can use numbers to symbolise the dynamic of the transcendent function, a movement from 1, a state of non-conscious being; to 2, a state of conscious being and therefore conflict, a tension of opposites (conscious/unconscious; thesis/antithesis); to 3, the new, unanticipated 'third thing' that arises out of the unconscious and transcends the opposition of stage 2; to 4, which restores homeostasis, balance, and provides a synthesis of the previous stages. Then, the whole process begins again with the '4' becoming the '1' of a new movement and development of psyche. By extension, this sequence, repeated time and time again, describes the process of individuation, a cumulative product of the repetitive action of the transcendent function, the natural activity of the psyche—simply, the way it 'works.' We turn now to Marie-Louise von Franz, who continued the work on the significance of numbers which Jung had started, as she explains that our 'use' of numbers to describe psychic dynamics needs to be *qualitative* rather than *quantitative* (i.e., the usual way in which we are taught to think of numbers). Von Franz explains that if we look at numbers as *qualitative*,

> as for instance, the Chinese use them, then the 1, 2, 3, 4 are not different quantities but [...] time sequences of the same thing [...], (as a series or continuum). The continuum is the continuation of the number one through the whole series, different aspects of the same number, always the same, [...]. I am describing a different idea of the continuum from the one found in books of mathematics. This [...] view of the continuum we know already from the famous alchemical saying of Maria Prophetissa, which runs: 'One becomes two, two becomes three, and out of the third comes the one as the fourth.' You see she counts up to three and then says, but those are really all the one—she reconceives the oneness of the three and then puts them together as four. Our minds run progressively, for when we normally count, 1, 2, 3, 4, 5, we make a chain, while when we count qualitatively [...] the four is really the one continuum in the three, so I go backwards: four is the oneness of three, and I add that oneness to the three and make four (von Franz 1980, pp. 90-91).

Hmmmm. How might this way of understanding the meaning of numbers relate to Jung's theory of synchronicity? (It seems that the closest we get to it in the Western Christian tradition is in the idea of the Trinity as 'Three in One and One in Three'). In the previous section on The Transcendent Function, we quoted Jung as saying that when psychic energy is blocked, it regresses; the blocked libido "streams backwards, as it were, to its source [...] (and causes) an activity of the unconscious [...] where all contents exist in a state of promiscuity" (CW6:824). Jung also held that "the deepest layers of the unconscious [...] are relatively timeless, i.e., outside time and space" (von Franz 1980, p.95). So we might deduce from all of this that in the 'promiscuous' continuum of the psychoid substratum of the collective unconscious, outside of the strictures of time and space (and the principle of causality) as it is, content is liable to emerge in the individual and/or collective psyche when the libido is blocked, or desperately one-sided in its focus, when there is a stalemate between opposing forces, or when the conscious attitude purposefully and openly turns towards the unconscious. And this content will be experienced as chance, coincidence or anomaly by some, and as meaningful and potentially transformative synchronicity by others.

And then we discover that number in the form of proportion and pattern describes and symbolises the way in which life forms, both organic and inorganic, are structured, come into being, and evidence the 'promiscuous' creativity of the psychoid unconscious:

It is said that the Buddha once gave a sermon without saying a word; he merely held up a flower to his listeners. This was the famous "Flower Sermon," a sermon in the language of patterns, the silent language of flowers. What does the pattern of a flower speak about?

If we look closely at a flower, and likewise at other natural and man-made creations, we find a unity and an order common to all of them. This order can be seen in certain proportions which appear again and again, and also in the similarly dynamic way all things grow or are made—by a union of complementary opposites.

The discipline inherent in the proportions and patterns of natural phenomena, and manifest in the most ageless and harmonious works of man, are evidence of the relatedness of all things. It is through the limits of discipline that we can glimpse and take part in the harmony of the cosmos—both in the physical world and in our way of life. Perhaps the message of the Flower Sermon had to do with how the living patterns of the flower mirror truths relevant to all forms of life (Doczi 2005, p. 1).

So number points and gives symbolic expression to the archetype of the Self, the creative, ordering principle of the psyche. What about the conscious psyche, and the elemental human need to find meaning in life, a need that is inseparable from psychic, subjective experience? Jung proposes that to the paradigm of time, space, and causality which has for so long described 'reality' be added synchronicity, to include the irrational, the emotional, and meaningful. Human consciousness has the capacity to perceive the ordering principle at work in the cosmos, and order, relatedness, and connectedness confer a sense of meaning. In this way, Jung is promoting a paradigm shift, a radical transformation in the way in which we see ourselves, and ourselves in relation to others and to the world, by proposing 'acausal orderedness,' synchronicity, as an underlying principle in the laws that structure all of life on earth and in the cosmos. This demands a re-evaluation of history, the conflicts of the past and the present, the crises that demand global action, and our aspirations, as a species, for the future. No easy task but a necessary one, nonetheless.

The final word, from Jung: "Synchronicity is no more baffling or mysterious than the discontinuities of physics. It is only the ingrained belief in the sovereign power of causality that creates intellectual difficulties and makes it appear unthinkable that causeless events exist or could ever occur. But if they do, then we must regard them as *creative acts,* as the continuous creation of a pattern that exists from all eternity, repeats itself sporadically, and is not derivable from any known antecedents" without, of course, "thinking of every event whose cause is unknown as 'causeless.'" (CW8:967).

DREAMS

Neither Freud nor Jung was the first to value dreams and consider the interpretation of dreams important to the psychological health of the dreamer! The earliest reference to dream interpretation is found in the Sumerian *Epic of Gilgamesh*, dating from the 4th millennium B.C.E., and first translated from the cuneiform (wedge-shaped) script of the stone tablets on which it was inscribed in 1872. In the epic, Gilgamesh, the tyrannical ruler of Uruk (Biblical Erech), dreams a star falls to the ground at his feet. The star is too heavy for him to lift. His mother interprets the star as, we would now say, a symbol of the Self, and the dream both as compensating for Gilgamesh's inflated conscious attitude and as a sign of his destiny. The result? The hero's journey and, after many 'tests,' the transformation of Gilgamesh! (Kluger 1991). Humankind has been fascinated by dreams and dreaming for thousands of years but Freud and Jung were able to introduce the importance of the dream as the *via regia* (royal road) to the unconscious, and bring it into the consulting room. Jung writes:

> Apart from the efforts that have been made for centuries to extract a prophetic meaning from dreams, Freud's discoveries are the first successful attempt in practice to find their real significance. His work merits the term 'scientific' because he has evolved a technique which not only he but many other investigators assert achieves its object, namely the understanding of the meaning of the dream.
>
> (CW8:447)

However,

> I was never able to agree with Freud that the dream is a 'façade' behind which its meaning lies hidden—a meaning already known but maliciously, so to speak, withheld from consciousness. To me dreams are a part of nature, which harbors no intention to deceive, but expresses something as best it can, just as a plant grows or an animal seeks its food as best it can. These forms of life, too, have no wish to deceive our eyes, but we may deceive ourselves because our eyes are shortsighted. [...] Long before I met Freud I regarded the unconscious, and dreams, which are its direct exponents, as natural processes to which no arbitrariness can be attributed, and above all no legerdemain (trickery). I knew no reasons for the assumption that the tricks of consciousness can be extended to the natural processes of the unconscious. On the contrary, daily experience taught me what intense resistance the unconscious opposes to the tendencies of the conscious mind.
>
> (1961/63, pp. 161-62)

So Jung disagreed with Freud on the purpose and meaning of the dream. For Jung, the dream works in a compensatory relation to consciousness, and plays a role in rectifying the one-sidedness of the ego attitude to restore the psyche to a state of homeostasis. "If we want to interpret a dream correctly, we need a thorough knowledge of the conscious situation at that moment, because the dream contains its unconscious complement, that is, the material which the conscious situation has constellated in the unconscious" (CW8:477).

In other words, "[t]he dream rectifies the (conscious) situation. It contributes the material that was lacking and thereby improves the patient's attitude. That is the reason we need dream-analysis in our therapy" (*ibid.*:482).

An Aside—Two Thoughts

- How important, then, to record the *context* (what is going on in your life) when you record your dream; the dream is the psyche's symbolic 'response' to the conscious situation.
- Jung's statement, "If we want to interpret a dream correctly," might suggest there is a right and wrong way to interpret a dream, and that the dream has *one* unequivocal meaning. But we have taken Jung's words out of the context of his essay, the very 'sin' he warns against when approaching the dream! And this is often the reason why Jung's theory is misunderstood, misquoted, and misused: we dip into *The Collected Works* and pick out a juicy morsel, thinking that is Jung's last word on the subject, only to find it means something quite different once returned to its context (not always! but most often!).

The compensatory role of dreams shows us the transcendent function at work in the psyche, both in the dream itself, and as crystallised in the unifying symbol the dream presents to the ego. As Jung writes: "Dreams are the direct expression of unconscious psychic activity" (CW7:295). The very *fact* of a dream suggests as much. The energy essential to the creation of the dream is generated by the tension between the conscious situation and what that situation constellates in the unconscious. As the 'third thing' that arises from the tension, the dream itself presents as a unifying symbol (of the conscious situation and what it constellates in the unconscious). The symbolic value of the imagery *in* the dream constitutes another product of psychic activity, as it serves to transcend the conflict inherent in the original conscious situation. Below is an example of the symbol-creating transcendent function of the unconscious psyche, provided by Anthony Stevens:

An introverted man, somewhat intimidated by his business colleagues and his formidable wife, was very apprehensive about having to address a difficult shareholders' meeting. Objectively, he need not have worried because he was extremely bright and industrious, a man of rare integrity with a strong flair for business. But although he was conscious of his good qualities, this awareness did little to calm his fears.

During the night before the dreaded meeting, he dreamed that he was entering the hall in which he was due to make his speech. A woman approached him, whom he did not recognize, yet who struck him as attractively familiar. She pressed a ring into his hand and, closing his fingers over it, said conspiratorially, "Hold on to it, and don't lose it." He passed on into the hall, aware that his apprehension had gone.

Before he left home the next morning, he telephoned his analyst to report the dream. It seemed the anima had come to his assistance and wished to lend him the support that his wife was incapable of giving. The ring was a magic gift, a symbol of union, a talisman with protective power. The analyst suggested that when the man rose to address the meeting, he should forget his audience and not give a moment's concern to the content of his address [...] but should think only of the golden ring the anima had given him: "Hold on to it, and don't lose it."

This seems to have been a great help to him. After his speech, his colleagues and shareholders gave him virtually unanimous backing, and he even received congratulations from his wife. With this dream, and the subsequent success, something changed in him and he began to feel more assured in all his dealings with people.

[...] Experiences like this are in accord with Jung's dictum that: "dreams are our most effective aid in building up the personality" (CW7, para. 332) (Stevens 1990, pp. 50-51).

We all know how difficult it often is to 'catch' a dream before it dissolves into mist or retreats to a dusty corner of the mind. Jung certainly appreciated the elusive quality of the dream: "You always have to imagine a dream as like a conversation you overhear on the radio or the phone. Somebody says something, you hear a sentence of conversation, then the conversation breaks off again, and now you should reconstruct what had been said. That's how you should think of dreams. It is always a 'listening in.' You just overhear something for a moment. Something becomes clear subliminally. You wake up with a sentence on your lips, but perhaps you've even forgotten the dream, too" (Jung 2008, p. 359).

As well as being elusive, a dream may appear totally opaque when one comes to work with it. This Jung seems to acknowledge and welcome when he speaks of the way in which we need to approach the dream:

> One would do well to treat every dream as though it were a totally unknown object. Look at it from all sides, take it in your hand, carry it about with you, let your imagination play round it, and talk about it with other people. [...] Treated in this way, the dream suggests all manner of ideas and associations which lead us closer to its meaning.
>
> (CW10:320)

Jung might well have used the plural, 'meanings,' as he wrote of the dream as a "living thing, by no means a dead thing that rustles like dry paper. It is a living situation, it is like an animal with feelers, or with many umbilical cords. We don't realize that while we are talking of it, it is producing" (1984, p. 44). In other words, the dream continues to act on us, and affect us, while we are working on it. This is why so many dreams bear revisiting. There are some dreams with which we are never 'done.' Each time we revisit a significant dream it seems to yield more possibilities of meaning, as though the creative activity of psyche were still at work—which it is, when we realise how energy is generated by the effect of our focus and interest on a product of the unconscious. Conscious/unconscious, dreamer/dream, and patient/analyst affect each other and, in so doing, activate the symbol-making genius of the psyche. And when no meaning emerges? When a dream remains opaque and we are unable to crack open its shell to expose the kernel of meaning, we may blame the dream for showing a 'false façade'; Jung suggests that "We say that the dream has a false front only because we fail to see into it. We would do better to say that we are dealing with something like a text that is unintelligible not because it has a façade—but simply because we cannot read it. We do not have to get behind such a text, but must first learn to read it" (CW16:319).

While Jung suggests that it is best to leave theory aside when approaching a dream, he did employ some theoretical parameters: "I call every interpretation which equates the dream images with real objects an *interpretation on the objective level*. In contrast to this is the interpretation which refers every part of the dream and all the actors in it back to the dreamer himself. This I call *interpretation on the subjective level*" (CW7:130, emphasis added). He also acknowledges that some theory is necessary in order to make things intelligible. "It is on the basis of theory, for instance, that I expect dreams to have a meaning. I cannot prove in every case that this is so, for there are dreams which the doctor and the patient simply do not understand. But I have to make such an hypothesis in order to find courage to deal with dreams at all" (CW16:318). Jung also speaks of understanding the dream as an inner theatre: "We apply a structure to the dream that corresponds to the pattern of a drama. We distinguish four elements: the *introduction* often specifies place and time, as well as the actors (*dramatic personae*) of the dream action. There follows the *exposition,* which unfolds the problem of the dream. It contains, so to speak, the theme, or maybe the question posed by the unconscious. From this arises the *peripeteia*: the dream action leads to increasing complexity, until it reaches a climax and changes—sometimes in the form of a catastrophe. Finally, the *lysis* gives a solution or the result of the dream" (2008, p. 236). Not all dreams, of course, give us the benefit of a full performance of all four acts! If and when they don't, it is often useful to engage in active imagination to 'dream the dream onwards' into the next act.

Jung developed a way of working with dreams in which "the dream symbols can no longer be reduced to personal reminiscences or aspirations, that is, when the images of the collective unconscious begin to appear" (CW7:122). He called the method amplification, and illustrates the method in an analysis of a woman's dream (*ibid.*:123-40). Amplification "is simply that of seeking the parallels" (CW18:173). The method entails the 'amplification' of dream imagery and symbols that can in no way be understood on the subjective, personal level. This is achieved by finding analogies in the ubiquitous, universal symbols of mythology, religion, art, and cultural history. Of the method, Jung (2008) writes:

> This method of amplification is an *expansion,* a conscious enrichment. I make the dreamer focus his interest on the image, and to bring up all associations linked to the image. This must not be confounded with *free association,* in which we glide from one association to another, without regard to the initial idea (or image). [...] In using this method, we are not necessarily bound to the concrete statement of the dreamer, but can amplify the dream images ourselves. In this, we have to revert to those images we all have in common, namely the *archetypal images,* of

the collective unconscious, as they are found in language, myths and so on. [...] [And] we must have a look not only at the dream by itself, but maybe also in the context of a whole series.

(pp. 237–38)

These 'objective' parallels then need to be 'synthesised' and integrated at the subjective, personal level. This allows the dreamer to recognise that his or her suffering is reflected in the myths and art of millennia, a discovery that can be healing and reassuring, as the dreamer then no longer feels alone but in the company of many who have gone before. Jung also applied the principles of amplification to the general theory of psychoanalysis when he came to the realisation that:

analysis, in so far as it is reductive and nothing more, must necessarily be followed by synthesis, and that certain kinds of psychic material mean next to nothing if simply broken down, but display a wealth of meaning if, instead of being broken down, that meaning is reinforced and extended by all the conscious means at our disposal—by the so-called method of amplification. [...] [T]he synthetic procedure integrates (fantasy-material) into a general and intelligible statement.

(CW7:122)

which may then be related back to the subjective experience of the dreamer.

Two final thoughts from Jung on the profound reach, significance, and creative autonomy of the dream in its capacity to evoke in the dreamer an intimation of the reality of psyche and cosmos that lies far beyond the purview of the conscious personality:

The dream is a little hidden door in the innermost and most secret recesses of the soul, opening into that cosmic night which was psyche long before there was any ego-consciousness, and which will remain psyche no matter how far our ego-consciousness extends. For all ego-consciousness is isolated; because it separates and discriminates, it knows only particulars, and it sees only those that can be related to the ego. Its essence is limitation, even though it can reach to the farthest nebulae among the stars. All consciousness separates; but in dreams we put on the likeness of that more universal, truer, more eternal man dwelling in the darkness of primordial night. There he is still the whole, and the whole is in him, indistinguishable from nature and bare of all egohood. It is from these all-uniting depths that the dream arises, be it never so childish, grotesque, and immoral.

(CW10:304-05)

And this leads to Jung's critical realisation of the essential role of dreams and dreaming in the development of the human personality: "This is the secret of dreams—that we do not dream, but rather we *are dreamt*" (2008, p. 159). If we are, indeed, dreamt into being, how important it is to dream the dream forward in a conscious endeavour to enhance consciousness, develop the personality, and engage life in as creative and meaningful way as possible!

TRANSFERENCE/COUNTER-TRANSFERENCE

Although transference and counter-transference were concepts that originated with Freud, Jung's personal experiences and the concepts he distilled from them as he developed his psychological theories led him to think very differently from Freud. Jung's subsequent contributions to the way in which analysts and therapists think about transference and counter-transference in the analytical relationship have been significant. Jung realised that transference was not always a factor: some patients have strong transferences towards the analyst; others do not, and it was certainly not a major factor in the outcome of an analysis. A mild transference allowed analyst and analysand to focus on the patient's unconscious material in a more collaborative way.

Jung's observations and study of the movement of *libido* in the psyche led him to move beyond Freud's idea that the contents of the patient's transference to the analyst consist of infantile incestuous fantasies concerning the child's relationship to the parent of the opposite sex. The differentiation of Jung's developing model of the psyche from his former mentor's is reflected in Jung's understanding of *libido*. The publication in 1912 of *Transformations and Symbols of the Libido* (in 1916, *Psychology of the Unconscious,* now CW5, *Symbols of Transformation*) introduced Jung's understanding of *libido* as a more general psychic energy, more akin to the life-force, the focus of which is by no means exclusively sexual. Although Jung never dismissed the value of a reductive (Freudian) analysis of infantile contents when they surface in the early stages of an analysis, he understood this to be a necessary *stage* in the analytical process which, in its aim, is essentially *synthetic* rather than *reductive,* with the analyst following the lead of the unconscious psyche in the patient's path towards a greater sense of wholeness and unity.

Jung did not, however, dismiss the importance of the transference, referring to it as "far from being a simple phenomenon with one meaning (i.e., sexuality)" (CW16:362). As his realisation of the reality of the objective, unconscious psyche grew through his own 'confrontation with the unconscious,' Jung came to understand that the fantasies projected onto the analyst in a transference are not simply those based on personal experience but contain an archetypal component. Not only is small 'f' father projected but also big 'F' father, the archetypal idea or image of Father! This means that the analyst can receive projections of the patient's experience of all that the *actual* father or mother failed to provide but also the *archetypal* expectations that have not been fulfilled. Both personal and archetypal content pull the strings of the transference.

It also became apparent to Jung that the analyst is deeply affected by unconscious content activated in the patient. The patient–analyst relationship then develops the potential to take on an undifferentiated, archetypal dimension that far exceeds the (then considered) normal bond of an analyst–analysand relationship. Recognition of this 'danger' is the origin of the emphasis in training programmes in analytical psychology on a thorough 'training analysis,' to ensure that the future analyst has as conscious as possible an understanding of his or her psychology or 'personal equation.' While the analyst's 'personal equation' is inevitably always a factor in the analytical relationship, the analyst's awareness of it can lessen the dangers of undermining the analytical alliance through unconscious collusion, etc. If the analyst is not sufficiently self-aware, he or she runs the risk that the patient, "by bringing an activated unconscious content to bear upon the doctor (analyst), constellates the corresponding unconscious material in him, owing to the inductive effect which always emanates from projections in greater or lesser degree. Doctor and patient thus find themselves in a relationship founded on mutual unconsciousness" (*ibid.*:364).

A very large part of the 'communication' between two individuals occurs unconsciously. Consequently, it is critical to understand that this is so in *any* relationship, but particularly in the heightened *temenos* ('container') of the analytical alliance. Jung's later exploration of the symbolism of the alchemical process, which serves as a potent metaphor for the transformation of the psyche through the process of individuation, led him to state:

> The transference [...] alters the psychological stature of the doctor [analyst], though this is at first imperceptible to him. He too becomes affected, and has as much difficulty in distinguishing between the patient and what has taken possession of him as has the patient himself. This leads both of them to a direct confrontation with the daemonic forces lurking in the darkness. The resultant paradoxical blend of positive and negative, of trust and fear, of hope and doubt, of attraction and repulsion, is characteristic of the initial relationship. [...] The activated unconscious appears as a flurry of unleashed opposites and calls forth the attempt to reconcile them [...]
>
> (*ibid.*:375)

Jung did not adopt Freud's practice of sitting behind the patient who lay prone on the couch. Instead, he felt it important to sit face to face with his analysand—in a meeting of two psyches, two souls. "The doctor," Jung writes in "The Psychology of the Transference," "must go to the limits of his subjective possibilities, otherwise the patient will be unable to follow suit. Arbitrary limits are no use, only real ones. It must be a genuine process of purification [...]" (*ibid.*:400). Unless both are affected, analyst and analysand, little is achieved. This emphasises the importance of the analyst's recognition of and working through the counter-transference, and of his or her reactions to and participation in the process. It is not solely about the analysand; it is about both partners in the alliance, as in any relationship—"When two chemical substances combine, both are altered. This is precisely what happens in the transference" (*ibid.*:358). "The transference of these (infantile fantasies) to the doctor draws him into the atmosphere of family intimacy, and although this is the last thing he wants, it nevertheless provides a workable *prima materia* (the original, chaotic elements of the analysand's 'problem'). Once the transference has appeared, the doctor must accept it as part of the treatment and try to understand it, otherwise it will be just another piece of neurotic stupidity" (*ibid.*:420).

Jung's most significant contribution to the transference/counter-transference conundrum is, perhaps, his insistence on the analyst's commitment to the process, as well as that of the analysand. In observing and analysing his or her own counter-transference, the analyst suffers and is transformed, supporting the suffering and transformation of the analysand in the process. In the end, it comes down to the fact that the growth of consciousness can never happen at the level of the collective but solely in the individual, in and through relationship. Only a collective of conscious individuals has the power to effect change:

> [...] [T]he bond established by the transference—however hard to bear and however incomprehensible it may seem—is vitally important not only for the individual but also for society, and indeed for the moral and spiritual progress of mankind. So, when the psychotherapist has to struggle with difficult transference problems, he can at least take comfort in these reflections. He is not just working for this particular patient, who may be quite insignificant, but for himself as well and his own soul, and in so doing he is perhaps laying an infinitesimal grain in the scales of humanity's soul. Small and invisible as this contribution may be, it is yet an *opus magnum*, for it is accomplished in a sphere (the psyche) but lately visited by the *numen*, where the whole weight of mankind's problems has settled. The ultimate questions of psychotherapy are not a private matter—they represent a supreme responsibility.
>
> (*ibid.*:449)

SUMMARY

- Jung's development of Active Imagination as a technique to work with images and figures from the unconscious by engaging in the 'theatre' of one's own inner drama
- Active Imagination as a technique to activate the Transcendent Function of the psyche
- Jung's warning of activating "the same psychic material which is the stuff of psychosis"
- The Transcendent Function of the psyche as a natural, dynamic process which can be activated through active imagination
- The Transcendent Function as the creative activity of the unconscious, generating unifying symbols to compensate the one-sidedness of the conscious attitude
- Healing symbols generated by the activity of the Transcendent Function can move ego-consciousness out of a position of conflict and 'stuckness,' into one of possibility

- A summary of Jung's key statements on the nature of the symbol
- The Transcendent Function promotes the process of Individuation
- "The aim of individuation is nothing less than to divest the self of the false wrappings of the persona [...], and of the suggestive power of primordial (archetypal) images [...]" (CW9i:269). Jung's statement describes the two stages of the process of Individuation
- Individuation is a natural process of development moving the individual towards the achievement of personality or individuality
- Individuation is a process that "does not shut one out from the world, but gathers the world to oneself" (CW8:432)
- The development of Jung's Theory of Synchronicity (with case study and examples)
- Synchronicity: "The simultaneous occurrence of a certain psychic state with one or more external events which appear as meaningful parallels to the momentary subjective state" (CW8:850). *Acausal meaningful coincidence*, usually between an inner psychic event and an external event
- Jung's broader definition of Synchronicity promotes a paradigm shift, proposing *acausal orderedness* or synchronicity in the laws that structure all of life and the cosmos
- A short discussion of the Dream. Importance of understanding the 'context' or conscious situation to which the dream (i.e., the unconscious) is responding
- Jung's advice to approach a dream as one would a text, by first learning to read it
- *Objective* and *subjective* interpretation of dream
- Jung's development of the method of amplification to expand and consciously enrich a non-personal dream image through analogies in mythology, culture, history, and the arts
- The 'objective' parallels discovered through amplification need to be synthesised and integrated at the subjective, personal level
- Transference/Counter-Transference: Jung's focus on the *synthetic* rather than the purely *reductive* model of analysis. Jung understood transference as a complex phenomenon, involving archetypal as well as personal content and affecting both patient and analyst
- Jung's contention that unless both patient and analyst are affected, nothing is achieved; the analyst must be fully committed to the process. This is perhaps Jung's most significant contribution to the on-going debate about the value and uses of transference

⊕

REFERENCES

Doczi, G. (2005) *The Power of Limits: Proportional Harmonies in Nature, Art, and Architecture*. Boston, MA: Shambhala.

Jung, C. G. (1953/75) *C. G. Jung Letters, Vol. 2*. G. Adler and A. Jaffé (Eds.). R. F. C. Hull (Trans.). Princeton, NJ: Princeton University Press.

Jung, C. G. (1953–83) *The Collected Works of C. G. Jung*, 20 vols. W. McGuire, H. Read, M. Fordham, G. Adler (Eds.). R. F. C. Hull (Trans.). London: Routledge & Kegan Paul; Princeton, NJ: Princeton University Press.

Jung, C. G. (1961/63) *Memories, Dreams, Reflections*. Recorded and edited by A. Jaffé. R. and C. Winston (Trans.). New York: Pantheon Books.

Jung, C. G. (1984) *Dream Analysis: Notes of the Seminar Given in 1928–1930*. W. McGuire (Ed.). London: Routledge.

Jung, C. G. (2008) *Children's Dreams: Notes from the Seminar Given in 1936–1940*. Princeton, NJ: Princeton University Press.

Kluger, R. S. (1991) *The Archetypal Significance of Gilgamesh: A Modern Ancient Hero*. Einsiedeln: Daimon Verlag.

Shakespeare, W. (1984) *Complete Works of William Shakespeare*. P. Alexander (Ed.). London: HarperCollins.

Stein, M. (1998) *Jung's Map of the Soul: An Introduction*. Chicago, IL: Open Court.

Stevens, A. (1990) *On Jung*. London: Routledge.

Von Franz, M. L. (1980) *On Divination and Synchronicity: The Psychology of Meaningful Chance*. Toronto: Inner City Books.

Table 5.1 Active Imagination

TOPIC/ KEYWORDS	LOCATION	DESCRIPTOR
Defining active imagination	CW6:712-13 (1921/1923)	Distinction between *active* and *passive* fantasy. Active fantasies are products of intuition which are then examined by consciousness. What emerges from the unconscious is subjected to amplification, which brings content into clearer focus in the form of images.
	CW18:397 (1935)	Active imagination confirms that images have a life of their own; consciousness must allow the free development of the psychological 'drama' but must interpret it.
"The Transcendent Function"	CW8:131-93 (1916/1958) (esp. paras. 166 *ff*)	Writing, visualising, and art can be used to make that which is unconscious, conscious, thereby facilitating transcendent function. Expression of mood or fantasy through creative free play, e.g., painting, helps activate transcendent function; aesthetic quality of work not important.

(Continued)

Table 5.1 (Continued)

TOPIC/ KEYWORDS	LOCATION	DESCRIPTOR
"The Technique of Differentiation between the Ego and the Figures of the Unconscious"	CW7:341-73 (1916/1928) (esp. paras. 343 *ff*, 366 *ff*)	Two case studies, one of which details method of active imagination (366 *ff*), presented. Emphasis placed on actively engaging fantasies.
"The Aims of Psychotherapy"	CW16:66-113 (1931) (esp. paras. 101-06)	Unconscious may be engaged through a patient's fantasies, which can find expression through painting. Such activities facilitate development of conscious maturity and independence but must be accompanied by synthetic interpretation to achieve both intellectual and emotional understanding.
"The Tavistock Lectures" (Lect. V)	CW18:390-415 (1935)	Discussion following lecture: term "active imagination" introduced; technique described through case studies
"On the Nature of the Psyche"	CW8:397-404 (1954) (esp. paras. 400-02)	Active imagination described. Fantasies produced shaped by artistic talents of a patient. Frequency and intensity of dreams diminishes, reflecting the extent to which unconscious has been integrated by ego-consciousness (400).
"A Study in the Process of Individuation"	CW9i:525-626 (1950)	Case study of a female patient undergoing individuation, which is expressed through a series of paintings. Each painting analysed in turn.
"Therapeutic Principles of Psychoanalysis" in *The Theory of Psychoanalysis*	CW4:407-57 (1955)	Section "Active Participation in the Fantasy" explores active imagination. Jung's vs. Freud's view of unconscious fantasies. Freud's view: patient cured when free of them. Jung's view: fantasies are products of creative unconscious and of great therapeutic use (415-18).
Mysterium Coniunctionis	CW14:705-11; 749-56 (1955-56)	Process of "dream[ing] with open eyes." Centrality of active engagement expressed through metaphor of theatre (706). Alchemical operation analogous to active imagination (749). By actively engaging in process and realising that inner images are "acting and suffering figure[s] in the drama of the psyche" (753), patients eventually gain independence from analyst (754). Recommendation of method not without reservations (755).

(Continued)

Table 5.1   (Continued)

TOPIC/ KEYWORDS	LOCATION	DESCRIPTOR
Description of the method	CW7:323 (1916/1928)	Description of the method.
	CW14:706 (1955–56)	Description of the first stage of active imagination.
	CW14:753	Second stage of active imagination described.
Purpose and impact of active imagination	CW7:358 (1916/1928)	Impact of sustained practice of active imagination is explained. Case example.
	CW8:414 (1954)	Through active imagination we discover the archetype "without sinking back into the instinctual sphere […]."
	CW14:754 *ff* (1955–56)	Active imagination describes purposeful engagement with unconscious processes and contents compensating conscious situation. Purpose of active imagination is "to integrate the statements of the unconscious, to assimilate their compensatory content, and thereby produce a whole meaning which alone makes life worth living and […] possible at all" (756).
Active imagination and the anima	CW7:323 *ff* (1916/1928)	Technique of active imagination described in the context of respecting, and engaging with, the anima as autonomous personality.
	CW9ii:39 (1951)	Anima/animus, appearing in dreams and other forms, can be made conscious through active imagination.
Active imagination and individuation	CW14:753 (1955–56)	What is created during active imagination is "the beginning of individuation, whose immediate goal is the experience and production of the symbol of totality."
Active imagination and Alchemy	CW14:749 (1955–56)	Parallels and connections made between alchemical operation and active imagination.
Dangers of active imagination	CW18:399 (1935)	Method does not work for everyone. Technique often used in later stage of analysis, replacing reliance on dreams. Method may quicken analytical process.
	CW14:753 *ff* (1955–56)	Consciousness endangered if one becomes victim of one's own fantasy. Active imagination is difficult and should not be taken lightly. Only recommended to patients who have attained high degree of self-knowledge. Dangers of active imagination include psychosis in those psychopathically disposed (755).

Table 5.2 Transcendent Function

TOPIC/ KEYWORDS	LOCATION	DESCRIPTOR
Defining the transcendent function	CW6:184 (1921/1923)	Function that mediates between opposites, a "combined function of conscious and unconscious elements […]."
	CW6:825 *ff*	"From the activity of the unconscious there now emerges a new content, constellated by thesis and antithesis in equal measure and standing in a *compensatory* […] relation to both. It thus forms the middle ground on which the opposites can be united." If ego succeeds in holding the middle position without siding with a particular viewpoint, the third 'thing' (symbol) that arises is superior to the original, opposing views held in tension (826). New content shapes a more holistic attitude that ends division and channels psychic energy towards a common goal (827). *Transcendent function:* "a complex function made up of other functions, and 'transcendent' not as denoting a metaphysical quality but [facilitating] a transition from one attitude to another." A "living symbol" arises from tension of opposites (828).
"The Transcendent Function"	CW8:131-93 (1916/1958)	Centrality of transcendent function to progressing individual therapy.
Bridging polarities	CW8:145 (1916/1958)	Conscious and unconscious together comprise the transcendent function which facilitates a transition from one attitude to another.
Conscious and unconscious	CW8:181	Importance of ego in mediating and tolerating the tension that is the result of 'activation' of transcendent function.
	CW7:121 (1917/1926)	Transcendent function as process of coming to terms with the unconscious, necessitating both action and suffering. Method entails reconciliation between real and imaginary, rational and irrational. A natural process that arises from tension of opposites.
	CW6:169 (1921/1923)	Opposites cannot be united by rationality alone. Something new arises between conscious and unconscious which, "although different from both," has power "to take up their energies in equal measure as an expression of both and of neither."

(Continued)

Table 5.2 (Continued)

TOPIC/ KEYWORDS	LOCATION	DESCRIPTOR
	CW9i:524 (1939)	Emerging from union of opposites are new situations and attitudes. How this tension is held and moderated specific to each individual and not pre-determined.
	CW14:257 *ff* (1955-56)	"This continual process of getting to know the counter-position in the unconscious I have called the 'transcendent function,' because the confrontation of conscious (rational) data with those that are unconscious (irrational) necessarily results in a modification of standpoint. But an alteration is possible only if the existence of the 'other' is admitted […]."
Transcendent function and individuation	CW7:186 (1917/1926)	Transcendent function proceeds with a teleological purpose. End goal is the realisation of original, potential wholeness (individuation and Self) and is expressed in symbols (i.e., quaternity, circle, mandala).
	CW6:759 (1921/1923)	Transcendent function as psychic process central to individuation.
The third Tertium non datur	CW6:824	"For this collaboration of opposing states to be possible at all, they must face one another in the fullest conscious opposition." When there is "full parity of the opposites," individual will is suspended and a "new, uniting function that transcends them" is produced.
	CW9i:285 (1951)	Third thing produced is irrational in nature.
	CW14:705 (1955-56)	Conflict and disorientation essential to making that which is unconscious, conscious. Solution can never be based purely on rationality but requires "a third [irrational] thing [symbol]" which facilitates synthesis.
The transcendent function and active imagination	CW8:181 *ff* (1916/1958)	Transcendent function may arise in practice of active imagination.

(Continued)

Table 5.2 (Continued)

TOPIC/ KEYWORDS	LOCATION	DESCRIPTOR
The transcendent function expressed in alchemy	CW7:360 (1916/1928)	"This remarkable capacity of the human psyche for change, expressed in the transcendent function, is the principal object of late medieval alchemistic philosophy, where it was expressed in terms of alchemical symbolism."
	CW14:676 (1955-56)	"[…] [T]he alchemists […] sought to find ways […] to produce that substance in which all opposites were united."
	CW14:790	The goal of alchemy is the emergence of a transcendental symbol.

Table 5.3 Individuation

TOPIC/ KEYWORDS	LOCATION	DESCRIPTOR
Defining individuation	CW7:266 (1916/1928)	"Individuation means becoming a single, homogenous being, and, in so far as 'individuality' embraces our innermost, last and incomparable uniqueness, it also implies becoming one's own self." Individuation as "'coming to selfhood' or 'self-realization.'" Process by which an individual develops psychologically and becomes differentiated. Individual is distinct from general, collective psychology.
	CW6:757 *ff*	Individuation as development of consciousness out of an original unconscious state (762).
	CW9i:490 (1939)	"I use the term 'individuation' to denote the process by which a person becomes a psychological 'in-dividual,' that is, a separate, indivisible unity or 'whole.'"
	CW8:430 (1954)	A necessary (albeit rare) developmental process of transformation entailing conscious integration of unconscious contents. Development of a strong-enough ego to engage unconscious contents. Emergence of a new centre-point of the personality (Self). Goal of individuation is wholeness.

(Continued)

Table 5.3   (Continued)

TOPIC/ KEYWORDS	LOCATION	DESCRIPTOR
"Two Essays on Analytical Psychology: Adaptation, Individuation, Collectivity"	CW18:1084–1106 (1916)	Call to individuation often met with resistance. Relationship between individuation and responsibility to the collective explored.
"The Relations Between the Ego and the Unconscious, Part II: Individuation"	CW7:266–406 (1916/1928)	The aim of individuation is to divest oneself of the false wrappings of the persona and the suggestive powers of primordial images. Case studies illustrate compensatory relationship between conscious and unconscious. Importance of anima/animus in the individuation process underscored. Anima/animus stand in a compensatory relationship to persona. Individuation occurs when self-regulation achieved through balancing an interplay of opposites. Active imagination offered as method to dialogue with, and transform relationship to, anima/animus. Dangers of greater self-knowledge articulated, in particular, the inflation that may accompany an approach towards, and meeting with, the mana personality. Further differentiation from mana personality leads to engagement with the archetypal Self.
"Conscious, Unconscious, and Individuation"	CW9i:489–524 (1939)	Individuation is a process by which a person becomes whole by successfully navigating dangers of individuation and learning to hold tension between opposites (conscious and unconscious), which may be facilitated through analysis.
"Concerning Rebirth: Natural Transformation (Individuation)"	CW9i:234–39 (1950)	Natural individuation process may occur spontaneously, evidenced in dreams symbolising rebirth and encounters with an other.
"A Study in the Process of Individuation"	CW9i:525–626 (1950)	Detailed case study of patient undergoing individuation facilitated through art therapy. Symbols of Self are created (particularly mandalas) in patient's art. Analyst's task is to help the analysand understand material and avoid dangerous misinterpretations.

(Continued)

Table 5.3   (Continued)

TOPIC/ KEYWORDS	LOCATION	DESCRIPTOR
"Transformation Symbolism in the Mass: The Mass and the Individuation Process"	CW11:424–48 (1954)	Christ symbolises total personality (Self). Paradoxical nature of Christ (as man and God) accentuated, within whom polarities are reunited. The symbol of the cross also carries opposing meanings, i.e., as both instrument of torture and divine symbol. The cross also gives birth to a third possibility. The act of making that which is unconscious, conscious is epitomised in the Mass by crucifixion and redemption.
Individuation and instincts	CW9i:660 (1950)	Conscious engagement with instincts is prerequisite for individuation.
Individuation vs individualism	CW7:267 (1916/1928)	"Individualism means deliberately stressing and giving prominence to some supposed peculiarity, rather than to collective considerations and obligations. But individuation means precisely the better and more complete fulfilment of the collective qualities of the human being [...]"
	CW6:761 (1921/1923)	Individualism has nothing to do with individuation; latter entails carving out an individual path that is still in harmony with society, but not completely governed by it.
Individual and collective	CW18:1095 *ff* (1916)	Personal benefits of individuation are offset by one's duty to bring forth new values benefitting collective.
Relational understanding of individuation	CW6:758 (1921/1923)	"As the individual is not just a single, separate being, but by his very existence presupposes a collective relationship, it follows that the process of individuation must lead to more intense and broader collective relationships and not to isolation."
	CW6:760 (1921/1923)	Individuation cannot be the sole aim of psychological education. Adaptation to collective expectations must be an initial priority.
	CW16:448 (1946)	Individuation is both an internal process and mechanism for enhancing objective relationships.
	CW8:432 (1954)	"Individuation does not shut one out from the world, but gathers the world to oneself."

(Continued)

Table 5.3   (Continued)

TOPIC/ KEYWORDS	LOCATION	DESCRIPTOR
Individuation and the persona	CW7:269 (1916/1928)	"The aim of individuation is nothing less than to divest the self of the false wrappings of the persona on the one hand, and the suggestive power of primordial images on the other."
Individuation and the child archetype	CW9i:278 (1951)	Appearance of the child paves way for future change of personality. In individuation, child archetype anticipates the figure that arises from synthesis of conscious and unconscious (Self). Child archetype mediates, initiates healing, and can make things whole.
Individuation and the Self	CW12:330 (1944/1952)	Every life is the realisation of a whole, i.e., the Self. Individuals are vessels through which individuation may be achieved. Every 'carrier' charged with an individual destiny; life only makes sense when individual destinies achieved.
	CW11:755 (1952)	Individuation entails making that which is unconscious, conscious, and finding balance between the two. Symbols (of the Self) produced spontaneously to express this union of opposites.
	CW8:432 (1954)	Individuation is more than ego-centredness; necessitates relationship to the Self and all other selves.
Individuation and the transcendent function	CW7:186 (1917/1926)	Transcendent function proceeds with a purpose. Natural process that may operate unconsciously. End goal is the revelation of an original potential for unity.
	CW6:759 (1921/1923)	Individuation closely aligned with the transcendent function. *Symbols of Transformation* recommended for further reading.
Natural individuation **Biological process**	CW7:187 (1917/1926)	Individuation as a natural process.
	CW11:233 (1948) CW11:460 (1952)	The goal of both psychological and biological development is individuation. "In so far as [individuation] [...] runs its course unconsciously as it has from time immemorial, it means no more than the acorn becomes an oak, the calf a cow, and the child an adult."

(Continued)

Table 5.3 (Continued)

TOPIC/ KEYWORDS	LOCATION	DESCRIPTOR
	CW11:755 *ff* (1952)	"The difference between the 'natural' individuation process, which runs its course unconsciously, and the one which is consciously realized, is tremendous. In the first case consciousness nowhere intervenes; the end remains as dark as the beginning. In the second case so much darkness comes to light that the personality is permeated with light, and consciousness necessarily gains in scope and insight. The encounter between conscious and unconscious has to ensure that the light which shines in the darkness is not only comprehended by the darkness, but comprehends it (756)."
	CW18:1641 (1955–56)	"*[I]ndividuation* is a natural phenomenon [...] It is not invented by man, but Nature herself produces its archetypal image."
Individuation as religious process	CW11:233 (1948) CW18:1624 (1956–57)	Self indistinguishable from the God-image. Self-realisation amounts to God's incarnation. "*Individuation is the life in God*, as mandala psychology clearly shows."
Individuation as synthesis and/ or balance of opposites	CW11:755 (1952)	Logic alone cannot achieve balance between conscious and unconscious (individuation). A seemingly irrational union of opposites is made possible by symbols produced by the unconscious and amplified by consciousness.
	CW11:400 (1954)	Individuation as synthesis of new unity which previously consisted of scattered parts.
Individuation as differentiation	CW8:111 (1948)	Every advance in culture is an extension of consciousness achieved through greater differentiation. Every advance begins with an individual's individuation.
Dangers of individuation	CW16:448 (1946)	First, individuation may be used as "a pretext for evading [...] deeper human responsibilities, and for affecting a certain 'spirituality' which cannot stand up to moral criticism [...]" Second, emergence of archetypal material may drag relationships to a less developed level.
	CW8:430 fn 128 (1954)	If ego is overpowered by Self, the latter will remain fixed at a lower tier of development, and liable to express itself through archaic symbols.

(Continued)

Table 5.3 (Continued)

TOPIC/ KEYWORDS	LOCATION	DESCRIPTOR
Individuation vs imitation	CW7:242 (1916/1928)	Imitation of strong personalities may only lead to outward distinction in very limited circles.
Individuation as ultimately unattainable	CW14:792 (1955–56)	No single individual may ever realise the richness and scope of development found in alchemical symbolism (by extension, individuation).
As arduous task	CW18:1641 (1956–57)	Matthew 22:14 cited: "Many are called, but few are chosen."
Individuation and consciousness	CW11:746 (1952)	The task of consciousness is to decipher symbols of individuation stemming from the unconscious. If it cannot, individuation continues, but individuals then become victims rather than conscious participants.
Individuation and alchemy	CW12:40 (1944/1952)	"What the symbolism of alchemy expresses is the whole problem of the evolution of personality [,] […] the so-called individuation process."
	CW12:564	Alchemists projected individuation into phenomena of chemical change.
	CW14:792 (1955–56)	Alchemy provides "material in which [Jung's] experience could find sufficient room" to describe individuation "in its essential aspects."

Table 5.4 Synchronicity

TOPIC/ KEYWORDS	LOCATION	DESCRIPTOR
Defining synchronicity	CW8:826 *ff* (1952b)	Based on experience of chance groupings, case is made for meaningful coincidences that are acausally connected and numinous in nature.
	CW8:840	Synchronicity is "a psychically conditioned relativity of space and time."
	CW8:849 *ff*	Coincidence in time of two or more causally unrelated events which have same or a similar meaning. Simultaneous occurrence of a psychic state with one or more external events which appear as meaningful parallels to momentary subjective state (850).

(Continued)

Table 5.4 (Continued)

TOPIC/ KEYWORDS	LOCATION	DESCRIPTOR
	CW8:858	The meeting of an unconscious image and an objective situation that coincides with the unconscious content.
	CW8:984 (1952a)	Three major categories of synchronicity: "1. The coincidence of a psychic state in the observer with a simultaneous, objective, external event that corresponds to the psychic state or content [...]. 2. The coincidence of a psychic state with a corresponding (more or less simultaneous) external event taking place outside the observer's field of perception, i.e., at a distance, and only verifiable afterward [...]. 3. The coincidence of a psychic state with a corresponding, not yet existent future event that is distant in time and can likewise only be verified afterward."
"On Synchronicity"	CW8:969-97 (1952a)	1951 lecture. Synchronicity defined and examples given (Rhine experiments, analysis of astrological experiment).
"Synchronicity: An Acausal Connecting Principle"	CW8:816-968 (1952b)	Synchronicity evidenced by Jung's clinical experience of meaningfully connected events. Ideas anticipating concept examined. Space and time, when considered in relation to the psyche, are "elastic." Introduction of acausality brings greater equilibrium to trinity of space, time, and causality by creating an intellectual terrain where psychoid aspects of experience are appreciated and not routinely dismissed.
"An Astrological Experiment"	CW18:1174-92 (1958)	Astrological experiment to ascertain if typical oppositions and conjunctions occur in natal charts of married partners.
"Letters on Synchronicity"	CW18: 1193-1212 To Markus Fierz (1950, 1954)	Jung questions Fierz about his mathematical analysis of Jung's comparison of horoscopes of 400 married pairs. Jung reiterates that his astrological experiment not intended to confirm astrology's veracity but to demonstrate "meaningful coincidences."
	To Michael Fordham (1955)	Synchronicity says something about psychoid nature of the unconscious and archetypes.

(Continued)

Table 5.4 (Continued)

TOPIC/ KEYWORDS	LOCATION	DESCRIPTOR
"Foreword to the *I Ching*"	CW11:964–1018 (1950)	Chinese 'synchronistic' approach distinguished from Western causal approach. Two experiments involving I Ching conducted and analysed.
Space and time	CW8:855 (1952b)	Synchronistic phenomena show "space and time can be reduced almost to zero," with causality disappearing.
	CW8:948	'Absolute knowledge' stemming from synchronistic phenomena point to meaningful existence that is transcendental (not confined by space and time).
	CW8:440 (1954)	Synchronicity made possible if "psychically relative space-time continuum" assumed.
Archetypes	CW8:840 *ff* (1952)	Archetypal material may emerge at a "favourable opportunity to slip" into consciousness.
	CW8:845 *ff*	Meaningful coincidences rest on an archetypal foundation (i.e., scarab example) (846).
	CW8:440 (1954)	Non-psychic aspects of archetype—supported by synchronistic occurrences—contemplated.
Physics and psychology	CW8:440 (1954)	A "genuine and authentic relationship of complementarity" between physics and psychology postulated; reference to work of C.A. Meier and Wolfgang Pauli.
Psychic and non-psychic	CW8:418 (1954)	Psyche and matter two sides of the same coin.
Acausality	CW15:81 (1957)	Conditions that led to Jung's conviction of acausality's importance are detailed (Orig. 1930).
Simultaneity	CW8:840 (1952b)	Limitations of causal explanations lead to contemplation of acausal connection, "a falling together in time, a kind of simultaneity."
Subjectivity and personal investment	CW8:838 (1952b)	In Rhine's ESP and PK experiments, successful 'hits' tend to decline after first attempt. Lack of interest and boredom are negative factors. The more invested we are in noticing synchronicities, the more likely they will be found.
	CW8:856	"Every emotional state produces an alteration of consciousness [...]; there is a certain narrowing of consciousness and a corresponding strengthening of the unconscious [...] The tone of the unconscious is heightened, thereby creating a gradient for the unconscious to flow towards the conscious."

(Continued)

Table 5.4 (Continued)

TOPIC/ KEYWORDS	LOCATION	DESCRIPTOR
Absolute knowledge	CW8:948 (1952b)	Knowledge stemming from synchronicity described as 'absolute knowledge.'
Scarab example (case of Maggy Reichstein)	CW8:843 *ff* and 982 *ff*	Central case study used as example of the first 'category' of synchronicity.
Extensions of synchronicity	CW8:850 (1952b)	Possibility of synchronistic meeting of two external states, without intervention of an inner state.
	CW8:855	Simultaneous occurrence of two different psychic states.
	CW15:81 (1957)	Synchronicity may include a simultaneous meeting of external events and internal, psychic states (Orig. 1930)
Synchronicity and science	CW8:864 (1952b)	Although science seeks to understand the whole, it imposes conditions that result in confirmation bias. For a truly holistic view, "we need a method of inquiry which imposes the fewest possible conditions […] and then leaves Nature to answer out of her fullness."

EPILOGUE

In our introduction, we quoted Jung as saying:

> Since it is a characteristic of the psyche not only to be the source of all productivity but, more especially, to express itself in all the activities and achievements of the human mind, we can nowhere grasp the nature of the psyche *per se* but can meet it only in its various manifestations.
>
> (CW15, p. 85)

And:

> The individual mind cannot be understood by and out of itself. For this purpose a far more comprehensive frame of reference is needed; in other words, investigation of the deeper-lying psychic strata can be carried out only with the aid of other disciplines.
>
> (CW3:551)

That is, with the aid of our study of the arts, culture, history, mythology, philosophy, science, religion, politics, education, and, importantly for Jung, the symbolism of alchemy ….

We have endeavoured to introduce you to the main concepts of Analytical Psychology and suggested where you may track Jung's development and discussion of them in *The Collected Works*. We have also highlighted techniques developed by Jung to aid the analytical process and the activation of unconscious material: amplification, active imagination, and attention to transference/counter-transference; and what Jung observed to be the natural dynamics of the psyche leading towards the growth of consciousness and enhancement of the personality: the transcendent function and individuation. We saw that Jung's contribution through his theory of synchronicity was to propose an acausal orderedness to all things, an hypothesis reflected in cultures worldwide in, for example, religious belief, philosophical conjecture, and divinatory practices such as the Chinese *I Ching* or Book of Changes, astrology, and the Tarot. We have seen how Jung developed his hypotheses and techniques empirically, through close observation of the products of his own psyche, the psyches of others, and the symbolic expressions of the human psyche discoverable in everything from religious rite to architecture to philosophical, scientific, and artistic endeavour. His psychological theory, together with the invaluable contributions of scholars and practitioners of analytical psychology since Jung's death in 1961, now provides an investigative tool to deepen our study of both the products of the human mind and the invisible substrata that underlie individual and collective life, our histories and cultures, and the cosmos in which we find ourselves.

The editors of *The Collected Works* have, for the most part, designated specific volumes to Jung's 'application' of his thinking to various disciplines and fields of study, e.g., CW11, *Psychology and Religion: West and East,* CW13, *Alchemical Studies.* Here is what you will find in volumes that fall outside of the scope (and word-count!) of this book:

1. CW3, *The Psychogenesis of Mental Disease*, covers essays dating from 1907 to 1958, and addresses topics such as "The Content of the Psychoses" and "On the Importance of the Unconscious in Psychopathology." The last two essays on schizophrenia (1957 and 1958) are of particular interest as Jung argues that students and doctors of the "physiology and pathology of the brain (need to work with) the psychology of the unconscious" (CW3:584) in the treatment of schizophrenia as the disease has both physiological and psychological aspects: "The problem (of schizophrenia) has two aspects, physiological and psychological, for the disease, so far as we can see today, does not permit of a one-sided explanation. Its symptomatology points […] to an underlying destructive process, possibly of a toxic nature, and […] to a psychic factor of equal importance" (CW3:552).

2. CW4: *Freud and Psychoanalysis.* We have already pointed (in Chapter 2) to CW4 as the volume comprising Jung's writings on Freud and psychoanalysis, dating from 1906 and ending with the 1929 essay, "Freud and Jung: Contrasts."

3. CW10: *Civilization in Transition* contains essays which bring Jung's archetypal hypothesis to bear on a wide range of questions in history and culture from "The Role of the Unconscious"

(1918); through discussions of WWII Europe ("Wotan"—1936, "After the Catastrophe"—1945); to two essays on India (1939) influenced by Jung's travels to that country; "Flying Saucers: A Modern Myth" (1958); and "A Psychological View of Conscience" (1958).

4. CW11: *Psychology and Religion: West and East* includes a number of essays on Christianity: "A Psychological Approach to the Dogma of the Trinity," "Transformation Symbolism in the Mass," and Jung's famous "Answer to Job," as well as his explorations of Eastern Religion: "Yoga and the West," "The Psychology of Eastern Meditation," etc. The basis of Jung's interest in religious dogma, ritual, and symbolism lay in his realisation that no civilisation has ever *not* had some form of religious belief and ritual. He posited, therefore, a 'religious instinct' in human beings that speaks to an innate need to relate to some higher power than transcends human experience and limitations. Jung's focus was on the symbolic and psychological significance of *all* religious experience and ritual as a manifestation of the collective unconscious.

5. CW12: *Psychology and Alchemy.* While Jung saw the dynamics of the psyche reflected in mythology and folk- and fairy-tale, art, literature and culture in general, in the second half of his life, he discovered the symbolism of alchemy as a nuanced and precise metaphor for the psycho-spiritual development of the personality, which he referred to as the process of individuation, and for the stage of transformation that occurs in the course of a thorough analysis. CW12 and the other two texts that focus on the symbolism of the alchemical process (CW13 and CW14) are difficult, to say the least, but they provide a symbolic language that perhaps better than any other, even poetic language, describes philosophical, psychological, and spiritual experience.

6. CW13: *Alchemical Studies* contains three specific textual studies: the Chinese alchemical text, "The Secret of the Golden Flower"; the visions of the medieval mystic, Zosimos; and *De Vita Longa* ('On Long Life'), in "Paracelsus as a Spiritual Phenomenon." "The Spirit Mercurius" is an easier read as Jung introduces and interprets a folktale about Mercurius; "The Philosophical Tree" is not so accessible but, with the other essays, forms a significant contribution to Jung's understanding of the psycho-spiritual relevance of alchemical symbolism.

7. CW14: *Mysterium Coniunctionis* bears the subtitle: "An Inquiry into the Separation and Synthesis of Psychic Opposites in Alchemy." This volume contains Jung's last published work. It focuses on the central problem of both the alchemical process and the process of individuation: the union of opposites. This volume is not an easy read because, in his characteristic way, Jung draws from obscure references ranging from medieval philosophy, Christianity, and mythology to the symbolic value of salt and numbers. Not for the faint-hearted but full of riches.

8. CW15: *The Spirit in Man, Art, and Literature.* The subjects of most of the essays in CW15—from medieval Swiss physician, Paracelsus, through Freud, sinologist Richard Willhelm, to Picasso and James Joyce—are figures Jung considered pioneers in their respective fields. All the essays were written between 1929 and 1932, including the two theoretical contributions, "On the Relation of Analytical Psychology to Poetry," and "Psychology and Literature." While Jung's foray into literary and art criticism may be disappointing, given his reliance throughout *The Collected Works* on references to art and literature, his archetypal hypothesis, together with his development of active imagination, identification of the processes of the transcendent function of the psyche, and individuation, provide invaluable analytical tools for art and literary critics.

9. CW16: *The Practice of Psychotherapy* is divided into two sections: "General Problems of Psychotherapy," covering such topics as "The Aims of Psychotherapy," "Medicine and Psychotherapy"; and "Specific Problems of Psychotherapy," addressing "The Therapeutic Value of Abreaction," "The Practical Use of Dream-Analysis," and the difficult but invaluable essay, "The Psychology of the Transference," in which Jung uses the symbolism of the alchemical process to elucidate the transformational relationship between analyst and analysand that promotes individuation. A 'must' for all (and aspiring) analysts and therapists; and a deep well to which to return time and time again.

10. CW17: *The Development of Personality* contains the little that Jung wrote on developmental and child psychology: "Psychic Conflicts in a Child," "Analytical Psychology and Education," "Child Development and Education," "The Gifted Child," "The Significance of the Unconscious in Individual Education," and "The Development of Personality" (see also CW4, "A Case of Neurosis in a Child"). Jung argued that while the unconscious

conflicts of parents have a significant impact on the child, 'development' (or individuation) is a life-long process. While he wrote quite extensively on the 'mother,' Jung wrote very little on the 'father' (see CW4, "The Significance of the Father in the Destiny of the Individual").

Well! We have come to the end of our little book. We hope to have introduced you to the still largely unacknowledged significance of Jung's contributions and worldview. In particular, we aimed to stress the importance of Jung's archetypal hypothesis, not only for psychotherapy but also for its validation of a symbolic attitude to life, relationship, and world—a way of seeing that helps us all to penetrate beneath the surface to the very heart of things, to the dynamics motivating human behaviour, to "the real, subterranean life of the psyche" (CW5, p.xxvi), and to an appreciation of Jung's argument for a unitary substratum, a continuum of creativity and principle of orderedness, underlying all being (CW8:962).

FURTHER SECONDARY SOURCE READINGS ON JUNGIAN CONCEPTS

GENERAL INTRODUCTIONS

Casement, A. (2021) *Jung: An Introduction*. London: Phoenix Publishing House.

Fordham, F. (1966) *An Introduction to Jung's Psychology*. Harmondsworth: Penguin.

Harris, A. S. (1996) *Living with Paradox: An Introduction to Jungian Psychology*. London: Brooks/Cole Publishing Company.

Humbert, E. (1998) *C. G. Jung: The Fundamentals of Theory and Practice*. Wilmette, IL: Chiron Publications.

Jacobi, J. (1951) *The Psychology of C. G. Jung: An Introduction with Illustrations*. London: Routledge & Kegan Paul.

Stein, M. (1998) *Jung's Map of the Soul*. Chicago, IL: Open Court.

Stevens, A. (1990) *On Jung*. Princeton, NJ: Princeton University Press.

DEEPENING YOUR UNDERSTANDING OF KEY CONCEPTS AND JUNGIAN ANALYSIS

Cambray, J. and Carter, L. (Eds.) (2004) *Analytical Psychology: Contemporary Perspectives in Jungian Analysis*. London: Routledge.

Papadopoulos, R. (Ed.) (2006) *The Handbook of Jungian Psychology*. London: Routledge.

Stein, M. (Ed.). (1984) *Jungian Analysis*. Boulder: Shambhala.

Winborn, M. (2019) *Interpretation in Jungian Analysis*. London: Routledge.

Young-Eisendrath, P. and Dawson, T. (2008) *The Cambridge Companion to Jung*, 2nd Edition. Cambridge: Cambridge University Press.

AN INTRODUCTION TO POST-JUNGIAN THOUGHT

Kirsch, T. (2004) "History of Analytical Psychology" in J. Cambray and L. Carter (Eds.), *Analytical Psychology: Contemporary Perspectives in Jungian Analysis*. Hove: Brunner-Routledge, pp. 5–31.

Papadopoulos, R. K. (1992) *Carl Gustav Jung: Critical Assessments* (4 vols.). London: Routledge.

Samuels, A. (1985) *Jung and the Post-Jungians*. London: Routledge.

——. (1996) "The Future of Jungian Studies: A Personal Agenda" in M. Stanton and D. Reason (Eds.), *Teaching Transference: On the Foundations of Psychoanalytic Studies*. London: Rebus.

——. (2017) "The Future of Jungian Analysis: Strengths, Weaknesses, Opportunities, Threats ('SWOT')" in *Journal of Analytical Psychology*, 62(5), pp. 636–49.

PSYCHOLOGICAL TYPES

Beebe, J. (2016) *Energies and Patterns in Psychological Type*. London: Routledge.

Myers, S. (2019) *Myers-Briggs Typology vs Jungian Individuation*. London: Routledge.

COMPLEXES

Brinton Perera, S. (1986). *The Scapegoat Complex*. Toronto: Inner City Books.

Jacobi, J. (1959) *Complex/Archetype/Symbol in the Psychology of C. G. Jung*. R. Manheim (Trans.). Princeton, NJ: Princeton University Press.

Lu, K (2013) "Can Individual Psychology Explain Social Phenomena? An Appraisal of the Theory of Cultural Complexes" in *Psychoanalysis, Culture & Society*, 18(4), pp. 386–404.

Shalit, E. (2002) *The Complex: Path of Transformation from Archetype to Ego*. Toronto: Inner City Books.

Singer, T. and Kimbles, S. L. (2004) "The Emerging Theory of Cultural Complexes" in Joseph Cambray and Linda Carter (Eds.), *Analytical Psychology: Contemporary Perspectives in Jungian Analysis*. Hove: Brunner-Routledge, pp. 176–203.

ARCHETYPES

Colman, W. (2018) "Are Archetypes Essential?" in *Journal of Analytical Psychology*, 63(3), pp. 336–46.

Knox, J. (2003) *Archetype, Attachment, Analysis*. Hove: Brunner-Routledge.

Pietikainen, P. (1998). "Archetypes as Symbolic Forms" in *Journal of Analytical Psychology*, 43(3), pp. 325–43.

Roesler, C. (2012) "Are Archetypes Transmitted more by Culture Than Biology? Questions Arising from Conceptualizations of the Archetype" in *Journal of Analytical Psychology*, 57(2), 223–46.

Stevens, A. (2002) *Archetype Revisited: An Updated History of the Self*. London: Brunner-Routledge.

SHADOW

Perry, C. and Tower, R. (2023) *Jung's Shadow Concept: The Hidden Light and Darkness within Ourselves*. London: Routledge.

Zweig, C. and Abrams, J. (Eds.). (1991) *Meeting the Shadow*. New York: Jeremy P Tarcher.

PERSONA

Hopcke, R. (1995) *Persona: Where Sacred Meets Profane*. Boston: Shambhala.

Sauder MacGuire, A. (2017) "Embodying the Soul: Towards a Rescuing and Retaining of Persona" in *Jung Journal*, 11(4), pp. 45–80.

ANIMA/ANIMUS

Hillman, J. (1985) *Anima: The Anatomy of a Personified Notion*. Dallas, TX: Spring Publications.

Jung, E. (1957) *Animus and Anima*. New York: Analytical Psychology Club of New York.

Kast, V. (2006) "Anima/animus" in R. K. Papadopoulos (Ed.), *The Handbook of Jungian Psychology*, London: Routledge, pp. 113–29.

Rowland, S. (2002) "The Goddess and the Feminine Principle" in *Jung: A Feminist Revision*. Malden, MA: Blackwell, pp. 47–71.

INDIVIDUATION

Edinger, E. F. (1972) *Ego & Archetype: Individuation and the Religious Function of the Psyche*. Boston: Shambhala.

Saban, M. (2019) *Two Souls Alas: Jung's Two Personalities and the Making of Analytical Psychology*. Asheville, NC: Chiron Publications.

Stein, M. (2006) *The Principle of Individuation: Toward the Development of Human Consciousness*. Wilmette, IL: Chiron Publications.

SELF

Colman, W. (2006) "The Self" in R. K. Papadopoulos (Ed.), *The Handbook of Jungian Psychology*. London: Routledge, pp. 153–74.

Redfearn, J. (1977) "The Self and Individuation" in *Journal of Analytical Psychology*, 22(2), pp. 125–41.

Young-Eisendrath, P. and Hall, J. (1991) *Jung's Self-Psychology: A Constructivist Perspective*. London: Guilford.

Zinkin, L. (2008) "Your Self: Did You Find it or Did You Make It?" in *Journal of Analytical Psychology*, 53(3), pp. 389–406.

SYNCHRONICITY

Aziz, R. (1990) *C. G. Jung's Psychology of Religion and Synchronicity*. Albany, NY: SUNY Press.

Cambray, J. (2009) *Synchronicity: Nature & Psyche in an Interconnected Universe*. College Station, TX: Texas A & M University Press.

DeMoura, V. L. (2019) *Two Cases from Jung's Clinical Practice*. London: Routledge.

Main, R. (2004) *The Rupture of Time*. Hove: Brunner-Routledge.

——. (2006) "The Social Significance of Synchronicity" in *Psychoanalysis, Culture & Society*, 11(1), pp. 36–53.

GLOSSARY

Active Imagination: Dreaming with open eyes. A method of actively engaging with unconscious material usually reserved for the latter stages of analysis. Dialoguing with fantasy images and paying critical attention to how one interacts with and experiences the inner 'landscape' creates a new relationship of conscious to unconscious.

Alchemy: Refers to an ancient art and practice of turning base metals into something more valuable, such as gold. Jung recognised the symbolic importance of alchemy, understanding the alchemical process as a metaphor for the transformation of the personality, the goal of individuation and the 'gold' of the unconscious, often referred to as *the philosopher's stone* or *the elixir of life*.

Amplification: An interpretative method used to 'amplify' personal imagery through analogies to collective and universal imagery. Amplification of dreams seeks mythic, historic, and cultural parallels with the dream imagery; this produces a synthesis of personal and collective patterns and meaning.

Anima and animus: In classical Jungian psychology, the anima denotes the image of the archetypal feminine in the male psyche, the animus the image of the archetypal masculine in the female psyche. Anima and animus form a bridge between ego-consciousness, the collective unconscious, and the Self.

Archetypal image: Archetypal images 'personify' various aspects of the archetypes. These images are in turn shaped by the personal, social, and cultural contexts in which they arise. Jung's distinction between the archetype and archetypal image preserves a delicate tension between saying something general ('archetype,' 'collective unconscious' and 'Self' remain hypotheses) and something specific about human experience.

Archetype: The archetype is an hypothesis. The concept denotes the 'contents' of the collective unconscious: innate, instinctual processes and patterns of behaviour, thought, imagination, and relationship that are common to all human beings. An archetype is irrepresentable in itself but something of its nature may be deduced from the way in which it manifests to consciousness in an archetypal image. An archetype is psychosomatic, linking instinct and image, body and psyche.

Collective unconscious: Jung's hypothesis of a collective, impersonal level of the unconscious, often referred to as the *objective psyche* because its content is irrepresentable as it denotes the bases of archetypal processes and the instinctual roots of all of humanity. Manifestations of the collective unconscious appear in images that are universal, numinous and irreducible.

Compensation: The self-regulatory dynamic process through which the psyche seeks homeostasis or balance. The compensatory relationship between conscious and unconscious enables the process of individuation, the movement of the psyche towards wholeness, and the growth of consciousness.

Complex: A feeling-toned content of the personal unconscious. Complexes are clusters of feelings, thoughts, and memories that accrue around a personal experience, often a traumatic event. The nucleus of a complex is archetypal and the complex may be understood as the 'flesh' or personification of the archetype.

Consciousness: Our awareness. Consciousness comprises readily accessible memories, thoughts, and feelings. The centre of consciousness is the ego, the core of which is one's sense of 'I.'

Ego: The centre of the field of consciousness. The seat of intention and will.

Enantiodromia: Originating with Heraclitus, the term means 'running contrariwise.' A psychological 'law' that maintains that everything can turn into its opposite. If an extreme attitude develops in consciousness, its powerful opposite will accumulate in the unconscious in compensation.

Extraversion: One of the two 'attitudes' that characterise one's conscious orientation to the world. Extraversion draws the subject to the object, the outer world and away from introspection and subjectivity (see *introversion*).

Imago: An individual's subjective image of an 'object,' for example, a parent, which is *not* the actual object. Siblings may have very different *imagos* of the same parental figure.

Individuation: A life-long process of psychic development that may lead to a conscious realisation of one's innate potential or individuality. The goal of individuation is not perfection, but wholeness. It is not about individual*ism*, but becoming a conscious, discrete individual.

Inflation: An identification with contents of the collective psyche leading to either a feeling of power and 'specialness' or one of worthlessness (negative inflation).

Instinct: An innate, physical source of libido (psychic energy). Instinct is closely related to archetype, which gives the dynamism of the instinct shape and structure.

Introversion: One of the two attitudes that characterise one's conscious orientation to the world. Introversion draws the subject to inner objects and to relate to experience subjectively. Each individual will favour one attitude over the other, although both are available to everyone.

Libido: Originally used by Freud to denote sexual energy, *libido* for Jung is a form of life-energy or psychic energy that is neutral and may be directed to creative, relational, and spiritual ends.

Mana personality: Attributed to magicians, priests, doctors, saints, etc., mana is an extraordinary, quasi-divine power that may be used destructively or for healing purposes. Inner mana personalities present to consciousness in the form of the anima/animus, the wise old man, the great mother.

Mandala: The Sanskrit word for 'magic circle,' which is usually accompanied by a division into four or a multiple of four. Mandalas are symbols of wholeness, of the psyche as microcosm. Mandala imagery typically represents the archetype of the Self and may occur in dreams and fantasies to compensate a fragile ego-consciousness.

Numinous: A term originally coined by Rudolph Otto to denote an inexplicable experience of great magnitude and transformative significance that destabilises the ego's centrality, offering instead an insight into the possible existence of a force that is mysterious, meaningful, and beyond oneself. 'Numinous' derives from the Latin word *numen* meaning deity or spirit.

Persona: The social masks one wears that usually represent particular roles or 'parts' one plays in life. The persona is a functional complex of collective adaptation, linked to the ego. It enables one to interact in the world. The persona is an archetype, meaning it is a psychic structure found to be universal. The ego's identification with the persona is a hindrance to individuation.

Personal unconscious: The level of the unconscious that is shaped by individual experiences and circumstances. It serves as a storehouse for memories, traits unacceptable to the ego and persona, all that bypasses consciousness, is repressed or not yet conscious. The personal unconscious rests upon the collective unconscious.

Possession: A psychological state where ego-consciousness is gripped, held, or controlled by psychological contents, including complexes and archetypes. In such a state, agency and free will are lost, and one-sidedness may ensue.

Projection: Unconscious aspects of the personality (which may include positive attributes) are projected onto others. The aim of the therapeutic process is to build sufficient ego-strength so that projections may be recognised, withdrawn from the 'other,' and owned in the interests of greater self-knowledge and psychological equilibrium.

Psyche: From the Greek word meaning 'soul.' Jung uses the term to denote the entirety of the personality, conscious and unconscious.

Psychoid: Refers to the quasi-psychic level of the collective unconscious and unknowable aspect of the archetypes. The psychoid signifies that which will forever remain inaccessible to consciousness.

Quaternity: An image of a fourfold structure that symbolises wholeness.

Religious Function of the Psyche: The human psyche's capacity and need for religious and/or numinous experiences. A living connection with that which is deemed spiritual and beyond oneself can strengthen one's capacity to live a meaningful life.

Self: The central archetype driving the individuation process, and which represents the quintessential wholeness and uniqueness of the individual personality. The Self may be experienced as a 'new' or second centre of the psyche by a personality transformed through the process of individuation. The Self comprises the totality of the psyche, conscious and unconscious.

Self-Regulating Psyche: Like the body, the psyche is a self-regulating system in which ego-consciousness and the unconscious seek a state of balance or homeostasis. The psyche self-regulates through the dynamic of compensation.

Shadow: The traits and aspects of the personality unacceptable to the ego and persona. Usually understood as the dark side of the personality, the shadow also harbours unlived potential. Shadow contents are unconsciously projected onto others. The shadow is the first archetype that is met in analysis. Jung differentiates between personal and archetypal shadow (absolute evil).

Soul: Jung uses the term 'soul' to express a distinct functional complex best described as a 'personality.' Jung's concept of soul is connected to his understanding of *anima/animus*—the soul of a man has a feminine character, while the soul of a woman has a masculine character. Soul has to do with experiencing psyche in depth.

Symbol: Jung distinguishes between a sign (when something points to something else) and a symbol, which is the representation of an intuitive idea that cannot be formulated in any different or better way.

Synchronicity: An acausal connecting principle. A meaningful coincidence between two events, one outer and physical, the other inner and psychic, that are not causally connected.

Teleology: Jung attributed a *teleological function* to the Self (and therefore to individuation), meaning that the Self demonstrates the innate characteristic of seeking its own fulfilment.

Transcendent Function: The psyche's capacity to mediate opposites—conscious–unconscious. 'Holding the tension' between opposites (thesis–antithesis) results in the realisation of a symbol, a 'third' thing that offers the possibility of synthesis. Through the 'new' symbol, the original conflict is 'transcended.' Jung understood the transcendent function as a natural process operating in the psyche, underpinning the development of consciousness and individuation. It may intentionally be activated through active imagination.

Transference: In therapy, the unconscious 'transfer' or projection onto the therapist of both personal material (experiences, thoughts, and feelings connected to previous relationships and outer world events) and archetypal content (saviour, mother). *Counter-transference* is the reverse—the analyst's unconscious projections onto the analysand—and also the analyst's response to the unconscious influence of the patient. This is why Jung insisted that all analytical psychologists must themselves engage in a 'training analysis' before working with patients, as it is important for analysts to understand the impact of their counter-transference on the analytical process.

Typology: Jung's theory of personality types that illustrates how consciousness functions in practice. Typology shows why and how consciousness functions differently in different people, shaping the way we engage with others and the world around us. Jung's original, eight-type model describes conscious orientation as a combination of one's predominant attitude (*introversion* or *extraversion*), and one's dominant (preferred), auxiliary, and 'inferior' (far less conscious) functions (thinking, feeling, intuition, and sensation). An individual's type is not fixed; the development of previously auxiliary or inferior functions enhances the functioning and growth of consciousness.

Unus mundus: Meaning 'one world' or 'unitary world.' The idea that all levels of existence are ultimately interconnected. Synchronicities emerge because of the interrelation of psyche and matter.

Wholeness: The realisation of, and conscious relationship to, the complexity and integrity of the psyche. The approach to a sense of completion that may emerge in the course of a lifetime.

INDEX

9 781138 667013